D1480567

THE GREAT AMERICAN GUN DEBATE

ESSAYS ON FIREARMS & VIOLENCE

Don B. Kates, Jr.
and
Gary Kleck

PACIFIC RESEARCH INSTITUTE FOR PUBLIC POLICY
San Francisco, CA

ISBN 0-936488-39-5

Printed in the United States of America
10 9 8 7 6 5 4 3 2 1

PACIFIC RESEARCH INSTITUTE FOR PUBLIC POLICY
755 Sansome Street, Suite 400
San Francisco, CA 94111
(415) 989-0833
www.pacificresearch.org

Distributed to the trade by National Book Network, Lanham, MD.

Library of Congress Cataloging-in-Publication Data

Kates, Don B., 1941-
    The great American gun debate : essays on firearms & violence /
Don B. Kates and Gary Kleck, with James R. Boen and John K. Lattimer.
        p.   cm.
    Includes bibliographical references and index.
    ISBN 0-936488-39-5
    1. Gun control—Government policy—United States. 2. Firearms
ownership—Government policy—United States. 3. Firearms—Law and
legislation—United States. 4. Gun control—United States—Public
opinion. 5. Violent crimes—United States. 6. Public opinion—
United States. I. Kleck, Gary, 1951-   . II. Title.
HV7436.K37   1997
363.3'3'0973—DC21   97-23009
                                                                                        CIP

Sales Manager: *Victoria Douglass*
Production Manager: *Kay Mikel*
Cover Design: *Colleen Dillon*
Interior Design: *Kay Mikel*
Index: *Kay Mikel*
Printing and Binding: *Data Reproductions Corporation*

Contents

About the Authors

■ **Don B. Kates, Jr.**
*is a criminologist and civil liberties lawyer in Novato,
California, and is the author of numerous articles and books
on the gun controversy.*

■ **Gary Kleck**
*is professor at the School of Criminology and Criminal Justice,
Florida State University, and the author of several books,
including* Point Blank.

■ Chapters 2 and 5 were co-authored with Don Kates by:
James R. Boen, *Associate Dean and Professor of
Bio-Statistics* at the University of Minnesota School of
Public Health, and
John K. Lattimer, *Professor Emeritus* at Columbia
University College of Physicians and Surgeons.

Acknowledgments

Don Kates wishes to acknowledge the special assistance of
Mr. C. B. Kates.

Gary Kleck would like to recognize Professor Marc Gertz for
his contributions to the field work for the National Self-Defense
Survey discussed in Chapters 6 through 8.

PART I

GUN CONTROL
&
CRIME RATES

Chapter 1

Introduction

Don B. Kates, Jr.

This book seeks to redress a remarkable dissonance that exists in the American gun control debate. On many issues the conventional wisdom is substantially, or even diametrically, inconsistent with criminological, legal, and other scholarship. Contrast conventional wisdom, as revealed in the editorials and columns of our leading newspapers and magazines, with the following summary statements from the social scientific literature: Repudiating his own prior support for banning handguns, Prof. Hans Toch of the School of Criminology, State University of New York (Albany), concludes that the best available current evidence shows that

> when used for protection firearms can seriously inhibit aggression and can provide a psychological buffer against the fear of crime. Furthermore, the fact that national patterns show little violent crime where guns are most dense implies that guns do not elicit aggression in any meaningful way. Quite the contrary, these findings suggest that high saturations of guns in places, or something correlated with that condition, inhibit illegal aggression.[1]

From an article analyzing violent crime patterns in Canada and the United States by Prof. Brandon Centerwall of the School of Public Health, University of Washington:

If you are surprised by my findings, so am I. I did not begin this research with any intent to "exonerate" handguns, but there it is—a negative finding, to be sure, but a negative finding is nevertheless a positive contribution. It directs us where not to aim public health resources.[2]

From an article on urban youth violence by Dean Joseph Sheley of the School of Social Science, California State University at Sacramento, and his colleagues:

[The problem of urban youth violence] will not yield to simplistic, unicausal solutions. In this connection, it is useful to point out that everything that leads to gun-related violence is already against the law. What is needed are not new and more stringent gun laws but rather a concerted effort to rebuild the social structure of inner cities.[3]

Substantially similar views are expressed by Dean Alfred Blumstein of the Heinz School of Public Policy and Management at Carnegie-Mellon University.[4] (At a February 1996 symposium presentation of this paper he added jocularly that banning guns or handguns to the general public is "like trying to stop sexually transmitted disease by forbidding sex."[5]) Last but not least, here is how the Wisconsin State Legislative Reference Bureau parses the attitudes of social scientists working on firearms issues today:

It is difficult to make rational decisions in an atmosphere where absolute moral values are assigned to an inanimate object. A gun, while powerful and often destructive, is *no more than a tool controlled by the person who uses it.* . . . And measures that attempt to restrict access to firearms without reference to drugs, poverty with its attendant lack of educational and employment opportunities, clogged courts and overcrowded prisons are bound to have only marginal effects on firearm crime.[6]

Our goal is to acquaint readers who do not regularly peruse scholarly journals with the findings that are so little reported, particularly in the major popular news sources. If I seem derisive about the conventional wisdom, it may be because my co-author and I (respectively) began working in this area under its influence. Laboring under that same misleading influence, lay readers are unlikely even to know of the vast gap that exists between the conventional wisdom and modern scholarly findings. So let me begin with some glaring examples of how thoroughly those findings discredit the conventional wisdom conveyed by the popular media.

Gun Accidents versus Self-Defense

How often is a small child killed in a handgun accident? From the national publicity such deaths often receive, lay readers are likely to assume them to be as frequent as they are tragic. In fact, handgun accidents kill only 10 to 15 children under age 6 each year. Tragic as each such death is, they are only about as numerous as the equally tragic deaths of children that age who are poisoned by ingesting iron supplements, which look like candy and are often prescribed for mothers after birth. Indeed, handgun accidents kill only about half as many children under age 6 annually as does the ingestion of common household poisons (roach spray, lighter fluid, ammonia, iron supplements, ant poison, and so forth).[7]

As to how many children of all ages die in gun accidents, the truth, "Contrary to impressions generated by the news media, [is that] gun accidents almost never involve preadolescent children. There were 142 fatal gun accidents, with about 50-60 of them involving handguns, involving children under 13 in the entire nation in 1991."[8] Yet *USA Today* editorializes that accidental gun deaths kill fourteen thousand Americans (of all ages) each year. In fact, the number is only fourteen hundred.[9] In comparison, as many as 3 million victims use guns to defend against crime each year (see discussion and evidence presented in Chapter 6).

Only a tiny proportion of such defense incidents are reported in the press. Nevertheless the total number of defense uses is so large that the tiny proportion reported still constitute a goodly number. But consumers of the popular media are unlikely to realize how common such incidents are because even when defense uses are reported locally, they are never reported nationally, unlike the (far, far fewer) instances of children being killed in gun accidents.

The one exception is that if a defensive gun use goes wrong

(or seems to have done so) then it may somehow become nation-wide news. It was nationwide news, for instance, when a Louisiana man mistakenly killed a Japanese student who menaced him in a Halloween prank; and also when a Texan who had received a concealed handgun carry license under Texas' new right to carry law killed a man who attacked him in a traffic dispute. (In fact, both shooters were cleared, the Texan because he fired in reasonable fear of death or great bodily harm from his larger and younger attacker.[10]) Those who get their information from the popular media are unlikely to realize that erroneous killings (which the Texas case was not) by civilians total only about 30 per year; even less likely is the average person to know how favorably this compares to the police who erroneously kill 5 to 11 times more innocent people each year.[11]

The nonreporting of successful victim self-defense incidents lends spurious credence to another aspect of conventional wisdom on guns that dates back to early in this century. The conventional wisdom holds that guns are not useful for self-defense – defensive gun ownership is a "dangerous self-delusion."[12] Epitomizing this, Handgun Control, Inc. advises victims who are attacked by a rapist, robber, or other felon that "the best defense against injury is to put up no defense – give them what they want or run."[13]

This conventional wisdom persists only because the definitive contrary facts receive little or no attention in the popular media. Criminological data and studies have definitively established that, compared to victims who resisted with a gun, *victims who submitted were injured about twice as often*; also, of course, nonresisters were much more likely to be raped or robbed.[14]

Nevertheless, until quite recently the sparsity of statistical information made it possible to still argue that guns are rarely used for self-defense.[15] But a series of seminal studies by my co-author, Gary Kleck, have now demonstrated beyond peradventure that handguns are actually used by victims to repel crime far more often than they are used by criminals in committing crimes – as much as three times more. I shall not review the evidence here as Kleck does so in Chapters 6, 7, and 8. I raise the point only because Kleck's studies either go unreported in the nation's press or are derided. This media dubiety contrasts strikingly with a remarkable accolade accorded the Kleck and Gertz study on defensive gun use by the doyen of American criminologists, University of Pennsylvania professor Marvin Wolfgang. Despite a deep antipathy to guns, Prof. Wolfgang offered what he himself described as a tribute:

> I am as strong a gun control advocate as can be found among the criminologists in this country. If I [had the power] . . . I would eliminate ALL guns from the civilian population and maybe even from the police. I hate guns — ugly, nasty instruments designed to kill people. . . .
>
> Nonetheless the methodological soundness of the current Kleck and Gertz study is clear. I cannot further debate it. . . .
>
> The Kleck and Gertz study impresses me for the caution the authors exercise and the elaborate nuances they examine methodologically. I do not like their conclusions that having a gun can be useful, but I cannot fault their methodology. They have tried earnestly to meet all objections in advance and have done exceedingly well.[16]

I can only speculate as to why the popular media omits any mention of this tribute even as they continue to ignore Kleck's work or treat it as dubious. What can be said is that here again the popular media is suppressing scholarly research that contradicts conventional wisdom.

In this connection it is interesting to contrast the treatment the popular media gave to two very different studies of the effects of laws passed by 31 states to allow qualified civilians to carry concealed handguns for self-defense.[17] Though these laws had been enacted in a number of more urbanized states for five or more years when it was done, the first of these studies was limited to just five selected cities in Florida, Oregon, and Mississippi.[18] In none of these cities had a murder been committed by a permit-holder. Yet this small, city-level study concluded that widespread carrying of concealed guns had not reduced crime and perhaps even had increased gun homicides in three of the five cities whose data were examined. But these conclusions are an artifact of the use of urban data exclusively and of the cities selected. Had the study looked at state level data — even for just the three states selected — it would have found that overall homicide declined. Nevertheless, the *New York Times,*[19] among others, gave extensive space to this study whose validity has been disputed, *inter alia,* because of the severely limited data set on which its momentous conclusions rest. The authors themselves caveat their results, though neither those caveats nor criticisms by other scholars have received attention in popular media reports of the study.[20] (It may be coincidental that the authors' conclusions here dovetail with the hypothesis they have advanced elsewhere — that self-defense is not a personal right but rather a social evil that ought to be eliminated insofar as possible.[21])

Contrast the *New York Times'* total silence of a later study, which differed from the earlier study in being data-rich. Done by University of Chicago economists, its findings reflected data from almost all 3,054 of the nation's counties. Perhaps more important to the *Times,* however, was that that data showed that liberal allowance of concealed handgun carry by 31 states had coincided with a reduction of thousands of murders, rapes, and other violent crimes in those states. The authors tentatively concluded that adoption of such policies by the other 19 states would save many more lives and prevent thousands more violent crimes.[22] The popular media did not follow the *New York Times* in completely blacking out the University of Chicago study. But insofar as it was reported, the results were denigrated by falsely reporting that the study had been sponsored by the gun industry.[23] (In turn, these falsehoods led to editorials denouncing the study as a fraud.[24])

Similar contrasts are endless. For instance, to their credit, the *New York Daily News* and several other New York City papers have noted that the New York City police, having unfettered discretion under New York law, issue concealed handgun carry licenses only to specially influential people, including Donald Trump, numerous Rockefellers and DuPonts and a raft of politicians, millionaires and celebrities. Perhaps because its own publisher has a carry license, the *New York Times* has never found this story "fit to print." Oddly, in lieu of such information, the *Times* gives readers editorials asserting that "The urban handgun offers no benefits," *inter alia,* because "most civilians, *whatever their income level* are likely to lack the training and alertness" required to "use a gun to stop an armed criminal."[25]

Returning to the issue of accidental child death, a child under age 6 is 25 times more likely to drown in an unattended swimming pool or bathtub than to be killed in a handgun accident and 10 times more likely to so drown than to be accidentally killed with any kind of firearm.[26] Editorialists often assert that no one really needs a handgun. It would be more accurate to say that no one, except the disabled, needs a bathtub (as opposed to a shower) and that in most areas even Olympic swimmers do not need home swimming pools. Does it follow that home swimming pools and bathtubs should be subject to a licensing system under which they are forbidden to all except the disabled and anyone else who can satisfy the authorities that they have a pressing need that cannot otherwise be met? (Of course, handguns and swimming pools are very different things, which may require very different policy responses. A vital difference, for instance, is that it cannot be seriously suggested that swimming pools prevent millions of violent crimes annually. See evidence as to defensive use of handguns in Chapter 6.)

The Character of Gun Owners

Another example of how far conventional wisdom differs from sociological fact is depiction of the character of the approximately 50 percent of the American populace who own a firearm, particularly those who keep it for home defense. News columnists, cartoonists, and the media in general contemptuously dismiss such people as deluded, uneducated, intellectually and socially backward, and morally obtuse. In general, American news media do not air indiscriminate stereotypical condemnations of entire groups. But to this general rule there is one exception. As a class, gun owners are routinely reviled by editorials, columns, and cartoons characterizing them as "gun lunatics who silence the sounds of civilization," "gun nuts," "gun fetishists," "traitors, enemies of their own *patriae*," "anti-citizens," "terrorists," sexually warped "bulletbrains," Klansmen, thugs, and vigilantes who represent "the worst instincts in the human character."[27]

Contrast this with the facts sociological and psychological research reveal about the character of gun owners as a class (as summarized by Kleck and in studies sponsored by the National Institute of Justice):

> Middle and upper income people are significantly more likely to own [firearms] than lower income people. . . .

Gun owners are not, as a group, psychologically abnormal, nor [do attitude surveys show them to be] . . . more racist, sexist, or violence-prone than nonowners. . . . Gun owner- ship is higher among middle-aged people than in other age groups, presumably reflecting higher income levels and the sheer accumulation of property over time. Married people are more likely to own guns than unmarried persons.

Probably fewer than 2% of handguns and well under 1% of all guns will ever be involved in even a single violent crime. Thus, *the problem of criminal gun violence is concen- trated within a very small subset of gun owners.*[28]

Most private weaponry is possessed for reasons of sport and recreation... Relative to non-owners, gun owners are disproportionately rural, Southern, male, Protestant, *afflu- ent and middle class.* . . .There is no evidence suggesting them to be an especially unstable or violent or maladapted lot; *their "personality profiles" are largely indistinct from those of the rest of the population.*[29]

It is clear that only a very small fraction of privately owned firearms are ever involved in crime or [unlawful] violence, the vast bulk of them being owned and used more or less exclusively for sport and recreational purposes, or for self- protection.[30]

Studies find gun owners do differ from nonowners in some ways. Gun owners are more likely to approve "defensive" force, that is, force used to defend victims; in contrast, those with "violent attitudes" (they approve of violence against social deviants or dissenters) are no more likely to own guns than not.[31] A study of citizens who rescued crime victims or arrested violent criminals found these Good Samaritans were two-and-half times more likely to be gun owners than nonowners.[32]

In sum, the conventional wisdom about gun owners perpe- trated by their enemies (among which the popular media must be counted) is a bigoted stereotype that would be recognized and denounced as such if directed against gays, Jews, African Ameri- cans, or virtually any group other than gun owners. This bigotry is particularly hard to dispel because the generally good-hearted, progressive liberal people who perpetrate it are wholly incapable of imagining that any opinion they fervently embrace could be bigotry.

The Character of Murderers

This brings me to a related character issue, the conventional wisdom that most murders are perpetrated by ordinary people, and only because they had a firearm available in a moment of ungovernable anger. The endlessly repeated argument for banning firearms is that "[M]ost murders are committed by *previously law abiding* citizens where the killer and the victim are related or acquainted"; "*previously law abiding* citizens [are] committing impulsive gun-murders while engaged in arguments with family members or acquaintances."[33] "That gun in the closet to protect against burglars will most likely be used to shoot a spouse in a moment of rage. . . . The problem is you and me—law-abiding folks."[34]

If this were true, it would seem that widespread gun ownership is indeed a prime cause of murder and that banning and confiscating guns from the ordinary citizenry would reduce it. But every local and national study of homicide shows that murderers are far from being "ordinary citizens" or "law-abiding folks." Rather, they are extreme aberrants, their life histories being characterized by felony records, psychopathology, alcohol and/or drug dependence, and often irrational violence against those around them.

This point is discussed at some length in Chapter 2, but it is so misunderstood, and so crucial to the gun debate, that I want to address it here as well, particularly because after that chapter was written, information of a generally new and critically important character has become available. The data set out in Chapter 2 show that—unlike ordinary gun owners—roughly 90 percent of adult murderers have prior adult crime records, with an average adult criminal career of six or more years, including four major adult felony arrests. All the foregoing was set out, with exhaustive supporting references, in a recent article I co-authored with a biostatistician from North Carolina State University and three professors from Harvard and Columbia Medical Schools.[35] We noted that the prior records of juvenile murderers were generally unavailable but that such information as is available shows that they often "have histories of committing personal violence in childhood, against other children, siblings, and small animals."[36]

Based on the foregoing, we predicted two things: if the prior juvenile records of minors who murder were available, they would show such minors to have long juvenile crime careers; and, by the same token, if the juvenile records of adult murderers were available, their total criminal careers, as juveniles and as adults, would probably average much more than four major felonies. Since those predictions were made, I have been given access to an almost unique data set that amply fulfills them. David Kennedy of the Kennedy (no relation) School at Harvard has graciously provided me with the results of a study of juvenile murderers (and victims) in Boston done by him and his associates.[37] Reviewing gun and knife murders of, or by, persons under 21 in Boston over the years 1990-94, they found:

> ♦ at least 60 percent of those homicides were by or among gang members. ("This is a conservative estimate, since [it did not include] cases in which the circumstances were unknown or ambiguous.")
>
> ♦ these murders were committed by "a relatively. small number of very scary kids." Overall, in just their years as minors these 125 murderers had run up records that averaged 9.7 prior offenses per murderer. Adding their records together, these 125 murderers had previously been charged with: 3 murders, 160 armed violent crimes, 151 unarmed violent crimes, 71 firearms offenses and 8 involving other weapons, 248 property offenses, and 141 drug offenses.
>
> ♦ their victims were remarkably similar. Seventy-five percent of the victims had prior crime records, many of them being only somewhat less serious than the killers'. Together, "more than 40% of killers and victims known to the criminal justice system before the incident had ten or more prior arraignments" for a criminal offense.

Those who think most murders occur because ordinary people have access to guns are likely to envision "acquaintance homicide" as killings arising out of neighborhood or family disputes among previously law-abiding people. Consider instead a real example of acquintance homicide that Kennedy, et al. cite as typical:

> [A] long time gang member was wounded by his best friend's sister's boyfriend [in the culmination] to a dispute that had run on for the better part of two years. The sister would feud with her brother, and call her boyfriend in for help; the boyfriend and brother would argue; the gang member would get involved out of solidarity with his friend; that made the boyfriend his enemy, and the boy-friend and the gang member had been shooting at each other for the duration of the [two-year] dispute. Wounded and on the mend, the gang member told his probation offi-cer he was going to kill the boyfriend. The probation officer offered police intervention as an alternative, which the gang member accepted.[38]

But the story does not end there. Not long thereafter, the gang member was found shot to death in his own bed. Who killed him? Maybe the boyfriend. Maybe some rival member of his own gang or of another gang. There is simply no way to know, given his extremely aberrant, extremely dangerous lifestyle.

Of course, the Boston statistics cannot be heedlessly assumed to be generalizable to every city in the nation. But they and other statistics clearly demonstrate that "acquaintance homicide" is not a crime of "ordinary citizens" or "law-abiding folks." Thus: 80 percent of homicides in Washington, D.C. are "drug-related"; 84 percent of 1990 homicide victims in Philadelphia had crime re-cords or showed ante-mortem use of illegal substances; 71 percent of Los Angeles child and teenage drive-by shooting victims are documented members of violent street gangs; 71 percent of shoot-ing victims in 1992 in Charlotte, N.C., had criminal records; trauma center studies show that recurrent gun and knife wounds are virtually a disease common to "unemployed, uninsured law breakers"; substance abusers, those with sub-par intelligence and those with major mental disorders are each several times more likely to commit a violent crime than are ordinary citizens.[39]

In sum, the possession of firearms by the responsible, law-abiding citizenry is not a cause of murder. On the contrary, murders are committed by "a relatively small number of very scary" aberrants. It is desirable to prohibit guns to such aberrants as our laws already do.[40] But it is unreasonable to think that any law can disarm such people. As the National Institute of Justice-funded evaluation of the pre-1980 literature on the criminology of firearms (hereinafter described as the NIJ Evaluation) puts it:

> There is no good reason to suppose that people intent on arming themselves for criminal purposes would not be able to do so even if the general availability of firearms to the larger population were seriously restricted. Here it may be appropriate to recall the First Law of Economics, a law whose operation has been sharply in evidence in the case of Prohibition, marijuana and other drugs, prostitution, pornography, and a host of other banned articles and substances, namely, that demand creates its own supply. There is no evidence anywhere to show that reducing the availability of firearms *in general* likewise reduces their availability to persons with criminal intent or that persons with criminal intent would not be able to arm themselves under any set of general restrictions on firearms.[41]

Likewise an English gun control analyst has commented that no matter how restrictive and severe its laws, in any society there will always be enough guns available to arm those who are willing to obtain and use them illegally.[42] Thus "conventional wisdom" is as wrong in thinking that gun laws (of any kind) can substantially reduce crime as in thinking that widespread gun ownership leads the law-abiding to murder.

The Second Amendment

Conventional wisdom on the constitutional right to arms is epitomized by the comment of Leonard Larsen of Scripps-Howard News Service: "Ordinarily, only gun nut simpletons, NRA propagandists and tinhorn members of Congress striving for careers at the public trough defend against gun controls on constitutional grounds."[43] A Knight-Ridder columnist, Don Shoemaker, endorsing stringent laws to "disarm the American people and keep them disarmed," dismissed any constitutional objection to such laws as "idiocy" that "thinking people" reject.[44] Though colorfully expressed, these comments are not any more dogmatic than the conventional wisdom regularly aired in the popular media that the Second Amendment doesn't guarantee individuals anything: "the Founding Fathers merely intended to guarantee *states* the right to arm their militia[s]."[45]

How this came to be conventional wisdom is suggested by the way the magisterial *New York Times* handled adverse scholarly reaction to a guest editorial it published to that effect. The author's qualifications for pontificating that individuals have no such right were that he had graduated from college and been accepted at a law school.[46] A distinguished legal historian and seven other law professors co-authored a letter to the editor refuting him. But theirs was yet another piece of information the *Times* deemed "not fit to print."[47]

Similarly, in a 21-part National Public Radio series on firearms, legal reporter Nina Totenberg informed listeners that there is no debate on the Amendment "in America's courts, its law schools, or its *scholarly legal journals. Indeed, even the NRA could not recommend for this broadcast a single constitutional law professor* who would defend the Second Amendment as conferring on individuals the right to bear arms" [emphasis added].

Ms. Totenberg is nearly right about the lack of meaningful debate, though not as she presented it. Of 60-plus law review articles treating the Amendment that have appeared since 1980, only a handful defend the position she presents as unquestioned — and that handful appears generally in minor journals authored by officers or lobbyists for anti-gun groups.[48] Even its most vehement opponents are compelled to recognize that the individual right view now represents the "standard model" among scholars writing on the Amendment.[49]

Unlike the opposing view, articles endorsing the standard model come from preeminent constitutional scholars, *regardless of their attitude toward firearms,* and appear in top journals. Authors include former ACLU national board member William Van Alstyne[50] (professor of constitutional law at Duke) and such other luminaries of liberal constitutionalism as Akhil Amar (professor of constitutional law at Yale) and Sanford Levinson (professor of constitutional law at the University of Texas)[51] — men who have never owned a gun or even fired one. Though he personally loathes guns and desires that the Second Amendment be repealed, Harvard law professor Alan Dershowitz (a colleague of Van Alstyne on the ACLU national board) chides:

> Foolish liberals who are trying to read the Second Amendment out of the Constitution by claiming it's not an individual right or that it's too much of a safety hazard. . . . They're courting disaster by encouraging others to use the same means to eliminate portions of the Constitution they don't like.[52]

(A succinct statement of the standard model that was endorsed by more than 75 academicians can be found in the notes.[53])

    The inconsistency of conventional wisdom with scholarship on the Amendment is both illustrated and explained by the disparate treatment accorded a recent Harvard University Press book that is generally recognized as the definitive historical treatment.[54] The author, historian Joyce Lee Malcolm, has little interest in the modern gun debate. Prof. Malcolm's specialty is the political and legal history of early modern England and colonial America and the early Republic. Her research was underwritten not by the gun lobby but by the Harvard Law School, the American Bar Foundation, and the National Endowment for the Humanities. Her book was the subject of rave reviews from English as well as American scholars, including one in the *London Times Review of Books.*[55]

    The one exception was a strikingly inaccurate diatribe in the *New York Review of Books* by Garry Wills, an eminent historian and nationally syndicated columnist.[56] Indicative of Wills' inability to address the issues fairly (or even rationally) are his constant denunciations of "gun nuts," "gun fetishists" as "anti-citizens," "terrorists," "sick," "traitors, enemies of their own *patriae,*" and of "individual self-protection" as "anti-social behavior" and so forth (see note 27). That the *New York Review of Books* would have Wills review a scholarly tome about an issue where his emotions run so high speaks for itself.[57]

A Brief History of the Modern Gun Debate

Having exemplified the dissonance between conventional wisdom and the fruits of scholarship, I refer readers to the detailed discussion of media bias in Chapter 3. Now I want to move on to describe the historical antecedents that helped form today's media-based conventional wisdom.

As early as 1976 it was estimated that more had been written on "gun control" than on all other crime-related topics combined.[58] Yet in this era, even the academic literature was both fundamentally flawed and severely biased. The bias arose from the crusading zeal of academics who, by their own admission, could "see no reason . . . why anyone should own a weapon in a democracy"[59] and felt that gun owners embodied an American soul that is "hard, isolate, stoic and a killer."[60] Naturally this led to gun ownership being discussed as a social pathology rather than as a value-neutral sociological phenomenon. The only admissible study topics were problematic ones: gun accidents, gun violence, and gun ownership by extremist groups.[61] Implicitly these problems were seen as fairly representing the 50 percent of American households that contain guns; nor did it occur to the crusading authors that gun ownership might present issues worthy of neutral or non-problematic study.[62]

Even within the limits of its problem-oriented approach, this early academic literature proved unpersuasive. Evaluating it in 1976, policy analyst Bruce-Briggs noted with astonishment that, despite the volume of academic writing, "no policy research worthy of the name has been done on the issue of gun control. The few attempts at serious work are of marginal competence and tainted by obvious bias."[63] Two authors of 1960s anti-gun work have themselves admitted: "In the 1960s, there was literally no scholarship on the relationship between guns and violence and the incidence or consequences of interpersonal violence, and no work in progress."[64] A sociologist has used this early academic literature on guns as a case study of Znaniecki's concept of "sagecraft," that is, the prostitution of scholarship by partisan "sages" who invent, select, or misinterpret data to validate preordained conclusions.[65]

Thus, until about the mid-1970s, academic writing about guns was virtually monopolized by crusaders seeking to validate their contempt and loathing for guns and gun owners. Neutral scholars eschewed the gun issue, and the gun lobby, although able to exert great pressure on legislators, was incapable of, and uninterested in, addressing intellectually sophisticated audiences.[66] But this intellectual default was a calamity for the gun lobby. It and its supporters may hold their views without feeling any need for factual or scholarly support, but the biased, problem-oriented pre-1976 literature indelibly shaped a conventional wisdom that many humane and responsible citizens who do not own guns embrace and that the popular media continue to dispense. In 1978 the National Institute of Justice funded a review of the whole corpus of then-extant literature on gun control. Its senior authors began with the expectation that it would confirm the anti-gun views they admittedly shared. Instead the NIJ Evaluation provided almost unrelieved condemnation of the one-sided problem-oriented literature of the 1960s and early 1970s.[67] As discussed in Chapter 5, articles on firearms published in medical and public health journals are, if anything, even less trustworthy than the academic literature of the 1960s and early 1970s. Amusingly, seven years after its initial publication, the NIJ Evaluation occasioned a new instance of this lamentable pseudo-scholarship. An article by several of the most prolific anti-gun medical journal writers actually cited the NIJ Evaluation as supporting their view that "restricting access to handguns could substantially reduce our annual rate of homicide."[68] What the NIJ Evaluation had in fact said was:

> It is commonly hypothesized that much criminal violence, especially homicide, occurs simply because the means of lethal violence (firearms) are readily at hand, and, thus, that much homicide would not occur were firearms generally less available. There is *no persuasive evidence* that supports this view.[69]

Fortunately the 1980s and 1990s have seen a vast quantity of honest, unbiased and competent research. A host of scholars have contributed, but undoubtedly the most important, and the most prolific, single contributor is my co-author on this volume, Gary Kleck. The culmination of his 1980s research is *Point Blank: Guns and Violence in America* (1991), hailed by the American Society of Criminology and reviewers alike as the benchmark and starting point "for any serious scholar working in the area."[70]

In the five years since *Point Blank*, Kleck has made other very important contributions to the criminology of firearms, and so have many other scholars.[71] This book's purpose is to make up-to-date information of the scholarship in this area available to scholars and lay persons not otherwise familiar with it, thereby helping to bridge the vast gap between scholarly understanding of firearms issues and how they are generally reported and discussed in the popular media.

Notes

1. From an article co-authored with his colleague Prof. Alan J. Li-
    zotte, "Research and Policy: The Case of Gun Control," in *Psychol-
    ogy and Social Policy*, edited by Peter Sutfeld and Philip Tetlock
    (NY Hemisphere, 1992).
2. Brandon Centerwall, "Homicide and the Prevalence of Handguns:
    Canada and the United States, 1976 to 1980," *American Journal of
    Epidemiology*, v. 134 pp. 1245-65 (1991).
3. Joseph F. Sheley, et al, "Gun-Related Violence in and Around In-
    ner-City Schools," 146 *American Journal of Diseases of Children* 677,
    682 (1992).
4. Alfred Blumstein, "Youth Violence, Guns and the Illicit-Drug In-
    dustry," 86 *Journal of Criminal Law and Criminology*, 10-36 (1995).
5. Symposium sponsored at Northwestern University School of Law
    in Chicago by the Journal of Criminal Law & Criminology. The
    comment was made at a panel presentation on which I was a dis-
    cussant.
6. State of Wisconsin Legislative Reference Bureau, "The Gun Con-
    trol Debate — An Update," *Informational Bulletin* 94-3 (Oct., 1994),
    p. 30.
7. Compare National Safety Council, *Accident Facts* (1994) p. 22 (child
    deaths from firearms accidents in 1991) to the following figures for
    accidental poisoning of children under age 6 in the same year: 24
    died from ingesting hydrocarbons (lighter fluid, kerosene) or pesti-
    cides; 11 died from ingesting iron supplements; 10 from antide-
    pressants. "Iron Pills Lead List in Killing the Young," *New York
    Times*, June 9, 1992.
8. Gary Kleck, "Guns and Violence: An Interpretive Review of the
    Field", 1 *Social Pathology*, 12, 29-30 (1995).
9. Compare *Social Pathology* and *Accident Facts*, above, and Don B.
    Kates, Henry E. Schaffer, et al., "Guns and Public Health: Epi-
    demic of Violence or Pandemic of Propaganda", 62 *Tennessee Law
    Review*, 513-596 (1995) at table 2, to *USA Today* editorial "Stop the
    Madness; Pass Sane Gun-Control Laws" Oct. 17, 1991 at 10A.
10. See *Odessa (TX) American*, March 21, 1996, p. 3B and Lori Shawn,
    "Violence Shoots Holes in USA's Tourist Image," *USA Today*, Sept.
    9, 1993, 2A.
11. John R. Lott, Jr. & David B. Mustard, "Crime, Deterrence, and
    Right-to-Carry Concealed Handguns," 26 *Journal of Legal Studies*
    1–68 (1997) (police erroneously kill 11 times more often than do ci-
    vilians, based on 1993 figures); Don B. Kates, "The Value of Civil-
    ian Arms Possession as Deterrent to Crime or Defense Against

Crime", 18 *American Journal of Criminal Law,* 113-167 (1991) at p. 130 (5.5 times more erroneous police shootings, based on 1970s figures).

12. Father Drinan coined the term "dangerous self-delusion" in his article, "Gun Control: The Good Outweighs the Evil," 3 *Civil Liberties Review,* 4 (1976). Early claims to this effect are found in W. McAdoo, *When the Court Takes a Recess,* 131 (1921) and "Causes and Mechanisms of Prevalent Crimes" 24 *Scientific Monthly,* 415, 419 (1927), Hoffman, "Homicide by Means of Firearms," reprinted in H. Wilson, *Outlawing the Pistol,* 22-3 (1925) and M. Kavanagh, *The Criminal and His Allies,* ch. 25 (1927). For more modern claims see the next note.

13. The language quoted is from then Handgun Control, Inc. Chairman Nelson "Pete" Shields: *Guns Don't Die, People Do,* 124-25 (N.Y.: Arbor House, 1981). To the same effect see, e.g. M. Yeager, et al., *How Well Does the Handgun Protect You and Your Family?* (Handgun Control Staff of the U.S. Conference of Mayors, 1976), Franklin E. Zimring & Gordon Hawkins, *The Citizen's Guide to Gun Control,* 32 (1987). These and other arguments against defensive gun ownership appear in Patti J. Patterson & Leigh R. Smith, "Firearms in the Home and Child Safety," 141 *American Journal of Disabled Children,* 221, 223 (1987); Daniel Webster, et al. "Reducing Firearms Injuries," *Issues in Science and Technolgy,* Spring, 1991; Douglas S. Weil & David Hemenway, "Loaded Guns in the Home: Analysis of a National Random Survey of Gun Owners," 267 *JAMA* 3033, 3037 (1992); Daniel W. Webster & Modena E. H. Wilson, "Gun Violence Among Youth and the Pediatrician's Role in Primary Prevention," 94 *Pediatrics,* 617 (1994).

14. In addition to the evidence discussed in Chapters 6, 7, and 8 of this book, see discussion and references in Don B. Kates, Henry E. Schaffer, et al., "Guns and Public Health: Epidemic of Violence or Pandemic of Propaganda," 62 *Tennessee Law Review* (1995), at 538–39.

15. See, e.g., Philip J. Cook, "The Technology of Personal Violence," in M. Tonry (ed.) 14 *Crime and Justice: An Annual Review of Research,* (1991) and David McDowall & Brian Wiersema, "The Incidence of Defensive Firearm Use by US Crime Victims, 1987 Through 1990," 84 *AM. J. PUB. H.* 1982 (1994).

16. Quoting from several pages in Marvin E. Wolfgang, "A Tribute to a View I Have Long Opposed," 86 *Journal of Criminal Law and Criminology,* 188 (1995).

17. For a description of these laws and their operation, see Clayton E. Cramer & David B. Kopel, "'Shall Issue': The New Wave of Concealed Handgun Permit Laws," 62 *Tennessee Law Review,* 679 (1995).

18. David McDowall, Colin Loftin, & Brian Wiersema, "Easing Concealed Firearms Laws: Effects on Homicide in Three States," 86 *Journal of Criminal Law and Criminology*, 193-206 (1995).
19. Nov. 2, 1995, *New York Times*, A-16; March 15, 1995, A23.
20. Compare McDowall, Loftin & Wiersema, above, to the critique by Daniel D. Polsby, "Firearms Costs, Firearms Benefits and the Limits of Knowledge," 86 *Journal of Criminal Law and Criminology*, 207-220 (1995) and the additional discussion between them at 221-230; see also Lott & Mustard, above.
21. David McDowall & Colin Loftin, "Collective Security and the Demand for Legal Handguns," 88 *American Journal of Sociology*, 1146 (1983).
22. Lott & Mustard, above.
23. Typically, the AP and the newspapers that ran its story simply accepted the false claims of anti-gun lobbying groups — though they would never have published a pro-gun lobby group press release without checking its accuracy. Checking would have been easy in this case. As any reporter could have discovered by calling the University of Chicago, Professor Lott holds a professorship that the Olin Foundation had endowed decades ago. Lott is just a successor to earlier holders of the same endowment. The Olin Foundation had no part in Lott's selection nor in the funding for his study. For an account by a *Chicago Tribune* columnist who did check, see Stephen Chapman, "Taking Aim: A Gun Study and A Conspiracy Theory," *Chicago Tribune*, Aug. 15, 1996, p. 31.

   As any reporter could have discovered by calling the Olin Foundation, it is entirely independent of the Olin Corporation. The Foundation was established in John Olin's will decades ago, and the corporation has no control over the Foundation or connection to it. See the Foundation chairman's letter to the editor: William Simon, "An Insult to Our Foundation," *Wall Street Journal*, September 6, 1996, p. A15.
24. See, e.g. *Chicago Sun-Times* editorial, August 11, 1996, p. 35.

   When Lott published a brief popular article on his results in the *Wall Street Journal* (Aug. 28, 1996 "More Guns, Less Violent Crime," p. A13), Rep. Charles Schumer (D-N.Y.) wrote a letter to the editor repeating the falsehood. "Gun Control Thesis Is a Shot in the Dark," *Wall Street Journal*, Sept. 4, 1996. Perhaps aware of the falsity, Mr. Schumer carefully attributed this disinformation to the Associated Press' false report of the matter. Nevertheless, the *Wall Street Journal* later printed both a retraction and a letter to the editor by former Treasury Secretary William Simon, the chairman of the Olin Foundation. (See note 23.)

25. Don B. Kates, "Handgun Prohibition and the Original Meaning of the Second Amendment," 82 *Michigan Law Review*, 203-73 (1983) at p. 208 and footnotes 16 and 17.

26. Compare figures on child firearms accidents discussed on page 5 to National Safety Council, *Accident Facts – 1988* (350 drownings of such children annually).

27. These are direct quotations from: Braucher, *Miami Herald*, July 19, 1982, "Gun Lunatics Silence [the] Sounds of Civilization"; Lewis Grizzard, "Bulletbrains and the Guns That Don't Kill," *Atlanta Constitution*, Jan. 19, 1981; the *Washington Post* editorial, "Guns and the Civilizing Process," Sept. 26, 1972 and a series of columns by Garry Wills including, "The Terrorists Who Pack an NRA Card," *Albany New York Times Union*, April 22, 1996; "NRA is Complicit in the Deaths of Two Children," *Detroit Free Press*, September 6, 1994; "Or Worldwide Gun Control," *Philadelphia Inquirer*, May 17, 1981; "Handguns that Kill," *Washington Star*, Jan. 18, 1981; and "John Lennon's War," *Chicago Sun-Times*, Dec. 12, 1980. See also the following cartoons: *San Jose Mercury-News*, March 3, 1989 ("I.Q.-47"); Morin (*Miami Herald*) cartoon showing gun store with sign "drug dealers, gangs, welcome" appearing in the *Arizona Republic*, March 21, 1989, Herblock cartoon, *Washington Post*, March 21, 1989 ("these guys who want to spray the streets with bullets"); *Los Angeles Herald Examiner*, January 31, 1989 (showing "Crips, Bloods and NRA" as "Three Citizen Groups Opposed to Outlawing Assault Rifles"); Interlandi cartoon, *Los Angeles Times*, Dec. 16, 1980. Additional articles, editorials, and cartoons to the same effect are discussed in Chapter 4.

28. Gary Kleck, *Point Blank: Guns and Violence in America*, 22 and 47–48 (N.Y., Aldine, 1991) (emphasis added).

29. J. Wright, P. Rossi, & K. Daly, *Under the Gun: Weapons, Crime and Violence in the United States*(1983) at p. 122; see also pp. 107–08 (emphasis added).

30. J. Wright & P. Rossi, *Armed and Considered Dangerous: A Survey of Felons and Their Firearms*, 4 (N.Y., Aldine: 1986).

31. Alan J. Lizotte & Jo Dixon, "Gun Ownership and the 'Southern Subculture of Violence'," 93 *American Journal of Sociology*, 383 (1987).

32. Don B. Kates, "The Value of Civilian Arms Possession as Deterrent to Crime or Defense Against Crime," 18 *American Journal of Criminal Law*, 113, 125 (1991).

33. Quoting an undated, unpaginated, widely distributed, National Coalition to Ban Handguns pamphlet, "A Shooting Gallery Called America" (emphasis mine). A multitude of repetitions of the same claim will be found in the medical and public health literature on

firearms—even though empirical analyses of homicide data in that same literature reveals the falsity of the claim. See 62 *Tennessee Law Review* at 579-84, particularly the citations given and discussed in footnotes 279, 291, 292 and 304.

34. Kairys "A Carnage in the Name of Freedom," *Philadelphia Inquirer,* September 12, 1988 (emphasis added). See also *Washington Post* editorial "Run Down, Gunned Down," March 4, 1994, p. A22.

35. Don B. Kates, Henry E. Schaffer, et al., "Guns and Public Health: Epidemic of Violence or Pandemic of Propaganda", 62 *Tennessee Law Review,* (1995) at 579-84 and 587.

36. *Id.* at 581, quoting R. Holmes & S. Holmes, *Murder in America,* 8-9 (London, Sage: 1994).

37. The study, co-authored by David M. Kennedy, Anne M. Piehl and Anthony A. Braga, is forthcoming in *Law & Contemporary Problems.*

38. Ibid.

39. For these references see Don B. Kates, Henry E. Schaffer, et al., "Guns and Public Health: Epidemic of Violence or Pandemic of Propaganda," 62 *Tennessee Law Review* (1995) at 583*ff.*

40. Federal and state law generally bar gun ownership by felons, drug addicts, minors, and persons who have been formally committed to mental institutions. See, e.g., Title 18 USC § 922(g), Cal. Penal C. §§ 12021ff., 12072, 12076, 12100-1, 12551-2 and W & I. C. §§ 8100–8105 and other statutes cited in James B. Jacobs & Kimberly A. Potter, "Keeping Guns Out of the 'Wrong' Hands: The Brady Law and the Limits of Regulation," 86 *Journal of Criminal Law and Criminology,* 93–95 (1995).

41. J. Wright, P. Rossi & K. Daly, *Under the Gun: Weapons, Crime and Violence in the United States* (N.Y., Aldine: 1983), at 137-38; italics in original. Unless otherwise stated, all references to the "NIJ Evaluation" are to this, its commercially published version. The preliminary NIJ-published version is J. Wright, P. Rossi & K. Daly, *Weapons, Crime and Violence in America: A Literature Review and Research Agenda* (Washington, D.C., Gov't. Print. Off.: 1981).

42. Colin Greenwood in Colin Greenwood & Joseph Magaddino, "Comparative Cross-Cultural Statistics" in Don B. Kates, *Restricting Handguns* (1979).

43. National column, printed in the March 27, 1989, *Evansville (Indiana) Courier* as "Bush Quoting NRA Hogwash is Absurd"; see also Leonard Larsen "Gun Nuts Selective About Constitution," *Evansville Courier,* Dec. 5, 1990.

44. National column printed in the *Evansville (Indiana) Press,* Dec. 7, 1990, under the title, "A Nation of Guns: Alarming Murder Rates Justify Disarming the American People."

45. Quoting syndicated columnist Martin Schram, "Clash of Rights

Has Deadly Ring of Gunfire," *The Evansville Press,* June 18, 1991, (emphasis added). For innumerable other articles, editorials and comments to the same effect, see, e.g. *Los Angeles Times* editorial "Guns: A History Lesson," Aug. 17, 1988; Roger Rosenblatt, "The Bill of Rights," *Life* (Fall Special edition, 1991), p. 13; Tom Brokaw, NBC News: "America the Violent," June 5, 1992; Molly Ivins, "Ban the Things. Ban them All," *Washington Post,* March 16, 1993; John O. Craig, "There is No Constitutional Right to Bear Arms," *Pittsburgh Post,* May 8, 1993; *Los Angeles Times* editorial "Taming the Gun Monster: How Far to Go," Oct. 22, 1993; Tom Teepen, "James Madison's Call to the NRA," Cox News Service, Dec. 1, 1993; *Los Angeles Times* editorial "Taming the Monster: The Guns Among Us" Dec. 10, 1993; David G. Savage, "The Inherent 'Right' to Own A Gun Has Yet to Stand Up in Court," *Los Angeles Times,* June, 15, 1994, p. A5; Neil A. Lewis, "At the Bar," *New York Times,* May 5, 1995, A13; Herbert Mitgang, "What Right to Arms?" *New York Times,* May 5, 1995, A15.

46. Daniel Abrams, "What Right to Bear Arms," *New York Times,* July 20, 1989.

47. Personal communication from the author George Washington U. Law School professor Robert Cottrol.

48. See the next several notes and the discussion and full list of citations in Chapter 2 and the appendix thereto.

49. The phrase "standard model" originated in a review of the scholarly literature by an individual right theorist, University of Tennessee constitutional law professor Glenn H. Reynolds, "A Critical Guide to the Second Amendment," 62 *Tennessee Law Review,* 461 (1995). For its acceptance by vigorous opponents of that model see Garry Wills, "To Keep and Bear Arms," *New York Times Review of Books,* September 21, 1995, and Andrew D. Herz, "*Gun Crazy:* Constitutional False Consciousness and Dereliction of Dialogic Responsibilities," 75 *Boston University Law Review,* 57 (1995).

50. William Van Alstyne, "The Second Amendment and the Personal Right to Arms", 43 *Duke Law Journal,* 1236-1255 (1994).

51. Akhil Amar, "The Bill of Rights and the Fourteenth Amendment," 101 *Yale Law Journal,* 1193, 1205-11, 1261-2 (1992); Amar, A.R. "The Bill of Rights as a Constitution," *Yale Law Journal,* 1991; 100: 1131-1210 at 1165-8; and Levinson, S. "The Embarrassing Second Amendment," *Yale Law Journal,* 1989; 99: 637-659.

52. Interviewed by Dan Gifford and quoted in his "The Conceptual Foundations of Anglo-American Jurisprudence in Religion and Reason," 62 *Tennessee Law Review,* 759, 789 (1995).

53. More than 75 professors of law, history, political science, or phi-

losophy endorsed this version of the standard model when it was circulated by the group Academics for the Second Amendment:

"The view that the Second Amendment to the Constitution of the United States guarantees only the states' right to maintain formal militias has attained a surprising respectability. That may be more explicable as an expression of the hostility many academicians feel towards guns and their owners than as an unbiased constitutional interpretation. The Second Amendment does not guarantee merely a "right of the states," but rather a "right of the people," a term which, as used throughout the Bill of Rights (e.g. the First and Fourth Amendments), is widely understood to encompass a personal right of citizens.

"Moreover, the Amendment refers to the "militia", a term which in the 18th Century meant not a formal military unit like the National Guard, but a system under which every household and every man of military age was required to own a gun in order to defend the community against foreign invasion, tyranny and crime. The leading interpretations before Congress when it enacted the Bill of Rights affirmed that by the Second Amendment "the people are confirmed in their right to keep and bear their private arms" — "their own arms."

"Furthermore, the "individual right" component of Second Amendment thought became even more important in constitutional theory due to the transformation wrought by and through the debates in the [after the Civil War] Congress concerning the privileges and immunities of national citizenship. Many Congressmen pointed out that blacks in the South needed to be constitutionally protected in the citizen's individual right to bear arms in self-defense.

"Of course, the right to bear arms is no more "absolute" than is the right to speak, to publish, or to assemble. Hence, there is room for disagreement over the scope of Second Amendment rights, just as their currently exists legitimate disagreement over the scope of First Amendment rights of assembly and free speech. Nothing in this statement, therefore, is intended to deny either the constitutionality of, or the need for, sensible gun laws."

54. Joyce Lee Malcolm, *To Keep and Bear Arms: The Origins of an Anglo-American Right* (Harvard U. Press, 1994).

55. All the following concur that Prof. Malcolm's book "demolishes the notion that the framers envisioned the right to keep arms only in the context of organized militia bodies" [quoting Vanderbilt University legal historian James E. Ely, Jr., 52 WM. & M. Q. (3rd Series) 212 (1995)]. The lengthiest reviews are by David B. Kopel, "It Isn't About Duck Hunting: The British Origins of the Right to Arms," 93 *Michigan Law Review*, 1333 (1995); Robert J. Cottrol and

Raymond T. Diamond, "'The Fifth Auxiliary Right'," 104 *Yale Law Journal*, 995 (1994); and T. Markus Funk, "Is the True Meaning of the Second Amendment Really Such A Riddle?" 39 *Howard Law Journal*, 411 (1995). The shorter reviews are: David Wootton, "Disarming the English," *London Times Review of Books*, July 21, 1994 (English political scientist); Paul Smoler, *London Observer*, August 7, 1994 (English historian); Glenn H. Reynolds, *ABA Journal*, August, 1994, pp. 94-95 (American constitutional law professor); Jeremy Rabkin, "Constitutional Firepower: New Light on the Meaning of the Second Amendment," 86 *Journal of Criminal Law and Criminology*, 231 (1995) (American political scientist).

56. Garry Wills, "To Keep and Bear Arms," *New York Review of Books*, September 21, 1995.

57. Interestingly, reader response was so negative that the *New York Times Review of Books*, which had expected to devote several issues' letters columns to Wills review (as they told me), cut the letters off with a single issue. The most sympathetic letter there printed was from a law professor who described Wills' diatribe as "oversimplification, distortion and caricature" and regretted his departure from "his usual high standards" of scholarship, while observing that "our understanding of the Second Amendment will be no greater as a result of [Wills'] review — and neither will our manners." *New York Review of Books*, Nov. 16, 1995, pp. 61-62 (David Williams).

58. Bruce-Briggs, "The Great American Gun War," Fall, 1976, *The Public Interest*.

59. Sociologist Morris Janowitz, quoted in Tonso, "Social Science and Sagecraft in the Debate Over Gun Control," 5 *Law and Policy Quarterly*, 325 (1983).

60. Historian Richard Hofstadter, applying to gun owners D. H. Lawrence's denunciation of Americans in general. Hofstadter, "America As a Gun Culture" in *American Heritage*, Oct. 1970 at 82.

61. See e.g. G. Newton & F. Zimring, *Firearms and Violence in American Life* (1970) (hereinafter cited as Newton & Zimring), Geisel, Roll & Wettick, "The Effectiveness of State and Local Regulation of Handguns: A Statistical Analysis," 1969 *Duke Law Journal*, 647, Newton & Zimring n. 10 above, Seitz, "Firearms, Homicides and Gun Control Effectiveness," 6 *Law and Society Review*, 595 (1972).

62. Compare such more recent nonproblematic work as Brian J. Given, "Zen Handgun: Sports Ritual and Experience," 7 *Journal of Ritual Studies*, 139–161 (1993); Hummel, "Anatomy of A War Game: Target Shooting in Three Cultures," 8 *Journal of Sport Behavior*, 131 (1985); Olmsted, "Morally Controversial Leisure: The Social World of Gun Collectors," 11 *Symbolic Interaction*, 277 (1988); Lizotte & Bordua, "Firearms Ownership for Sport and Protection:

Two Not So Divergent Models," 46 *American Sociology Review,* 499 (1981); Lizotte & Bordua, "Firearms Ownership for Sport and Protection: Two Divergent Models," 45 *American Sociology Review,* 229 (1980); Bordua & Lizotte, "Patterns of Legal Firearms Ownership: A Situational and Cultural Analysis of Illinois Counties," 2 *Law and Policy Quarterly,* 147 (1979).

63. Bruce-Briggs, above.

64. F. Zimring & G. Hawkins, *The Citizen's Guide to Gun Control,* Introduction at xi (Macmillan, 1987). The authors' 1960s works, which are among the most scrupulous and accurate discussions by gun control advocates, include G. Newton and F. Zimring, *Firearms and Violence in American Life* (Eisenhower Commission Staff Report, 1969), N. Morris and G. Hawkins, *The Honest Politician's Guide to Crime Control* (U. Chi. Press, 1969) and Zimring, "Is Gun Control Likely to Reduce Violent Killings," 35 *University of Chicago Law Review,* 721 (1968).

65. Tonso, above, applying concepts based on F. Znaniecki, *The Social Role of the Man of Knowledge,* 72-4 (N.Y., Harpers, 1968).

66. As used herein "the gun lobby" means such organizations as the National Rifle Association, Citizens Committee for the Right to Keep and Bear Arms, Gun Owners of America, etc. that either formally lobby for "gun rights" or mobilize their members and other gun owners to lobby.

67. NIJ evaluation, note 30, especially pp. 321*ff.*

68. John Sloan, et al., "'Handgun Regulations, Crime, Assaults and Homicide: A Tale of Two Cities," 319 *New England Journal of Medicine,* 1256 (1988) at 1256, citing the 1983 version of the NIJ Evaluation, but without supplying any specific page citation.

69. I am here quoting (with emphasis added) from the Abstract to the "Executive Summary" of the original government published version of J. Wright, P. Rossi & K. Daly, *Weapons, Crime and Violence in American: A Literature Review and Research Agenda* (Washington, D.C., Gov't. Print. Off.: 1981) at p. 2, emphasis added. Note the various similar quotations from the 1983 version of the NIJ Evaluation scattered throughout this Introduction. Readers who are especially interested in the personal views of Wright, et al. should consult the extended disavowal of their own prior support for gun control at pp. 319*ff* of the 1983 version and two later articles by Wright: "Ten Essential Observations on Guns in America," 32 *Society,* 63 (1995) and "Second Thoughts About Gun Control," *The Public Interest* (v. 91; Spring, 1988).

70. Quoting from the review by H. Laurence Ross, 98 *American Journal of Sociology,* 661 (1992). See also Lawrence W. Sherman, 18 *The Criminologist,* 15 (1993) ("As a comprehensive reference, there is

nothing like it. It will stand for years as indispensable reading for anyone concerned about guns and violence.") and Philip J. Cook, Review, 330 *New England Journal of Medicine*, 374 ("Kleck is encyclopedic in covering the relevant literature, noting the shortcoming of others' research and providing careful explanations of his own original contributions.") In 1992 *Point Blank* received the American Society of Criminology's Hindelang Award, pronouncing it the most significant piece of criminological research over the past several years.

71. In addition to Toch & Lizotte, Sheley, et al., Blumstein, Lott & Mustard, and Polsby, and others cited above, see, Gary Kleck, "Crime, Culture Conflict and the Sources of Support for Gun Control," 39 *American Behavioral Scientist*, 387-404 (1996); Chester L. Britt, Gary Kleck & David J. Bordua, "A Reassessment of the D.C. Gun Law: Some Cautionary Notes on the Use of Interrupted Time Series Designs for Policy Impact Assessment," 30 *Law and Society Review*, 361-379 (1996); T. Markus Funk, "Gun Control and Economic Discrimination: The Melting-Point Case-in-Point," 85 *Journal of Crime and Criminology*, 764, 776-789 (1995); James B. Jacobs & Kimberly A. Potter, "Keeping Guns Out of the 'Wrong' Hands: The Brady Law and the Limits of Regulation," 86 *Journal of Criminal Law and Criminology*, 93 (1995); Gary Kleck and Marc Gertz, "Armed Resistance to Crime: The Prevalence and Nature of Self-Defense with a Gun", 86 *Journal of Criminal Law and Criminology*, 150 (1995); Gary Kleck, "Bad Data and the 'Evil Empire': Interpreting Poll Data on Gun Control," 8 *Violence and Victims*, 367 (1993); Kleck and DeLone, "Victim Resistance and Offender Weapon Effects in Robbery," 9 *Journal Quant. Criminology*, 55-81 (1993); Gary Kleck & Britt Patterson, "The Impact of Gun Control and Gun Ownership Levels on City Violence Rates," 9 *Journal Quant. Criminology*, 249-87 (1993); David B. Kopel, *The Samurai, The Mountie, and the Cowboy: Should America Adopt the Gun Control of Other Democracies?* (Prometheus 1992); Gary Mauser and Holmes, "Evaluating the 1977 Canadian Firearms Control Legislation: An Econometric Approach," 16 *Evaluation Research*, 603 (1992); Robert L. Ohsfeldt & Michael A. Morrisey, "Firearms, Firearms Injury and Gun Control: A Critical Survey of the Literature," 13 *Advances in Health Economics and Health Services Research*, 65 (1992); Gary A. Mauser and Michael Margolis, "The Politics of Gun Control: Comparing Canadian and American Patterns," *Government and Policy*, Vol. 10. pp. 189-209 (1992); Gary A. Mauser and David Kopel, "Sorry, Wrong Number: Why Media Polls on Gun Control Are So Often Unreliable," *Political Communication*, Vol. 9, pp. 69-92 (1992).

Chapter 2

Problematic Arguments for Banning Handguns

By Don B. Kates, Jr. J.D.
with John K. Lattimer, M.D., Sc.D.
and James R. Boen, Ph.D.

The American Academy of Pediatrics is only one entity in a long list of concerned physicians, public health professionals, and organizations to call for handgun prohibition.[1] This chapter reviews the relevant criminological literature to assess the likelihood that banning handguns would reduce crime. We focus on actual *control* of firearms, with the emphasis on identifying and disarming likely misusers. This differentiates us not only from decontrol advocates but also from utopians whose prohibitionist goals actually impede pragmatic *control* by alienating 65-plus million responsible firearm owners whose cooperation is essential if gun laws are to work.[2]

James R. Boen is *Associate Dean and Professor of Bio-Statistics* at the University of Minnesota School of Public Health.

John K. Lattimer is *Professor Emeritus* at Columbia University College of Physicians and Surgeons.

The Myth that Ordinary
Citizens Murder

Perhaps to dodge intractable enforcement problems, it has been claimed that most murderers are not criminals (who concededly would defy gun bans) but are otherwise "law-abiding citizens who might have *stayed* law-abiding if they had not possessed firearms."[3] This is contradicted by innumerable criminological studies showing murderers to be violent aberrants with extensive histories of felony, violence (mostly directed against relatives and acquaintances), mental imbalance, substance abuse, and firearms and car accidents.[4] (Incidentally, firearms accident perpetrators exhibit similar patterns of prior behavior—suggesting extraordinary indifference to human life, including their own.[5])

Thus, even assuming that ordinary citizens would surrender their handguns, there is no reason to think dangerous owners would. The sole empirical basis for the idea that ordinary citizens murder is a claim of FBI statistics showing 73 percent of murderers were previously "law-abiding citizens." This is apparently a misreading as the statistics actually show the reverse: The FBI publication for the year cited, and multi-year FBI data runs, show 67 to 78 percent of arrested murderers having prior records for a violent felony or burglary. They averaged four major prior felonies over a prior criminal career of at least six years. A National Institute of Justice-sponsored survey among 2,000 inmates of ten state prisons found those who sporadically or regularly used guns in crime to be the "hardest" felons. They had committed both more violent crimes per capita (including ones with weapons other than firearms) than other prison inmates and more crimes of all kinds.[6]

Yet these records (which don't even count juvenile arrests) are only the visible part of the iceberg. Deeper scrutiny reveals that murderers have life histories of violence that never resulted in charges, that violence having been directed against family and friends. The extent of such violence within a relatively short time frame is indicated by police records in Detroit and Kansas City: In 90 percent of domestic homicides, police had been called to the residence at least once in the two years prior; in 54 percent of the cases, they had been called five or more times.[7]

It is often implied that murderers *must* be ordinary citizens because victims are usually their relatives or acquaintances. This doesn't follow — unless one assumes that criminals have neither relatives nor acquaintances. *Family killings accounted for only 12 percent of U.S. homicides in 1994,*[8] and typical "acquaintance homicides" are mutual killings among rival gang members, drug dealers, or organized crime figures.[9] "The day-to-day reality is that most family murders are preceded by a long history of assaults." Studies "indicate that intrafamily homicide is typically just one episode in a long-standing syndrome of violence."[10]

The foregoing demonstrates the need for stringent controls targetted on dangerous owners. In theory, current state and federal law bar guns to felons, the unstable, and children. In fact, prisons are so overloaded that in many areas felons caught with guns face little penalty.[11] Thus, although gun laws could use fine-tuning, the real need is for the intensive enforcement resources necessary to deter or incarcerate dangerous owners.

The Threat of Long Gun Substitution

Indubitably, "*guns* are much more deadly than other methods of assault," but it is error to jump to the conclusion that "reducing the availability of [only] *hand*guns [our italics]" will reduce deaths, particularly if it is conceded that a handgun ban "will not reduce the number of violent confrontations."[12] The error lies in assuming that without *hand*guns attackers would use knives (weapons that kill only about 2.4 percent of those they wound, whereas handguns kill 10 to 15 percent). What if at least some assailants turn to rifles, weapons approximately 15 times more deadly than knives and, therefore, 5 to 11.4 times more deadly than handguns?[13] Or shotguns, which are so much deadlier yet that for medical purposes the wounds they cause ought not to be "compared with other bullet wounds . . . [A]t close range they are as deadly as a cannon."[14]

Criminological studies demonstrate "that anywhere from 54 percent to about 80 percent of homicides occur in circumstances that would easily permit the use of a long gun."[15] Kleck modeled what would happen if differing shares of prospective attackers, who otherwise would have used handguns, instead substituted long guns of differing lethalities. He showed that a net increase in homicide deaths as a result of long gun substitution was likely, and that the only way this could be avoided would be if there were some combination of optimistically low levels of substitution of long guns, or substitution of unusually low lethality long guns, for example, long guns being substituted that were only twice as deadly as handguns rather than four or five times as deadly, in combination with less than half of attackers substituting a long gun). Of the 2,000 felons queried in the National Institute of Justice felon survey: 82 percent concurred that "if a criminal wants a handgun but can't get one he can always saw off a long gun"; 87 percent of inmates who often used handguns in crime felt that sawing a long gun off to make it concealable for carrying would be "easy" — with which 89 percent of those who had often used shotguns criminally agreed.[16]

Based on these responses, Lizotte estimated that the murder rate would triple if a handgun ban were actually effective enough to make felons substitute long guns at the rates indicated.[17] Another NIJ-sponsored analysis facetiously concluded:

> If someone intends to open fire on the authors of this study, our *strong* preference is that they open fire with a handgun, and the junkier the handgun, the better. The possibility that even a fraction of the predators who now walk the streets armed with handguns would, in the face of a handgun ban, prowl with sawed-off shotguns instead, causes one to tremble. [Emphasis in original.][18]

Two Other Misconceptions

The widespread belief that firearm ownership causes increased violence is implausible because criminological studies commonly find either no relationship or a *negative* one (i.e., that areas with high firearms ownership suffer less violence than demographically comparable areas with lower ownership).[19] When studies have found a purportedly positive association, it is because of failure to take into account the possibility that high crime levels stimulated purchasing of guns rather than high gun ownership stimulating crime.[20] Once again, less than 2 percent of handguns are ever criminally misused.

Interestingly, despite fears that homicide would greatly increase, the adoption by over half the states of laws under which police must issue law-abiding, responsible applicants licenses to carry concealed handguns has not been accompanied by increased homicide. Indeed, adoption of these laws was accompanied by *declines* in homicides, and a decline in other violent crime as well—a finding based on a recent nationwide study by the University of Chicago's John Lott and David Mustard.[21]

Although one might question whether these declines really represented an impact of the easier access-to-carry permits, they clearly refute the claims of McDowall, Loftin, and Wiersema that the laws are followed by increased homicide rates,[22] claims that were for all practical purposes based on anecdotal information as they relied on analysis of just five unrepresentative counties. In sharp constrast, Lott analyzed crime data pertaining to every county in the nation for which data were available, more than 3,100 of them, finding the typical sequelae of the introduction of liberalized carry laws was a *decline* in homicide rates.[23]

Direct evidence that widespread gun carrying by the law-abiding does not cause homicide is provided by statistics from Florida, whose licensing agency meticulously tracks the licensing process and its results. Florida data for the five years since the liberal licensure law passed show not one unlawful killing by any of the approximately 186,000 responsible, law-abiding persons to whom licenses have been issued.[24]

It is equally wrong to attribute the much lower violence rates of some foreign countries to their banning handguns.[25] European violence was even lower *before* strict firearm laws. Those laws were not adopted to curb our kind of crime but as an antidote to political violence, an ill of which the United States has been uniquely free but which has always troubled Europe, regardless of firearm laws. Thus, firearm bans: (a) cannot claim credit for low levels of European apolitical violence—which long *preceded* their enactment; (b) have not stemmed the political crimes against which they were aimed; and (c) have not insulated Europe from the vast increase in apolitical violence that afflicted all Western nations in the post-World War II period.

Rates are actually rising faster in Europe than in the United States. They remain lower only because they started from a base that was so much lower—in the era before Europe adopted stringent gun controls.[26] At the same time, severe anti-gun laws have not prevented nations like Russia, South Africa, and Taiwan (where illegal firearm possession is a capital offense) from suffering apolitical homicide rates 100 to 150 percent greater than America's.[27]

One might generalize from the foregoing that peaceful nations do not need firearm laws and violent ones do not benefit from them. Although well-tailored firearm laws may have marginal benefits, the true determinants of criminal violence are socio-economic and cultural. This fundamental truth has been obscured in the gun control controversy by selectiveness and inaccuracy in describing foreign firearm policies. For instance, Switzerland and Israel are cited as among nations that "have strict handgun laws [and] report negligible deaths by handguns."[28] The "negligible deaths" part is true, but the "strict laws" is highly misleading.

Although a permit is required to own a handgun, "for a law-abiding citizen it is easy to get a permit," reports Israeli police lieutenant, criminologist (and lawyer) Abraham Tennenbaum. The same is true in Switzerland.[29] In Israel the permit allows the handgun to be carried concealed on the person, a practice Israel strongly encourages, contrary to American policy, which severely restricts it. Massacres in which dozens of unarmed victims are mowed down before police can arrive are inconceivable to Israelis. Consider, for example,

> what occurred at a Jerusalem cafe some weeks before the California MacDonalds massacre: three terrorists who attempted to machine-gun the throng managed to kill only one victim before being shot down by handgun-carrying Israelis. Presented to the press the next day, the surviving terrorist complained that his group had not realized that Israeli civilians were armed. The terrorists had planned to machine-gun a succession of crowd spots, thinking that they would be able to escape before the police or army could arrive to deal with them.[30]

The unimportance of firearm availability as a "cause" of violence is illustrated by differences in national policies concerning real assault weapons (i.e. fully automatic ones, not mere semi-automatic copies). Although banning some *semi*-automatics is now being fitfully attempted in the United States, fully automatic weapons have been banned or subjected to strict state and federal controls-cum-prohibitive taxation for 50-plus years. Regrettably, no reductive effect on American violence rates can be observed. In contrast, for military preparedness, Israel and Switzerland not only allow such weapons but distribute them to civilians by the millions—again without observable effect in raising those countries' "negligible deaths by" gun.

Also erroneous is the hailing of Canada's strict anti-handgun policy as effective, based on a short-term comparison between just two cities, Seattle and Vancouver.[31] Analyses of a decade of crime data for all Canada yield contrary evaluations.[32]

Evaluation by yet another Canadian criminologist, Stenning, yields the pessimistic assertion: "The Canadian experience shows gun control just doesn't work."[33] Indicating the unimportance of gun availability and the primacy of socio-economic and cultural factors is Centerwall's finding that Canadian provinces have far less handgun ownership—yet their homicide rates are almost identical to those of neighboring northern tier American states.[34]

Those who explain homicide in terms of firearm availability rather than socio-economic and cultural factors might usefully compare American to foreign suicide rates. Handgun availability is often seen as a cause of American suicide, the rates of which actually exceed our murder rates.[35] Indeed, the preceding and other articles argue that the magnitude of "the handgun problem" can best be measured if both homicides and suicides are totalled in one combined rate. [36] Yet if that approach is adopted in making foreign comparisons, the suicide rates of many foreign nations so far exceed the American rate that we fall below the median on the international combined murder-suicide rate table (see Table 2.1).

Note that such firearm-intensive countries as Australia and New Zealand fall even lower yet; and one of the most gun intensive of all, Israel, is the lowest of all. Why do European countries that virtually ban handguns have 33 percent to 500 percent more suicide than the United States where they are freely available to the general populace? Such comparisons only highlight the unimportance of firearms in comparison to socio-economic and cultural factors in explaining the social ills of diverse nations.

TABLE 2.1   International Suicide and Homicide Rates

Country	Suicide	Homicide	Combined Rate
Rumania (1984)	66.2	n.a.	66.2
Hungary (1991)	39.9	3.1	43.0
Finland (1991)	28.5	2.86	31.4
Denmark (1991)	24.1	4.8	28.9
France (1991)	20.9	4.36	25.3
Austria (1991)	23.6	1.6	25.2
Switzerland	24.45	1.13	25.58
Belgium	23.15	1.85	25
West Germany	20.37	1.48	21.85
United States (1985–88)*	12.5	8.3	20.8
Luxembourg	17.8	2.9	20.7
Norway (1991)	15.6	1.16	16.76
Canada	13.94	2.6	16.54
New Zealand (1991)	14.7	1.8	16.5
Australia	11.58	1.95	13.53
England/Wales**	8.61	0.67	9.28
Scotland** (1991)	10.5	1.7	12.2
Israel**	8.0	1.0	9.0

Notes: * These four-year averages are based on the suicide rates in Kleck (1986, table 6.5) and the homicide rates in Bureau of Justice Statistics (1989, p. 365, table 3.118); ** homicide rate does not include "political" homicides.

Source: Don B. Kates, Henry E. Schaffer, Edwin Cassem, John K. Lattimer, and George Murray (1995), "Guns and Public Health: Epidemic of Violence or Pandemic of Propaganda", *Tennessee Law Review*, 62, pp. 513–596.

Constitutional Restrictions

Gun control advocates minimize the Second Amendment to the United States Constitution as a mere "states' right" that guarantees nothing to individuals. This is often argued in the popular media, but law review articles endorsing it are limited to a handful by fervidly anti-gun authors, most being officers or paid employees of anti-gun groups, in mostly minor reviews.[37] Of more than 60 law review articles on the subject since 1980, less than ten endorse the states' right view. As Northwestern University law professor Daniel Polsby recently summarized the matter:

> almost all the qualified historians and constitutional-law scholars who have studied the subject [concur]. The over-

whelming weight of authority affirms that the Second
Amendment establishes an *individual* right to bear arms,
which is not dependent upon joining something like the National Guard.[38]

It bears emphasis that, unlike the scholarship on the other side,
this "overwhelming weight of authority" is wholly *non-partisan*.
Though a number of articles have been contributed by officers or
paid employees of pro-gun groups, many others are by distinguished constitutional scholars, many of whom were surprised
and dismayed at the conclusions forced upon them by the evidence. The authors include three of the major figures in liberal
American constitutionalism today.[39] The complete list of articles
is so extensive — even excluding those by gun lobby officers or
employees — that we consign it to an appendix.

But, as one of the authors has urged in debate with the NRA,[40]
the Amendment does not forbid firearm *control*, as opposed to
wholesale prohibition. Registration, licensing and numerous
other forms of regulation are permissible so long as they do not
restrict the availability of firearms to law-abiding adults or unreasonably hinder their ability to acquire firearms.

So far, gun laws have generally not been so extreme as to raise
serious questions under the Second Amendment. In the most
significant case the Supreme Court allowed individuals to challenge
gun laws under the Amendment, though holding that it protects
their possession of military type and quality weapons only. This
would seem to include high quality handguns and other firearms but
not shoddy or gangster-type weapons like "Saturday Night Specials,"
switch blade knives, blackjacks, and so forth.[41] Recent Supreme Court
authority implicitly rejects the claim that the right to arms applies
only to state militias. The Court emphasized that the Second
Amendment uses the term "right of the people" — a phrase consistently used throughout the Bill of Rights to denote the rights of
individuals.[42]

Conclusion

In 1978 the National Institute of Justice funded at the Social and
Demographic Research Institute a comprehensive analysis of the

role of firearms in violence. To their surprise, the researchers' review of the entire corpus of criminological literature yielded the following summary:

> There appear to be no strong causal connections between private gun ownership and the crime rate. . . . It is commonly hypothesized that much criminal violence, especially homicide, occurs simply because the means of lethal violence (firearms) are readily at hand, and thus, that much homicide would not occur were firearms generally less available. There is no persuasive evidence that supports this view.[43]

In an expanded commercial version published in 1983 they confessed that they began their research as proponents of severe controls; but "the more deeply we have explored" that, "the less plausible it has become."[44] As of 1988, co-author James Wright was of "the opinion that a compelling case for 'stricter gun control' *cannot be made*" (his italics).[45] In late 1991 Kleck published *Point Blank: Guns and Violence in America*. Already hailed as an "encyclopedic" treatment that seems destined to become the definitive work for decades to come, *Point Blank* endorses Wright's views, concluding that "gun controls only nibble at the problem [of violence] rather than striking at its core."

It bears emphasis that Kleck, Wright, and the authors of this chapter all support reasonable controls carefully tailored not to impose costs excessive to the marginal benefits to which firearm law is necessarily limited. What cannot be supported is unrealistic faith in utopian schemes of general disarmament that portend only massive diversion of scarce law enforcement resources in an effort that—even if it were not hopeless—cannot off-set the fundamental socio-economic and cultural factors promoting violence.

Appendix

Articles rejecting the states' right view of the Second Amendment (not including articles by officers or paid employees of the gun lobby) include:

▶ McAfee, T. and Quinlan, M.J. [SIU-Carbondale law professors], "Bringing Forward the Right to Keep and Bear Arms: Do Text, History or Precedent Stand in the Way?" 75 *U. N.C. L. Rev.* #3 (1977);

▶ Shalhope, R.E. [U. OK professor of history], "The Ideological Origins of the Second Amendment," 69 *J. Am. Hist.* 599–613 (1982);

▶ *The Right to Keep and Bear Arms,* Report of the Subcommittee on the Constitution, Senate Judiciary Committee (Washington: committee print; 1982);

▶ Kates, D.B. "Handgun prohibition and the original meaning of the Second Amendment," 82 *Mich. L. Rev. 203–273 (1983);*

▶ Malcolm, J.L. [Bentley College, professor of history] "The Right of the People to Keep and Bear Arms: The Common Law Tradition." 10 *Hastings Const. L. Q.* 285–314 (1983);

▶ Halbrook, S.P. *"That Every Man Be Armed": The Evolution of a Constitutional Right.* (Albuquerque: U. of NM Press; 1984);

▶ Levy, L.W, Karst, K.L, and Mahoney, D.J. *The Encyclopedia of the American Constitution* (New York: Macmillan; 1986) at v. 4, 1639-40;

▶ Curtis, M.K. [Wake Forest U. law professor], *No State Shall Abridge: The Fourteenth Amendment and the Bill of Rights* (Durham, Duke U. Press; 1986);

▶ Lund, N. [George Mason U. professor of law], "The Second Amendment, Political Liberty and the Right to Self-Preservation," 39 *Ala. L. Rev.* 103–130 (1987);

▶ Halbrook, S.P. *A Right to Bear Arms: State and Federal Bills of Rights and Constitutional Guarantees* (New York: Greenwood; 1989);

▶ Levinson, S. [U. TX professor of law], The Embarrassing Second Amendment. 99*Yale L. J.* 637–659 (1989);

▶ Walker, W.A. "Review, 88 *Mich. L. Rev.* 1409–14 (1990);

▶ Amar, A.R. [Yale U. professor of law], "The Bill of Rights as a Constitution." 100 *Yale L. J.* 1131–1210 at 1165-8 (1991);

▶ Cottrol, R.J. [George Washington U. professor of law], andDiamond, R.T. [Tulane U. professor of law] "The Second Amendment: Toward an Afro-Americanist Reconsideration." 80 *Georgetown L. J.* 310–361 (1991);

▶ Scarry, E. [Harvard U. professor of English], "War and the Social Contract: The Right to Bear Arms," 139 *U. PA. L. REV.* 1257–1316 (1991);

▶ Pope, J.G. [Rutgers U. professor of law], "Republican Moments: The Role of Direct Popular Power in the American Constitutional Order," 139 *U. Pa. L. Rev.* 287, 328 (1991);

▸ Kates, D.B. "The Second Amendment and the Ideology of Self-Protection." 9 *Const. Comm.* 87–104 (1992);

▸ Amar, A. [Southmayd professor of constitutional law at Yale] "The Bill of Rights and the Fourteenth Amendment," 101 *Yale L. J.* 1193–1284 at 1205–11, 1261–2 (1992);

▸ Bradley, G.V. [U. Il. professor of law], "The Bill of Rights and Originalism," *U. Illinois L. Rev.* 417, 434 (1992);

▸ Levin, S. "Grass Roots Voices: Local Action and National Military Policy," 40 *Buffalo L. Rev.* 321, 346-7 (1992);

▸ Aynes, R.L. [U. of Iowa professor of law], "On Misreading John Bingham and the Fourteenth Amendment," 101 *Yale L. J.* 57–104 at 84, 98 (1993);

▸ Yoo, J.S. [U. of CA-Berkeley professor of law], "Our Declaratory Ninth Amendment," 42 *Emory L. J.* 967 (1993);

▸ Malcolm, J.L. *To Keep and Bear Arms: The Origins of an Anglo-American Right* (Cambridge: Harvard U. Press; 1994);

▸ Cottrol, R.J. and Diamond, R.T. "'The Fifth Auxiliary Right'," 104 *Yale L. J.* 995-1026 (1994);

▸ Van Alstyne, W. [William & Thomas Perkins professor of constitutional law at Duke], "The Second Amendment and the Personal Right to Arms," 43 *Duke L. J.* 1236-1255 (1994);

▸ Vandercoy, D. [Valpariso U. professor of law], "The History of the Second Amendment," 28 *Valparaiso L. Rev.* 1006 (1994);

▸ Quinlan, M.J. [SIU-Carbondale law professor], "Is There a Neutral Justification for Refusing to Implement the Second Amendment or Is the Supreme Court Just 'Gun Shy,'" 22 *Capital U. L. Rev.* 641 (1995);

▸ Funk, T.M. "Is the True Meaning of the Second Amendment Really Such A Riddle?" 39 *Howard L. J.* 411 (1995);

▸ Reynolds, G.H. [U. TN professor of law] and Kates, D.B. "The Second Amendment and States' Rights: A Thought Experiment," 36 *WM. & M. L. R.* 1737–68 (1995);

▸ Funk, T.M. "Gun Control and Economic Discrimination: The Melting-Point Case-in-Point," 85 *J. Crim. & Criminol.* 764–789 (1995);

▸ Rabkin, J. [Cornell U. professor of political science], "Constitutional Firepower: New Light on the Meaning of the Second Amendment," 86 *J. Crim. L. & Criminol.* 231–246 (1995);

▸ Cottrol, R.J. and Diamond, R.T. "'Never Intended to Be Applied to the White Population': Firearms Regulation and Racial Disparity, The Redeemed South's Legacy to a National Jurisprudence?" 70 *Chicago-Kent L. Rev.* 1307 (1995);

▶ Johnson, N.J. [Fordham U. professor of law], "Shots Across No Man's Land: A Response to Handgun Control, Inc.'s Richard Aborn," 22 *Fordham Urban L. J.* 441–451 (1995);

▶ Reynolds, G.H. [U. TN professor of law], "A Critical Guide to the Second Amendment," 62 *Tenn. L. Rev.* 461–512 (1995);

▶ Barnett, R.E. [Boston University law professor] and Kates, D.B. "Under Fire: The New Consensus on the Second Amendment," 45 *Emory L. J.* 1139–1259 (1996);

▶ Larish, I.A. "Why Annie Can't Get a Gun: A Feminist Appraisal of the 2nd Am.," *U. Ill. Law F.* 467 (1996).

Notes

1. American Academy of Pediatrics, Policy Statement, *AAP News* 20–3 (January, 1992); Goldsmith, M.F., Epidemiologists Aim at New Target: Handgun Proliferation. *JAMA* 1989; 261: 675–6.
2. Kaplan, J. "The Wisdom of Gun Prohibition." *Annals Amer Acad Pol & Soc Sci* 1981; 455: 11–23; Kates, "Bigotry, Symbolism, and Ideology in the Battle Over Gun Control," *Pub Int L Rev* 1992; 31–46; Kessler, "Enforcement Problems of Gun Control: A Victimless Crimes Analysis," *Crim. L. Bull.* 1980; 16: 131–49; Moore, M., "The Bird in Hand: A Feasible Strategy for Gun Control, *J. Policy Admin. & Mngmt.* 1983; 2: 185–8 at p. 187–8; Wright, J.D. "Guns and Crime," in Sheley, J.E. *Criminology* (1991; Belmont, CA Wadsworth) 441–457.
3. Quotation from the National Coalition to Ban Handguns' undated, unpaginated pamphlet "A Shooting Gallery Called America," emphasis in original. See also Lindsay, J. "The Case for Federal Firearms Control," 1973; NY: New York City gov't. publication at p. 22; McNamara, J.D. *Safe and Sane* (1984; NY: Perigree) 59–75; Ruben, E.R., Leeper, J.D. "Homicide in Five Southern States: A Ffirearms Phenomenon," *Southern Medical Journal* 1981; 74: 272–277 at p. 276; Kairys, D. A. "Carnage in the Name of Freedom," *Philadelphia Inquirer,* (Guest Editorial) September 12, 1988; American Academy of Pediatrics, Policy Statement, *AAP News* 20-3 (January, 1992).
4. A large number of studies to this effect are cited in Don B. Kates, Henry E. Schaffer, et al., "Guns and Public Health: Epidemic of Violence or Pandemic of Propaganda," 62 *Tenn. L. Rev.* 513, 579*ff.* (1995); Chicago Police Department, Murder Analysis, mimeo, volumes for the years 1966, 1967, 1968, 1969, 1970, 1971, 1972, 1973, 1974, 1975, 1976 Chicago city publication. See also Hearings on S. 3691 etc. before the Sub-Committee to Investigate Juvenile Delinquency of the U.S. Senate Committee on the Judiciary, 19th Congress Second Session (1968; US GPO) Exhibit 7, pp. 75–6; D. Mulvihill, et al. *Crimes of Violence: Report of the Task Force on Individual Acts of Violence* (1969; Washington, D.C., US GPO), table at 532; *FBI Uniform Crime Reports* (1971; Washington, US GPO) at 38; R. Narloch, "Criminal Homicide in California" (1973; Sacramento: Cal Bur of Crim Stats) at 55–6; A. Swersey and E. Enloe, *Homicide in Harlem* (1975; NY: Rand) at 17ff; F.B.I. *Uniform Crime Reports* (1975; Washington, US GPO) at 42ff; Kleck, G. & Bordua, D.J. "The Factual Foundation for Certain Key Assumptions of Gun Control," *Law & Policy Q.* 1983; 5: 271–98 at 291–4; Howard, M. "Hus-

band-wife homicide: An essay from a family law perspective," *Law & Contemp Prob.* 1986; 49: 63–88 at 69-74; Straus, M.A. "Domestic Violence and Homicide Antecedents," *Bul NY Acad Med* 1986; 62: 446–465 at 454 and 457; Kleck, G. "Policy Lessons from Recent Gun Control Research," *Law & Contemp. Prob.* 1986; 49: 35–59 at 40-41; Kates, D. "The Value of Civilian Handgun Possession as a Deterrent to Crime or a Defense Against Crime," *Am J. Crim. L.* 1991; 18: 113–167 at 127-8; Kates, D. "The Law-abiding Gun Owner as Domestic and Acquaintance Murderer," in Nisbet, L. *The Gun Control Debate* (1990; Buffalo: Prometheus) 270–4; Wright, J.D. "Guns and Crime," in Sheley, J.E. *Criminology* (1991; Belmont, CA: Wadsworth) 441–457.

5.   Cook, P. "The Role of Firearms in Violent Crime: An Interpretative Review of the Literature," in Wolfgang, M. & Weiler, N. *Criminal Violence* (1982; London: Sage) 236–91 at 269; Kleck, G. *Point Blank: Guns and Violence In America* (1986; NY; Aldine) ch. 7; Lane, R. "On the Social Meaning of Homicide Trends in America," in Gurr, T.R., *Violence in America* (1989; London: Sage) 55–79 at 59 (v. 1); Kates, D., "Gun Accidents," in Nisbet, L. *The Gun Control Debate* (1990; Buffalo: Prometheus) 300–3.

6.   J. Wright, P. Rossi, *Armed and Dangerous: A Survey of Felons and Their Firearms* (1986; NY: Aldine) at 65–77.

7.   See Wright, J.D., "Guns and Crime," in Sheley, op. cit.

8.   FBI Uniform Crime Reports 1995, p. 19.

9.   Kates, D.B., Schaffer, E., et al.,"Guns and Public Health: Epidemic of Violence or Pandemic of Propaganda," 62 *Tennessee Law Review,* 513–596 (1995) at 582–83.

10. Straus, M.A. "Domestic Violence and Homicide Antecedents," *Bul NY Acad Med* 1986; 62: 446–465 at 454 and 457.

11. Kates, D.B. "Firearms and Violence: Old Premises and Current Evidence," in Gurr, T.R., *Violence in America* (1989; London: Sage) 197–215 (v. 1) at 210–11; Bendis, P. & Balkin, S. "A Look at Gun Control Enforcement," *J. Police Sci. & Admin.* 1979; 7: 439–78.

12. Christoffel, K.K., Christoffel, T. "Handguns: Risks versus Benefits," *Pediatrics* 1986; 77: 782-3; Baker, S. "Without Guns, Do People Kill People?" *Am. J. Pub. Health* 1985; 75:587.

13. Kleck, G. "Handgun-Only Gun Control: A Policy Disaster in the Making," in Kates, D. *Firearms and Violence: Issues of Regulation* (1984; Cambridge: Ballinger) 186–94; Fackler, M.L. "Physics of Missile Injuries," in McSwain (Jr.) N. & Kerstein, M. (eds.) *Evaluation and Management of Trauma* (1987; Norwalk, CO; Appleton-Century-Crofts).

14. Taylor, "Gunshot Wounds of the Abdomen," *Annals of Surgery* 1973; 177: 174–5.

15. Kleck, G. "Handgun-Only Control: A Policy Disaster in the Making," in D. Kates (ed.) *Firearms and Violence* (Cambridge, Ballinger, 1984) p. 189.]

16. J. Wright, P. Rossi, *Armed and Dangerous: A Survey of Felons and Their Firearms* (1986; NY: Aldine) at 221, table 11.3.

17. Lizotte, "The Costs of Using Gun Control to Reduce Homicide," *Bul N.Y. Acad Med* 1986; 62: 539–

18. J. Wright, P. Rossi, K. Daly, *Under the Gun: Weapons, Crime and Violence in the United Sstates* (1983; N.Y.: Aldine) at 322–3.

19. Kleck, G. *Point Blank: Guns and Violence in America* (1991; NY; Aldine) ch. 5; Murray, D.R. "Handguns, Gun Control Law and Firearm Violence," *Soc Prob* 1975; 23: 81-92; Bordua, D.J. and Lizotte A.J. "Patterns of Legal Firearms Ownership: A Cultural and Situational Analysis of Illinois Counties," *Law & Policy Q* 1979; 1: 147–75; Cook, P. "The Effect of Gun Availability on Robbery and Robbery Murder," in Haverman, R. & Zellner, B.B. *Policy Studies Review Annual* (1979; London: Sage) 743–81; Lizotte A.J. and Bordua, D.J. "Firearms Ownership for Sport and Protection: Two Divergent Models," *Am Soc Rev* 1980; 45: 229–44; Kleck, G. "The Relationship Between Gun Ownership Levels and Rates of Violence in the United States," in D. Kates (ed.) *Firearms and Violence* (1984; Cambridge: Ballantine) 99–133; Magaddino, J.P. and Medoff, M.H." An Empirical Analysis of Federal and State Firearm Control Laws," in Kates, D. *Firearms and Violence: Issues of Regulation* (1984; Cambridge: Ballinger) 101–12; McDowall, D. "Gun Availability and Robbery Rates: A Panel Study of Large U.S. Cities (1974–1978)," *Law & Policy Q* 1986; 8: 135-48; Bordua, D.J. "Firearms Ownership and Violent Crime: A Comparison of Illinois Counties," 156–88 in Byrne, J.M. and Sampson, R.J. (ed.) *The Social Ecology of Crime* (1986; NY: Springer-Verlag) 156–88; Eskridge, C.W. "Zero-Order Inverse Correlations Between Crimes of Violence and Hunting Licenses in the United States," *Soc Sci Res* 1986; 71:55–7.

20. See discussion and table in Gary Kleck & Britt Patterson, "The Impact of Gun Control and Gun Ownership Levels on City Violence Rates," 9 *J. Quant. Crimin.* 249–87 (1993) at 253–55.

21. John R. Lott, Jr. & David B.M. Mustard, "Right-to-Carry Concealed Handguns and the Importance of Deterrence," paper presented at the 1996 American Law & Economics Assoc. meetings — forthcoming in the Journal of Legal Studies.

22. John R. Lott, Jr. and David B. Mustard, "Crime, Deterence, and the Right-to-Carry Concealed Handguns," 26 *Journal of Legal Studies* 1–68 (1997).

23. Ibid.

24. See generally Clayton E. Cramer & David B. Kopel, "'*Shall* Issue': The New Wave of Concealed Handgun Permit Laws," 62 *Tenn. L. Rev.* 679 (1995). We are, however, informed by Kopel that a homicide outside the state was committed by a homeless person who had a Florida carry license.

25. Kopel, D.B. *The Samurai, the Mountie, and the Cowboy: Should America Adopt the Gun Control of Other Democracies* (1992: Buffalo; Prometheus—in press); Kates, D., "Comparisons Among Nations And Over Time," in Nisbet, L. *The Gun Control Debate* (1990; Buffalo: Prometheus) 187–94; Bruce-Briggs, B. "The Great American Gun War," *The Public Interest* 1976; 45: 37–62 at 52; Castberg, A.D. *Japanese Criminal Justice* (1990; NY: Praeger) at p. 126–7; Greenwood, C. *Firearms Control: A Study of Firearms Control and Armed Crime in England and Wales,* London: Routledge, Kegan Paul 1972; Wright, J.D. "Guns and Crime," in Sheley, JE. *Criminology* (1991; Belmont, CA Wadsworth) 441–457 at 449–50.

26. Gurr, T.R. "Historical Trends in Violent Crime: A Critical Review of the Evidence," in *Annual Review of Crime and Justice,* vol. 3 (Chicago: U Chi Press, 1981); Wright, J.D. "Guns and Crime," in Sheley, JE. *Criminology* (1991; Belmont, CA: Wadsworth) 441–457 at 450.

27. Compare the 1993 U.S. homicide rate of 9.5 per 100,000 {U.S. Federal Bureau of Investigation. *Crime in the United States 1994* (Uniform Crime Reports). Washington, DC: U.S. Government Printing Office} to the Russian rate of 19.7 {*The Economist* July 9, 1994: "Russia's Mafia: More Crime than Punishment"}. The former U.S.S.R.-controlled nation of Estonia, with similaly stringent gun bans, had a 1993 homicide rate of 17 per 100,000 population. {A.P. dispatch, 4/1/94: "Baltics Take Up Arms."} It bears emphasis that international homicide comparisons are inherently problematic due to data lacunae and definitional problems.

28. Shetky, D.H. "Children and Handguns: A Public Health Concern," 1985, *Am. J. Dis. Child.* 139: 229–231.

29. For discussion of Swiss law and policy see: David B. Kopel, "Peril or Protection? The Risks and Benefits of Handgun Prohibition," 12 *St. L. U. Public L. Rev.* 285, 299 (1993) and David B. Kopel, *The Samurai, the Mountie, and the Cowboy: Should America Adopt the Gun Control of Other Democracies?* ch. 8 (Buffalo: Prometheus 1992). For Israeli law and policy see Don B. Kates & Daniel D. Polsby, "Of Genocide and Disarmament," 86 *J. Crim. L. & Criminol.* 247, 252 (1995).

30. Ibid.

31. Sloan, J.H., Kellermann A.L., Reay, D.T., et al. "Handgun Regulations, Crime, Assault and Homicide: A Tale of Two Cities," *N Engl*

J Med 1988; 319: 1256–62; Houser, H.B., "Invited Commentary: Common Wisdom and Plain Truth.," *Am J Epidemiol* 1991; 134: 1261–3.

32. Mundt, R.J. "Gun Control and Rates Of Firearms Violence in Canada and the United States," 1990, Jan: *Can J Crim* 137–54; Mauser, G.A. & R. Holmes, "Evaluating the 1977 Canadian Firearms Control Legislation: An Econometric Approach," 16 *Evaluation Report* 603 (1992); see also note 34.

33. Comments made from the floor by Prof. Philip C. Stenning at the 1989 annual meeting of the Law & Society Ass'n., Berkeley, CA.

34. Centerwall, B.S. "Homicide and the Prevalence of Handguns: Canada and the United States, 1976 to 1980," *Am J. Epidemiol* 1991; 134: 1245–1260.

35. Kassirer, J.P. "Firearms and the Killing Threshold," *N Eng J Med;* 1991; 325: 1647–9; Kellermann, A.L., Lee, R.K., Mercy, J.A. et al. "The Epidemiologic Basis for the Prevention of Firearm Injuries," *Annual Review of Public Health* 1991; 12: 17–40; Webster, D.W., Chaulk, C.P., Teret, S.P. et al "Reducing Firearm Injuries," Issues in *Science and Technology*, Spring, 1991; Wintemute, G.J., "Firearms as a Cause of Death in the United States, 1920-82." J of Trauma 1987; 27: 532–536.

36. Prof. Stephen Teret quoted in Goldsmith, M.F "Epidemiologists Aim at New Target: Handgun Proliferation," *JAMA* 1989; 261: 675–6. Baker, S.P. "Firearm Mortality in the United States," a presentation to the 1984 annual meeting of the American Public Health Association, citing Baker, S.P., O'Neill, B. and Karpf, R. *The Injury Fact Book* (1983; Lexington, MA: Lexington).

37. Richard Aborn, "The Battle over the Brady Bill and the Future of Gun Control," 22 *Fordham Urb. L.J.* 417 (1995) (president of Handgun Control, Inc.); Carl Bogus, "Race, Riots and Guns," 66 *U.S.C. L. Rev.* 1365 (1993) (by member of the board of the Center to Prevent Handgun Violence), Ehrman and Henigan, "The Second Amendment in the 20th Century: Have You Seen Your Militia Lately", 15 *U. Dayton L. Rev.* 5 (1989) and Henigan, "Arms, Anarchy and the Second Amendment," 26 *Valparaiso U. L. Rev.* 107 (1991)—both written by general counsel of Handgun Control, Inc.; Spannaus, "State Firearms Regulation and the Second Amendment," 6 *Hamline L. R.* 383 (1983) (article by anti-gun politician); Fields, "Guns, Crime and the Negligent Gun Owner," 10 *N. KY. L. R.* 141 (1982) (article by non-lawyer lobbyist for the National Coalition to Ban Handguns).

38. *Atlantic Monthly*, June, 1994, p. 13, emphasis in original.

39. William Van Alstyne, William & Thomas Perkins professor of constitutional law at Duke, "The Second Amendment and the Per-

sonal Right to Arms," 43 *Duke L. J.* 1236–1255 (1994); Akhil Amar, Southmayd professor of constitutional law at Yale, "The Bill of Rights and the Fourteenth Amendment," 101 *Yale L. J.* 1193–1284 at 1205–11, 1261–2 (1992) and "The Bill of Rights as a Constitution," 100 *Yale L. J.* 1131, 1164ff. (1990); and Sanford Levinson [St. John Garwood professor of constitutional law at the University of Texas], "The Embarrassing Second Amendment," *Yale L. J.* 1989; 99: 637–659.

40. Kates, D.B. "The Second Amendment: A Dialogue," *Law & Contemp. Probs.* 1986; 49: 143–150; Halbrook, S.P., "What the Framers Intended: A Linguistic Analysis of the Right to 'Bear Arms,'" *Law & Contemp. Probs.* 1986; 49: 151–162.

41. *United States v. Miller*, 307 U.S. 174 (1939).

42. *United States v. Verdugo-Urquidez*, 110 S.Ct. 1056 (1990).

43. Wright, J.D., Rossi P.H., *Weapons, Crime and Violence in America: Executive Summary* (1981; Washington, D.C., US GPO).

44. Wright, J.D., Rossi, P.H., Daly, K. *Under the Gun: Weapons, Crime and Violence in the United States* (1983; NY: Aldine).

45. Wright, J.D. "Second Thoughts About Gun Control," *The Public Interest.* 1988; 91: 23–39.

PART II

MEDIA BIAS
&
PUBLIC OPINION

Chapter 3

Media Bias: Gun Control, Assault Weapons, Cop-Killer Bullets, the Goetz Case, and Other Alarms in the Night*

Gary Kleck

Most Americans receive the bulk of their information about crime and violence through the mass media rather than from direct personal experience. Does this information, as it pertains to guns and violence, neutrally reflect reality, or has it been shaped or managed to encourage some conclusions and discourage others? The premise of this chapter is that the nation's most important news sources do indeed shape information on gun issues in a way that encourages pro-control conclusions. The purpose of this chapter is to identify and illustrate the forms that this information shaping can take.

This assertion should not be viewed as being part of a broad accusation of liberal bias in the press or mass media generally. Survey evidence does indicate that reporters and editors are somewhat more liberal than the general public (*Los Angeles Times*

*Original paper presented at the annual meetings of the American Society of Criminology, San Francisco, November 20–23, 1991.

8-11-85), but newspapers, magazines, and television and radio stations and networks are owned by wealthy businessmen, and most wealthy businessmen are not liberals. It seems unlikely that these wealthy owners would consistently permit their property to be used to promote a liberal ideology they personally oppose.

Instead of pro-control bias being but one part of a general liberal bias on the part of news workers, bias on the gun issue is a thing apart, whose persistence may be possible partly because it does not conflict with any strongly held elements of the ideology of the owners of media corporations. Consequently, the gun issue may provide a fairly rare situation where purportedly "liberal" ideas can be repeatedly favored by reporters without provoking intervention from management.

It should also be stressed that it is not being argued that there is a consciously calculated or coordinated campaign to lie about or distort the gun issue. Rather, a variety of information management techniques may be used to produce impressions that news managers honestly believe to be accurate. It is thus not the sincerity of news workers that is in question. The content of news stories is what is at issue in this chapter, not the intentions of the stories' authors. Most news people probably sincerely believe that guns are a major cause of the nation's high rates of violence and that there would be less violence if there were more gun control and fewer guns. Therefore, to be pro-control or anti-gun is merely to be in accord with the facts, "biased" only in favor of the truth. From this viewpoint, news sources are merely accurately informing the public of a genuinely one-sided issue rather than slanting the news to create a one-sided picture of what is actually a multi-sided issue.

There are occasional outrageous and obvious "smoking gun" examples of anti-gun/pro-control bias, but these are exceptions to the general rule of more subtle information manipulation. For example, there was the presumably unusual case of a newspaper firing a staff writer for publicly expressing support for positions taken by the National Rifle Association (*Brown Deer [Wisconsin] Herald* 3-23-89). Sophisticated information management does not rely primarily on lies or crude censorship but rather on less obviously illegitimate or sloppy techniques.

First and foremost, news stories can shape the audience's views through the omission of accurate, relevant information that would tend to undercut the theme of the story. Biased exclusion of information is both more important and more effective in shaping public opinion than inclusion of inaccurate information. Lies do not further the interests of propagandists in a democracy in the long run, because they are vulnerable to exposure and threaten the future credibility (and possibly the profits) of the news outlet. Information that contradicts a news story's thesis can be excluded from a story either by a reporter or by an editor or producer. All news stories necessarily must exclude information in the interests of brevity, but exclusions are biased when they are patterned to consistently weed out information contradicting a theme or message favored by the producers of the news. The practice is especially pernicious because, unlike inaccurate or biased statements that are included in a story, excluded facts are generally invisible to the ordinary reader or viewer. Further, there rarely can be any "smoking gun" proving propagandistic intent because, ordinarily, no one could prove that a reporter was aware of the information in the first place.

Second, in deciding which bits of information to include, and, if included in the story, whether to treat information as factual, different levels of skepticism, and different standards for assessing importance, can be applied to information supporting the preferred view and to information contradicting it. Information contrary to the preferred view can be subjected to intense and searching scrutiny, or downplayed as unimportant or self-serving, while information supporting the preferred view is spared any comparable scrutiny and is presented to the audience without comment, or even with comments suggesting the information is credible and of great importance.

Third, differing amounts of "play" can be given to stories with pro- or anti-control implications. Stories with implications supporting the preferred view can be given coverage that is prominent (front page vs. inside page), extended (15 column inches vs. six), and prolonged (coverage on multiple days rather than just one), whereas stories with contrary implications can be given little play or ignored altogether.

Fourth, pro-control editorial positions prevail among the nation's major daily press outlets, and such positions can lend credibility and legitimacy to a pro-control stance as the preferred position of responsible and educated persons. (See Cohen and

Young 1981; Bagdikian 1987; Herman and Chomsky 1988 for general discussions of media influence on public opinion).

Sins of Omission — Exclusion Bias

Examples of biased exclusion of information are not hard to find in news stories on guns. It should be stressed that in each of the following examples, the omitted information was critical to judging the main theme of the story and could have been included in the story in a single sentence. Therefore, it cannot be argued that the omissions were due to either the information being irrelevant or unimportant or to space limitations making it impossible to include the information.

The major gun-related story of 1989–1991 was the alleged proliferation and criminal use of so-called "assault rifles" (ARs) or, more broadly, "assault weapons" (AWs), a vague category that encompassed handguns and shotguns as well as rifles. AWs are semi-automatic firearms with a "military-style" appearance. AWs were presented in the press as especially threatening to public safety mainly because they allegedly (1) were more lethal than their ordinary counterparts (especially ARs compared with civilian rifles), (2) had rapid rates of fire, and (3) had large ammunition capacities. The first claim was false, the second either false or barely true to a trivial degree, whereas the third was sometimes true but of limited significance for most incidents of violence, which rarely involve large numbers of rounds fired (Kleck 1991, pp. 70–82). News stories that addressed the rate-of-fire issue commonly hinted or stated that AWs either fired as rapidly as machine guns or that they might as well do so as they could easily be converted to fire like machine guns (e.g. *Newsweek* 10-14-85, pp. 48–9). The convertability claim was inaccurate and was apparently repeated by news sources simply because they did not, as the *New York Times* eventually did (4-3-89), check with the relevant authorities to see if it was true (but see also the contradictory editorial in the *New York Times*, 8-2-88). The implication that AWs could fire like machine guns was hinted at through descriptions of shootings in which the gunman allegedly "sprayed" an area with bullets from his AW. Without making the claim explicit, this wording strongly hinted that ARs were capable of fully automatic fire, that is, sending out a virtually continuous stream of bullets as long as the trigger was held down and ammunition remained. In fact, AWs can fire only in semi-automatic mode, that is, one shot is fired for each trigger pull, the same as is done with ordinary revolvers (Kleck 1991). Television network news programs also hinted at the same idea by overlaying reporters speaking about semiautomatic AWs with film of fully automatic weapons being shown on the screen.

Failing to make this distinction explicit could leave the average reader or viewer with the erroneous impression that AWs were machine guns, and that therefore machine guns were being legally sold without significant restrictions. In 1989, *most* news stories about AWs omitted this critical piece of information. A content analysis of a random national sample of 115 newspaper stories on guns and gun control indicated that nearly 80 percent of the 65 stories on ARs failed to distinguish fully automatic fire from semi-automatic fire, or to in any way indicate that ARs could not fire like machine guns (Etten 1991).

In 1985 and 1986, one of the major gun-related stories concerned armor-piercing ammunition. Numerous examples of biased exclusion of relevant information can be found in stories on these "cop-killer" bullets, projectiles capable of penetrating the body armor worn by police officers. Two facts were consistently omitted from stories on this issue: (1) supporters of restrictions had never documented a single case in which this ammunition actually killed a police officer by penetrating his body armor, and (2) many common types of rifle ammunition had always been capable of penetrating police body armor and had been commonly available for years. Leaving aside whether restrictions on this ammunition were advisable, these facts were obviously relevant to informed public debate about the issue, yet somehow they did not make it into print in the nation's leading newspapers (e.g. *New York Times* 7-20-85, p. 22; 9-27-85, p. A30; 3-7-86, p. A15; *Chicago Tribune* 3-7-86, p. 1–3; *Los Angeles Times* 12-19-85, p. II–6; 3-7-86, p. I–15; 8-15-86, p. I–2; 8-29-86, p. I–4). There was at least one exception—the *Los Angeles Times* did mention, in one article, that no police officer had ever been killed by the bullets. The diligent reader could find it on page 20, in the middle of the 12th paragraph of a 14-paragraph story (*Los Angeles Times* 8-29-86). Marginalizing the information in this way is only slightly better than omitting it altogether. Can it seriously be argued that it is not relevant and important that the "cop-killer" bullet had never killed a cop?

At the very least, the repeated use of an inflammatory and inaccurate term like "cop-killer bullet" was dubious journalistic practice. News sources uncritically accepted a label invented by pro-control activists for propaganda purposes. One presumed justification would be that this term had become the commonly used label for the ammunition in question. This is something of a circular justification as it became the commonly used term at least partly because news workers had chosen to accept and disseminate it. Although the ammunition certainly is capable of killing a police officer (or civilian for that matter), the term nevertheless is not very descriptive because the same is also true of any other firearms ammunition. The desire for a pithy, hard-hitting label apparently won out over a commitment to accuracy.

One of the difficulties in documenting specific instances of "sins of omission" is that it is usually impossible to be sure that the reporter knew about the information; therefore, one cannot be certain that the information had been deliberately excluded. Usually, one can only be sure that the reporter either did not make an effort to acquire the information *or* someone excluded it. There are, however, occasional exceptions.

I have given hundreds of interviews about gun issues, sometimes talking for as long as two hours at a time with reporters. Occasionally I have read the stories that print reporters prepared on the basis of interviews with me and others. It was often apparent that reporters had been assigned a story with a preset theme and charged with gathering relevant information. The nature of the theme sometimes became apparent during the course of an interview, and when it was inconsistent with what I knew, I would convey the contrary information to the reporter. Again and again I have had the experience of providing information that flatly contradicted a pro-control theme of the story as finally published, yet the contradictory information was neither rebutted nor mentioned in the story. Space (or time) limitations can account for omission of information that is marginal or irrelevant to a story, or whose accuracy has been put in doubt, but it cannot account for exclusion of unrebutted information that directly contradicts the principal claims or themes of the story.

The following examples are illustrative. On June 14, 1989, I

was interviewed by a reporter from *USA Today*. The story concerned child gun accidents and had been stimulated by five gun
accidents involving children in Florida, all occurring within a
week of each other. I told the reporter that unconnected accidents,
and rare events in general, occasionally cluster together in time,
that this is bound to happen somewhere, sometime, and that such
short-term clusterings were not a sound basis for concluding that
there was a significant trend developing. I then told her what the
actual national trends had been in recent years — the number of
fatal gun accidents involving children (under age 10) had dropped
sharply, from 227 in 1974 to about 92 in 1987, the latest year for
which data were available. (The same was true of accidents in all
age groups.) When the story appeared the next day (*USA Today*
6-15-89, p. 3A), it was a fairly long article (or as long as they get in
USA Today — 50 square inches including photo and charts), but
evidently not long enough to have room for either these facts or
any others I provided the reporter. The theme of the article was
the supposedly large number of recent child gun accidents, the
article's headline being "Spate of shootings spurs Florida to act."
The article had room for a statistic provided by a pro-control
advocacy group, to the effect that gunshot wounds to children had
increased by 300 percent (!) since 1986, in certain unspecified
"large urban areas." It did not, however, have room for the only
relevant national data available to the reporters and editors that
bore directly on the frequency of child gun accidents, data that
indicated that fatal gun accidents were sharply declining and had
been doing so for many years.

One might be tempted to dismiss this sort of selectivity on
this issue as characteristic only of a news outlet with a less-than-
lofty journalistic reputation. However, CBS News, the organization that Edward R. Murrow built, broadcast a story with the exact
same misleading theme, presented even more bluntly. On the CBS
evening news for October 11, 1989, anchorman Dan Rather read a
story on child gun accidents, describing the problem as "an epidemic that shows every sign of worsening." In fact, the only data
reliable for judging national trends in such accidents, mortality
statistics, had long indicated precisely the opposite. However, in
this case it is impossible to know whether CBS knew about, or
made any effort to discover, these figures.

In December of 1989 I gave an interview lasting about an hour to a reporter from the National Public Radio (NPR) affiliate in St. Paul, Minnesota. The interview was done as part of national effort by NPR affiliates to explore the gun issue, and the resulting reports were distributed to NPR member stations. The bulk of my remarks concerned the considerable evidence indicating the utility of guns for self-defense, as well as evidence indicating that most existing gun laws appear to be ineffective in reducing violence. I also very briefly (for a minute or two) noted the risks of keeping guns for defense in homes with children, and remarked that most crime victimizations occurred in circumstances that do not permit effective defensive use of a gun. When WETA-FM, the NPR affiliate in Washington, D.C., broadcast an excerpt of about 30 seconds from my interview, it was entirely taken from my brief remarks noting the limits and risks of keeping guns for self-defense. None of my extensive (and unrebutted) remarks noting the defensive effectiveness of guns were included. Further, the brief excerpts were placed in a section of the broadcast devoted to arguing a proposition—that keeping a gun for defensive purposes was irrational—which was clearly contradicted by both the bulk of my remarks and by the overwhelming weight of scholarly evidence (broadcast 12-17-89, as part of the "All Things Considered" program; compare with Kleck 1991, Chapter 4).

In June of 1989 I gave a series of interviews lasting over two hours to a reporter from *Time* magazine, in which I noted, among other things, that gun violence had been decreasing since the early 1980s. The magazine's story briefly noted, in the text, the decrease in gun deaths in the 1980s (p. 31), but this was undercut by their twice referring in large type to the "epidemic" of gun violence (pp. 3, 30). If "epidemic" does not mean an increasing or spreading problem, exactly what does it mean?

One section of this article pertained to suicides. Without mentioning any evidence rebutting that which I had discussed with the reporter, the article asserted that "most people who attempt to kill themselves do not really wish to die." I had told the reporter that although this claim was true of suicide attempters in general, there was good reason to believe it was *not* true of those who use guns. The article noted that only 1 in 20 suicide attempts results in death, whereas, according to one study, 92 percent of gun attempts are fatal. I had told the reporter that the fatality rate in suicide attempts with guns was indeed very high but that the rate was nearly as high in attempts using such likely substitutes for shooting as hanging, carbon monoxide poisoning, and drowning.

The article described a gun suicide in which the absence of a gun allegedly could have made a difference as to whether the attempter eventually survived. I had told the reporter that one reason few suicides could be prevented by removing guns was that the people who use guns in suicide typically have a more serious and persistent desire to kill themselves than suicide attempters using other methods. If denied guns, some or all of this group would substitute other methods and kill themselves anyway. The case the article cited seemed to provide the perfect illustration of my point, since the woman had suffered from "recurring depression" and had made at least three suicide attempts. Yet the article implied that the woman died only because she had found a "swift and certain" method of suicide and that her depression could have been cured before the next attempt had she not obtained a gun (*Time* 7-17-89, pp. 30–61).

In this 31-page article, as finally published, no experts on gun violence were quoted or explicitly cited, with the exception of a single remark by James Wright (p. 61). I have no idea how many other experts were consulted and provided *Time* reporters with information contrary to their preferred views, and I can only be sure that they excluded the information I provided. Professor Wright, however, was interviewed and was quoted in a context that inverted his remarks' original meaning. Wright was quoted as saying that "everyone knows that if you put a loaded .38 in your ear and pull the trigger, you won't survive." His intended meaning was that ambiguously motivated people intending only to make a "cry for help" do not make such attempts with guns. Only people who truly want to die use guns to attempt suicide, and these highly motivated persons would just use other means to kill themselves if guns were not available. Professor Wright has confirmed to me in a letter that this was indeed his meaning (Wright 1991a; see also Wright 1991b, p. 446 for his published views on this point). However, the remark was quoted in a context that suggested precisely the opposite, that gun victims *would* have survived had guns not been available, because guns are a uniquely lethal method of suicide.

This story illustrates another noteworthy pattern. Recent news stories that give very extended coverage of gun issues (e.g., feature-length newspaper or magazine stories or hour-long broadcast stories) usually make virtually no use of expert commentary. This raises the possibility that reporters did seek out expert information but could not find any acknowledged experts who would confirm the preset themes of the story. By defining the experts' unsupportive remarks as irrelevant or unimportant, reporters would be able to exclude them from the final story on grounds the reporters considered to be legitimate. This must necessarily remain a speculation, however, because news stories never report which experts were consulted but ignored.

A Speculation About How Exclusion Bias Works

Reporters and editors do not decide to exclude certain pieces of information from stories because they know them to be false but rather because they consider them to be suspect, trivial, or irrelevant to their stories. They are especially likely to arrive at such an assessment, however, when the data do not fit into their general worldview as it pertains to guns and gun control. Such information does not seem to jive with the rest of the information in their possession, leading to the suspicion on the reporter's part that the information may be inaccurate or tainted by the source's personal biases. The information is suspect because it deviates from the accepted orthodoxy, even if the reporter does not know of any solid facts that directly contradict the suspect claims.

Further, since the suspect information would be hard to integrate with the rest of the information in their story, the easiest way for the reporter to handle such anomalous data is simply to drop them from the story, a decision that also comports nicely with the general pressure to conserve print space or air time. This sort of decision to exclude can be done in good faith, for who can criticize excluding suspect information?

This process largely works on an individual, ad hoc basis, reporter by reporter, and story by story. However, if reporters for the major national news outlets generally share the same worldview on guns and gun control, they will also tend to reject the same kinds of troublesome information, without any coordinated conspiracy being needed to achieve this result. The result, nevertheless, is exactly the same as it would be if there *were* a calculated conspiracy.

Unfortunately, this phenomenon sets up a vicious circle. Because reporters are themselves consumers of news, they read other reporters' stories on guns, which, of course, excluded the same sorts of suspect information as their own stories did. This reinforces their skewed worldview, which then encourages their subsequent decisions to exclude the anomalous information.

Unbalanced Skepticism Applied to Pro and Con Information

Media bias often results from what might be termed "sloppiness in the service of bias." Because the people who produce and manage the news are operating under deadlines, and under limits on print space, air time, and resources of all kinds, a certain amount of sloppiness and imperfection in news coverage is unavoidable. Therefore, inevitable there are limits to the thoroughness with which reporters can evaluate debatable claims. However, it is illegitimate bias when reporters selectively direct their reportorial skepticism predominantly toward those advocating ideas with which they disagree, and devote the bulk of their limited resources to debunking such positions, while directing little skepticism at those who espouse more congenial views, and devoting little or no time to checking out the factual basis for those views.

Sloppiness in checking out technical claims made about guns is a chronic problem. Consider the case of a newspaper that published a mislabeled photograph to support their claim that a particular "assault rifle" was an unusually powerful and lethal rifle. On January 23, 1989, the *Los Angeles Herald-Examiner* (pp. A-1, A-6, ff.) printed a news story that focused on the "AK-47" (actually a semi-automatic civilian adaptation of the AK-47), the type of gun used in the 1989 Stockton, California, schoolyard killing of five children. The story was accompanied by a photo showing a melon being blown apart by a bullet supposedly fired from the "AK-47." The text made a number of perfectly accurate comments about the high penetrating power of the ammunition used in this gun, although it failed to note other attributes of the ammunition that tended to make it *less* lethal than other rifle rounds (see Fackler et al. 1990).

Unfortunately, the shot that had so dramatically blown up the melon had not come from the "assault rifle" in question, or indeed from any kind of rifle. A member of the Los Angeles County Sheriff's Department had initially been asked by a reporter to fire an "AK-47" round through the melon, which he did, using the fully jacketed, military-style 7.62 x 39 mm. ammunition type used in the Stockton shootings. Because the ammunition in question does not in fact create an unusually large wound cavity (Fackler et al. 1990), it failed to blow up the melon, creating a small hole and merely cracking the melon instead. For comparative purposes, the deputy sheriff was also asked to fire a police handgun round (a 9 mm. 115 grain jacketed hollow point) from a Beretta Model 92 pistol, which he did, causing the melon to blow up (Van Horn 1989).

That the rifle ammunition in question does not blow up melons as portrayed was substantiated by tests conducted by *Gun Week*, a weekly firearms newspaper (5-5-89, p. 1), and later in an ABC-TV documentary ("Peter Jennings Reporting: Guns," broadcast 1-24-90). Consequently, it was evidently a photograph of the effects of the police handgun round that was published in the newspaper and described in the picture's caption as portraying "the power of an AK-47." Apparently, the photographer or an editor mislabeled the photo of the melon being blown up by the handgun round, identifying it instead as portraying the effects of an AK-47 round. The reporter present at the scene could not be sure whether this was what had happened (Askari 1989), and the photographer never returned my phone calls. The *Los Angeles Herald-Examiner* has since gone out of business.

After the *Herald-Examiner* published this story, local television stations, including the Los Angeles ABC affiliate, KABC-TV, broadcast filmed demonstrations showing melons being blown up, supposedly by an "AK-47." Finally, one year after the Stockton shooting, the ABC-TV network broadcast an accurate demonstration in which the "AK-47" round merely put a small split in a melon, while ordinary civilian hunting rifle ammunition caused one to explode ("Peter Jennings Reporting: Guns," broadcast 1-24-90).

The KABC broadcasts become more understandable in the

context of the station's editorial stance. Bill Press, News Commentator for KABC-TV, testified to the U.S. Senate that his station's reports on AWs stemmed from a conscious decision on the part of the station to influence the public: "We have involved the public in this issue through our daily commentary. We are working every day with the Los Angeles Police Department. Every time there is an incident using a semiautomatic rifle in the city of Los Angeles, we report it on the news and we ask people to write to the State legislature to ban these weapons" (U.S. Congressional Research Service 1992, pp. 38–39).

Numerous other allegations about a variety of guns and ammunition have been made in various news stories, could easily have been checked out, but were not. The following claims (stated or implied) all had clear pro-control (or anti-gun) implications, all were false, and all could have been disconfirmed with a single phone call: (1) AWs are readily convertible to fully automatic fire like a machine gun, (2) ARs are more lethal than ordinary civilian-style hunting rifles, (3) AWs are the preferred weapon of criminals in general, or of drug dealers or youth gangs in particular, (4) large numbers of police officers have been killed with AWs, and (5) large numbers of police officers have been killed with "cop-killer" bullets. (See Kleck 1991, chapter 3, for documentation of the assertion that these claims are all inaccurate.)

Amount of "Play" — Extent and Prominence of Coverage

Bias can also be evident in the amount of "play" gun stories are given depending on whether their implications are pro- or anti-control, that is, the amount of space or air time devoted to a story and the prominence given it—front page versus inside page, lead story in a broadcast, or a later one. Major victories for the anti-control forces are sometimes downplayed, whereas pro-control victories are given disproportionately prominent coverage. Trivial pro-control victories such as the banning of nonexistent "plastic" guns, outlawing of "cop killer" bullets, and temporary federal import bans on "assault rifles" have been given front-page treatment, whereas more far-reaching anti-control victories such as the passage of state preemption bills have been virtually ignored.

A state preemption measure establishes that only the state may regulate guns, wiping out local gun controls and preventing local governments from passing further restrictions. The significance of these measures derives partly from the fact that rather than merely eliminating just one form of control, they commonly void entire broad categories of controls, usually virtually all forms of gun control. Further, this does not affect just a single local jurisdiction but hundreds of local jurisdictions in a given state. Finally, typical preemption measures not only strike down existing controls but also make local enactment of future controls impossible. All this is of special significance in light of the fact that the nation's strongest gun controls have all been imposed by local governments (Kleck 1991, Chapter 8). The NRA and other anticontrol forces have gained state preemption laws in at least 34 states, with at least 23 being passed or strengthened in the period from 1982 to 1987 (*U.S. News and World Report,* 4-25-88; NRA 1987). These victories were largely ignored by the national news media, usually being covered only within each affected state.

In sharp contrast, a minor bill allowing a commission to ban certain types of cheap handguns, passed in Maryland in 1988, was given front-page coverage in papers across the nation. (The low frequency of involvement of cheap handguns in crime is documented in Kleck 1991, Chapter 3). To establish the national newsworthiness of what seemed to be, disregarding the amount of news coverage itself, a minor local story in Maryland, news sources falsely claimed that this was "the first state law to outlaw the cheap handguns called Saturday Night Specials" (e.g. *Chicago Sun Times,* 5-29-88; see also *Washington Post,* 4-12-88). In fact, at least four other states already had similar statutes on the books: Illinois, Hawaii, Minnesota, and South Carolina. The first three banned both sale and manufacture of the guns, and the last banned only sale. The Hawaii statute was even stronger than the Maryland measure, banning most possession of the guns as well as sale and manufacture (Hawaii 1980, pp. 70–71). One major newspaper even made this "first in the nation" claim while directly contradicting itself in another story on the same page, by the same author, noting the existence of these "similar statutes" (*Chicago Sun Times* 5-29-88)! The only novel element of the Maryland law was the technical details of how authorities would determine which handguns would be prohibited.

Editorial Stances and Other Newspaper Policies

According to historians Kennett and Anderson, "three quarters of the nation's newspapers, and most of the periodical press" support gun control (1975, p. 237). These authors described the media as "mostly unsympathetic" to the pro-gun forces, stating that, in the 1960s, "large urban dailies with mass circulation—*The New York Times, Washington Post, Los Angeles Times,* and *Christian Science Monitor*—issued continual calls for new and tougher laws. With few exceptions the popular magazines followed suit." They noted that the *Washington Post,* in what may be a record, once published pro-control editorials on the gun issue for 77 consecutive days (pp. 239, 312). Perhaps the *Post* had moderated their views by 1988 when the Maryland handgun referendum was voted on—they published strongly worded pro-referendum editorials for only nine consecutive days before the vote (*Washington Post* 10-30-88 to 11-7-88).

News organizations regularly insist on the independence of their news coverage and their editorial stances, but media scholar Ben Bagdikian has stated that "studies throughout the years have shown that any bias in the news tends to follow a paper's editorial opinions" (1987, p. 100). This claim received support regarding the gun control issue in Etten's (1991) study of daily newspaper stories—papers with pro-control editorial policies were more likely to show pro-control bias in their new stories.

The general public apparently is sensitive to a pro-control slant in news stories about gun control. In a 1985 national *Los Angeles Times* poll, people were asked how they thought their daily newspapers felt about stricter gun laws. Among those who thought they knew their paper's stance, 62 percent felt that stance was pro-control. Further, among those who thought they knew their paper's stance, most said they knew this because of the way their paper covered *news stories* on gun control rather than from editorials (DIALOG 1990). Apparently, bias in news coverage of gun issues is sufficiently obvious to convey newspapers' gun control preferences even to large numbers of ordinary readers. Media bias is not exclusively exercised in the newsroom. Advertising industry publications have reported that the advertising departments of national publications, including *Newsweek, Time,* the *Christian Science Monitor,* and *Reader's Digest* magazines, as well as the NBC and CBS television networks, have refused to accept paid advertisements from the National Rifle Association (*Adweek* 6-26-89, p. 4). Consequently, gun owner groups are often in the position of not being able to even *buy* the opportunity to counter the claims of the news media.

Other Forms of Bias

Anti-gun bias can take even more subtle, sometimes subliminal, forms. In recent years, local television stations have taken to displaying a stylized handgun "insert" or "super" to introduce crime stories, including those not involving handguns. This is done even though less than 1 percent of all crimes, and only 13 percent of violent crimes involve handguns (Rand 1994). Thus, "crime" and "handgun" are repeatedly paired in the minds of viewers, even though handguns are neither a predominant nor even a very common element of crime. A practice that reinforces an association between handguns and violence is not questioned, perhaps because the contribution of handguns to violence, and the high frequency of their use in violent acts, are taken for granted as unquestioned facts, fixed elements of the "consensual paradigm" under which news workers operate (Young 1981).

A Case Study – A CBS Television Documentary

Close examination of a particular case will illustrate some common forms of news media bias as they pertain to gun issues. On March 16, 1989, the CBS television network broadcast an episode of its "48 Hours" news magazine program titled "Armed and Deadly." The program's purported topic was "assault rifles," defined in the documentary as military-style semi-automatic rifles. However, the focus often wandered to both fully automatic machine guns and to the broader category of "assault weapons," which includes handguns and shotguns.

Although no written analysis can fully convey the emotional and visual impact of a television documentary, the following description covers in some detail all of the major segments of the program, in their original sequence. The subheadings of paragraphs convey what seemed to be the main theme of each segment.

I will usually refer to assertions being made by CBS, rather than by particular reporters, to emphasize that the documentary was a collaborative product. (All assertions about what is actually true about ARs and AWs are documented in Kleck 1991, chapter 3).

Vivid Images of "Assault Weapon" Violence. The documentary opened with dramatic footage of a trauma center helicopter flying a gunshot victim to a Washington, D.C. hospital. Viewers heard a medical technician speaking to hospital staff over the helicopter's radio, saying the victim was shot five times with a "high caliber automatic pistol." As it turned out, this was inaccurate; the weapon was evidently an ordinary nine millimeter (9 mm.) semi-automatic pistol, that is, one that is neither automatic in fire nor large in caliber. Thus, in a documentary supposedly focusing on "assault rifles," the opening footage did not even pertain to a recent "assault rifle" killing, almost certainly because such events are so rare in any one city, even one as large as Washington, that CBS would have had to wait for months before they could have gotten footage on such a crime.

Perhaps to establish the relevance of footage on a handgun killing, rather than an "assault rifle" killing, a District of Columbia homicide detective was filmed at the hospital claiming that a 9 mm. semi-automatic pistol is "just as dangerous as any assault rifle," because it can carry 12 to 17 rounds at a time. CBS did not explicitly vouch for the validity of this claim, but simply broadcast the claim without criticism or commentary from gun or medical experts on the lethality of different types of firearms. The statement was incorrect regardless of how one might define dangerousness. The higher lethality of rifles in general (including "assault rifles") compared to handguns (including 9 mm. handguns) is one of the few traits that truly does make at least some assault rifles more dangerous than other guns. A 9 mm. pistol has neither the muzzle velocity nor maximum magazine capacity assault rifles commonly have. Thus, CBS conveyed both the message that "assault rifles" are especially dangerous guns, and the message that they are no more dangerous than very common semi-automatic handguns, with no evident awareness of the contradiction.

Persuading Viewers the Problem Affects Them Too. Next, the head of the hospital's trauma unit was interviewed, and he alluded to "this epidemic of violence," implying that criminal gun violence was rapidly increasing. Although this was true in the District of Columbia at that moment, it was not true nationally or in most local areas — the number and rate of gun homicides had been fairly stable for years. CBS neither noted this fact nor denied it but simply presented an unrebutted statement that surely would lead at least some viewers to draw the seemingly obvious, but erroneous, conclusion that the nation, and perhaps their own community, was also undergoing an "epidemic" of gun violence. In fact, the U.S. homicide rate (the most accurately measured violent crime rate) had fluctuated, without any consistent trend, within a narrow range between 7.9 and 8.6 from 1983 through 1988, and had declined sharply from its peak of 10.2 in 1980. Likewise, the share of homicides involving guns fluctuated very slightly between 58 and 61 percent from 1983 through 1988, down from the peak of 68 percent in 1974 (U.S. FBI 1990, p. 48).

A physician was then interviewed, and he argued that the ordinary medical patient might face a shortage of blood or might have important surgery delayed because of the heavy hospital gunshot caseload, and implied that trauma centers are closing down and are unavailable to treat automobile accident victims because of the increasing burden of gunshot cases. CBS anchorman Dan Rather asked the doctor whether some trauma centers have "been forced to close" because of "these new pressures," that is, the allegedly increasing numbers of gunshot wounds. The doctor replied "They have," citing unnamed trauma centers in Chicago, Los Angeles, the District of Columbia, and South Florida, which refused to "open their doors to the care of the injured." Note that this response did not actually answer Rather's question, since the doctor did not cite any specific cases of trauma centers *closing* but only some that restricted their services, nor did he explicitly claim that gunshot wounds were the sole or even the principal reason for even these limited restrictions. Rather did not inquire whether the well-known increases in medical malpractice insurance costs, the increasing difficulties of recouping payment from low-income patients, or troubles in finding physicians willing to work in urban emergency rooms might have been more important factors, and moved on to the next segment. Rather's hinted claim that gunshot wounds were responsible for the closing of urban trauma centers was highly implausible. Washington, D.C. had the highest homicide rate of any large U.S. city at the time, yet the hospital that treated 30 to 40 percent of the city's adult gunshot patients in the 1980s admitted only about four such patients a week even during the peak violence years of 1983–1990 (Webster et al. 1992, pp. 694, 695).

This Is a New Crisis, Not the Same Old Thing. Rather stated that only about 4,000 "military-style assault weapons" were imported into the United States in 1986, compared to the first few months of 1989, when over 100,000 importation applications had been submitted. The documentary never claimed that the mechanically identical civilian-appearing semi-automatic rifles are any less dangerous than their military-style counterparts or that imported "assault weapons" are more dangerous than domestically manufactured ones. (In fact, Rather later asserted that three out of four ARs in the U.S. were domestically made.) Therefore, it is unclear what the viewer was to learn from trends only in imports of the military-style weapons.

An "assault rifle" is basically a semi-automatic centerfire rifle. It was not mentioned that nonmilitary-style semi-automatic rifles had already been commonplace in the United States for decades, a fact anyone in the firearms industry could have told CBS. No basis was provided for believing that relative increases in the total sales of all semi-automatic centerfire rifles were anywhere as large as was implied by the import figures. In fact, it is not clear that the trend in total sales of these rifles was upward at all. In 1972, well before the popularity of "military-style" ARs began, 360,000 centerfire semi-automatic rifles were produced for civilian sale by domestic U.S. manufacturers, compared to only 149,000 in 1987, well after the increase in AR sales was supposed to have begun. Even taking into account the increase in rifle imports, total sales in semi-automatic centerfire rifles may well have *declined* between 1972 and 1987 (Kleck 1991, table 3.1). Although imports of *military-style* semi-automatic rifles did grow in the 1980s, there was little technically different in these few weapons from the much larger number of ordinary nonmilitary-style semi-automatic rifles that had already been common, and nothing at all of criminological significance in the fact that the weapons were imported. Citing the import figures appears to have served no other purpose than to impress the viewer with the contrast between the very large 100,000 figure and the very small 4,000 figure. In any case, this supposed trend was the synthetic product of an apples-and-oranges comparison between the number of guns actually imported in one period versus the number for which import applications had been filed. Because it costs an importer no more to apply for the importation of many guns than it does for few guns, the import application figures commonly are much higher than the numbers actually imported.

In the next segment, at a D.C. police firing range, an officer was shown firing first a bolt-action rifle, firing four shots in about nine seconds, and then an AR, firing five rounds in about five seconds, to demonstrate the higher rate of fire of ARs. Because bolt-action rifles are the slowest firing major type of multi-shot firearm, virtually *any* gun will fire more rapidly. Therefore, this exercise did not demonstrate any unique superiority peculiar to ARs. Then a policewoman was shown firing about 16 or 17 rounds from an AR in about eight seconds. No comparison was made with ordinary revolvers, which are the most common type of gun used by criminals, perhaps because such a comparison would have revealed little or no difference in rate of fire.

The police officer erroneously claimed on camera that "when you talk about semi-automatic weapons, you always talk about a large, a lot of, uh, a large capacity hold (sic) ammunition," holding up a magazine that appeared to be capable of holding about 30 rounds (she later referred to "32 rounds"). In fact, ARs are commonly sold with magazines holding only about five rounds; a 32-round magazine would be the largest magazine commonly sold with an AR, not the typical one (Warner 1988, pp. 293–302). Certainly ARs are not "always" sold or used with large magazines, and CBS cited no evidence they are even typically sold or used with large magazines. Again, CBS did not explicitly endorse the policewoman's claim; they merely presented it to viewers and allowed it to stand unquestioned.

"Assault Rifles" Are Machine Guns Waiting to Be Converted. In the next segment, reporter David Martin related how he found, in two hours, a gunsmith willing and able to convert an AR into a fully automatic weapon. He did not say how he located him, or whether the ordinary violent criminal would be able to locate such a person. The unnamed "gunsmith" was shown, in a series of

seven camera shots lasting a total of 15 seconds of air time, allegedly converting the gun. The editing of the sequence was rapid and unlike that in the rest of the program, evidently intended to convey the rapidity of the conversion. "Nine minutes later, he had turned it into an automatic rifle," said reporter Martin. Although Martin did not say one way or the other whether the man used any unusual, expensive, or specialized machine shop tools, the gunsmith was shown on camera using no tool more exotic than a pair of pliers. In most shots, he was shown using only his hands—he even held the rifle between his legs while working on it rather than using a vise. Likewise, there was no mention of the need for any additional, hard-to-obtain (or illegal) parts. The viewer was left with the distinct impression that the conversion could be done quickly, without special tools or parts.

According to Ed Owen, chief of the Bureau of Alcohol, Tobacco and Firearms (BATF) Firearms Technology Branch, it is unlawful to buy or otherwise transfer any guns that are readily convertible to automatic fire, since such guns are defined by BATF as machine guns. Thus, the semi-automatic guns legally on the market at the time of the documentary could not be "readily converted" to fully automatic fire, according to BATF standards. Owens' branch of BATF is charged with, among other things, determining whether guns are convertible to automatic fire. Owen had been supplied with a videotape of the CBS "conversion" sequence by an anti-gun control group, Gun Owners of America. After viewing the brief tape frame-by-frame, Owen said that although he could not conclusively say that a nine-minute conversion was impossible or whether it had in fact occurred, he "was not aware that a conversion could be done in the manner shown." Thus, one of the nation's leading authorities on conversions had never seen a conversion done in the manner supposedly performed in nine minutes by a gunsmith CBS was able to locate in under two hours (Owen 1989).

This becomes more interesting in light of the fact that no one was shown demonstrating the allegedly converted weapon's ability to fire in fully automatic mode. Casual viewers might be forgiven if they thought they *had* seen the weapon fired this way, since the documentary cut directly from the gunsmith segment to footage of Martin firing "an automatic rifle" at a firing range. If viewers were not paying very close attention, they would not have noticed that the gun fired was different from the rifle supposedly converted. Thus, juxtaposition of the sequences probably left some viewers with the impression that it was the converted weapon's fully automatic capabilities being demonstrated, without CBS actually saying so. The documentary never did say whether anyone checked to see if the "conversion" was successful. It is worth noting that if the conversion did indeed occur, CBS induced the gunsmith to commit a federal crime, assuming he was not licensed to manufacture machine guns (U.S. Bureau of Alcohol, Tobacco and Firearms [BATF] 1988, pp. 14–16).

Assault Rifles Are Especially Dangerous Firearms. In this sequence at the police firing range, reporter Martin fired a fully automatic rifle, noting that he could not fire the gun accurately, and then switched over to semi-automatic fire. He did not note the implication that this difficulty in controlling fire would presumably make the gun less useful for killing people, instead commenting only that "semi-automatic was all the firepower I needed." At this point, it became hard to understand what the purpose of the conversion sequence had been. If fully automatic fire does not provide any additional capability for harming people, what purpose was served by attempting to establish how easily ARs can be converted to fully automatic fire?

Martin and a police officer then examined the damage done to a wrecked car at which Martin had fired. The officer pointed to a hole in a side door of the car, saying "look at that—straight through the car." Neither he nor Martin noted that the same result could also have been achieved with most medium or large caliber bolt- or lever-action rifles, shotguns loaded with rifled slugs, or even a magnum revolver. The impression left with at least some viewers, but never explicitly stated by anyone, was that ARs have unique or unusually high penetrating or hitting power. In fact, ballistics data on the ammunition most commonly fired from ARs, the .223 round, indicate that it is smaller than average for a rifle round and imparts *less* energy than the average rifle round. Further, one of the principal military advantages of this ammunition is that it usually does *not* kill but rather wounds, thereby not only removing the wounded soldier from combat but also diverting enemy resources to evacuate and treat the wounded soldier.

The Pro-Control Forces Are Winning.   In the next segment, Dan Rather noted that many people had been urging President George Bush to do something about getting ARs "off the streets." At that point, CBS had not actually established that there *were* large numbers of ARs on the streets, but treated it as a given. In fact, even in areas supposedly heavily afflicted by ARs, such as Los Angeles, these guns are almost never used by criminals and are only a tiny fraction of firearms seized by police or linked to homicides. Dan Rather then discussed Bush's decision to temporarily ban importation of ARs.

Next, Rather reported the results of a CBS "48 Hours Poll" — 73 percent of the 663 respondents (Rs) supported a "total ban on military-style assault weapons," with 22 percent opposed, and 5 percent missing. The significance of these findings is impossible to gauge in the absence of any evidence indicating that Rs knew what interviewers meant by the term "assault weapons." It is likely that many, perhaps most, of the Rs believed that the guns referred to were capable of fully automatic fire; indeed, true military assault rifles *do* have this capability. The weapons available to civilians, however, do not. The contrary view was also encouraged by the aforementioned news stories that repeatedly blurred the distinction between automatic and semi-automatic fire and that inaccurately insisted that weapons currently on the market can be readily converted to fire like a machine gun. With this background, it would not be surprising that a large majority of Americans favor a ban on private possession of machine guns, especially since this is already the law of the land (U.S. BATF 1988). It was not clear whether Rs opposed weapons that have a military appearance, opposed semi-automatic weapons, understood what "semi-automatic" meant, or even knew that the weapons referred to in the question *were* semi-automatic. Given that even news sources were confused about the relevant distinctions, it cannot be assumed that the survey Rs understood what they were being asked about.

The "48 Hours" documentary itself wandered back and forth between machine guns, "assault weapons," "assault rifles," "military-style assault rifles" and even commonplace semi-automatic pistols. Like CBS, other prominent news sources also have asserted that semi-automatic weapons are little more than fully automatic machine guns waiting to be converted. For example, even though federal law bans guns readily converted to fully automatic fire and no weapons available for sale to the public had this property, the *New York Times* (8-2-88) insisted in an editorial that "many semi-automatics can be made fully automatic with a screwdriver, even a paperclip," a claim that their own reporters then contradicted just eight months later (4-3-89).

Survey researchers know that most respondents are reluctant to admit they do not know what a surveyor is asking about and will generally provide a response, however meaningless, to an opinion question. They will even "express an opinion about an issue they could not possibly know anything about, simply because they do not wish to appear empty-headed or uninformed." For instance, they will respond to questions asking about prejudice against imaginary ethnic groups or about nonexistent government officials invented by the surveyors (Lewis and Schneider 1982, p. 42). CBS presented the results without commentary, letting viewers draw the apparently obvious conclusion about the popularity of the restrictions in question.

The Violence Problem Is an Assault Rifle Problem.   The next segment was devoted to anecdotal information about the prevalence of ARs "on the streets" and among crime weapons. Two Boston police officers were shown on patrol; they offered the opinion that there were a lot of ARs "out there." Then a police detective was shown in a Fort Lauderdale police property room against a backdrop of dozens or hundreds of confiscated guns. CBS did not report what fraction of these seized guns were ARs. At least 36 reports on the prevalence of assault weapons among crime guns recovered by police, from at least 30 jurisdictions, indicate that less than 1 percent are "assault rifles" and only about 2 percent fall into the more broadly defined "assault weapons" category (Kleck 1996).

The detective described how he thought local drug gangs typically killed people—"they'll spray the area, just an indiscriminate shooting. . . . If they hit innocent bystanders along the way, no big deal." CBS did not ask how many times innocent bystanders had been killed in indiscriminate drug-relating shootings, did not ask the officer to relate even one such incident, and did not confirm that it had actually happened, even once. Fortunately, such incidents are in fact extremely rare. (Note again that the word "spray" could suggest, without anyone explicitly saying so, that the guns were capable of fully automatic fire.)

Late in the documentary, in a segment largely devoted to showing machine gun scenes from commercial films, the first and only scholarly expert of any kind to appear or even be cited on the program was interviewed. Professor David Malamud was questioned about the effect of media violence on real-life violence. None of the research he cited bore specifically on the significance of media portrayals of either weapons generally, or automatic (or semi-automatic) weapons specifically. No gun violence researchers of any kind were interviewed or cited in the program in connection with any of the issues addressed.

A live studio discussion followed, involving two persons: Larry Pratt, spokesman for Gun Owners of America, an organization even more strongly opposed to gun controls than the National Rifle Association, and a man named Joseph McNamara. Pratt was clearly identified as being a spokesman for an anti-control group, but McNamara was described only as chief of the San Jose police department. Some viewers might assume that McNamara had arrived at his views purely on the basis of his experience as a police officer familiar with violent crime. In fact, he is a gun control activist, a board member of The Handgun Information Center, a tax-exempt branch of Handgun Control, Inc., has frequently testified in favor of gun control before legislative bodies, and holds views arguably as extreme in support of AR restrictions as Pratt's are in opposition (*New York Times* 6-8-86, p. A26).

No police administrator was shown expressing skepticism about the likely efficacy of AR restrictions or the frequency of their involvement in crime. CBS did not overtly describe McNamara as a disinterested or representative spokesman for responsible law enforcement opinion; they merely presented his views without mentioning his affiliation with gun control lobbying groups and without any opposing law enforcement views. Because of his affiliation, Pratt's opinions could be easily dismissed by the viewer as the biased views of a mouthpiece for the gun lobby. But a spokesman clearly affiliated with the "gun lobby" was not "balanced off" by identifying the spokesman for Handgun Control as such. It is unlikely that spokespersons affiliated with advocacy groups and those not so affiliated would be perceived by viewers as equal credible.

The final sequence concerned the critical event that stimulated the movement to restrict ARs, the January 17, 1989, Stockton,
California, schoolyard massacre. Dan Rather stated that the killer,
Patrick Purdy, "brought his imported AK-47 to a school play-
ground in Stockton, California. He fired 106 bullets within 120
seconds. Five children were murdered, 29 wounded." The *Los
Angeles Times* (1989) reported that 110 shots were fired, in three to
four minutes. While both time estimates should be viewed skepti-
cally, the time difference is important. The *L.A. Times* figures implied
a rate of fire that was only half as rapid as that implied by the CBS
figures and that was no faster than that which can be easily sustained
by an ordinary revolver — about one shot every two seconds.

In this and many of the examples previously cited, there is
no reason to believe CBS knew they were misinforming their
audience. On the other hand, there is also little reason to doubt
that the documentary was intentionally constructed to persuade
viewers that ARs represented a major threat to public safety. Its
producers probably believed what they were attempting to persuade their audience to believe, even though their message was
largely without firm factual foundation. They did not discover this
because they failed to exercise sufficient journalistic skepticism or
diligence in seeking out potentially contrary information. They
did not bother to check out questionable claims or to seek out
expert opinion on dubious propositions, perhaps because they did
not seriously entertain the possibility that the assertions were
questionable or subject to dispute in the first place.

None of the information management strategies used by CBS
are unique to that organization. Other television documentaries
about guns have been equally unbalanced, sloppy, and manipu-
lative of viewers. The "48 Hours" program was not an unusual or
extreme case. For example, NBC TV's program, "Guns, Guns,
Guns" (broadcast in June of 1988), could easily have served as an
even more extreme example of shoddy coverage of the issue.

Newsweek and the Invention
of a Machine Gun Crisis

Magazines have also manipulated information to create a pro-
control impression. The *Newsweek* cover story of October 14, 1985,

on "machine guns" is a straightforward example. The cover headline was "MACHINE GUN U.S.A." with a subheadline claiming that "Nearly 500,000 Automatic Weapons Are Now in the Hands of Collectors—and Criminals." In fact, no one had any idea how many automatic weapons were in private hands, least of all *Newsweek.* The 500,000 figure was mentioned only once in the article itself, and then it referred neither to machine guns nor to fully automatic weapons but rather to semi-automatic "military-style assault guns" or "assault weapons" (Morganthau 1985, pp. 46, 49). These weapons fire only one shot per trigger pull, the same as revolvers. But even this number as it pertained to semi-automatic "assault weapons" was nothing more than a guess supplied by the general counsel of the National Coalition to Ban Handguns. *Newsweek* apparently saw nothing improper about using a guess from a gun-control lobbyist as the sole basis for a cover headline. No basis was ever provided for the claim of 500,000 machine guns.

The only numbers that did pertain to automatic weapons were the number of federally registered automatic weapons (116,000 at the time, according to BATF) and a guess by the gun control lobbyist that "perhaps 125,000" of the 500,000 "assault weapons" (a guess derived from a guess) had been converted to full automatic fire. In fact, only 40 percent of the federally registered automatic weapons were even in private hands at the time (*Los Angeles Times,* 11-16-86, p. D–4), implying about 46,000 registered machine guns in private hands. There was no factual basis whatsoever for the claim that a quarter, or even 1 percent, of "assault weapons" had been converted to full automatic status. Indeed, even among the guns confiscated by police (presumably more criminally involved than other guns, and thus more likely to have undergone an illegal conversion), semiautomatic "assault weapons" converted to fully automatic fire are virtually nonexistent (U.S. Congressional Research Service 1992, p. 18 [*none* of 3527 Washington, D.C. guns were converted]; U.S. Senate 1989, p. 379 [of over 4,000 Los Angeles guns, six had been converted]).

The article vaguely asserted that these weapons were somehow "raising the risks of criminal violence" (p. 46) yet never cited a single national or even local crime statistic to indicate that the frequency of crimes committed with either machine guns or "assault weapons" was increasing. Indeed, the authors came up with descriptions of a grand total of two fatal machine gun attacks, occurring in two different years. In lieu of any hard evidence on the prevalence of such incidents, Edward Conroy, a Miami BATF agent, was quoted as claiming that "South Florida is the mecca of illegal automatics, and machine-gun hits are almost commonplace. . . . There are even brazen attacks at stoplights, with grandma and the kiddies getting greased along with the target" (p. 48). In fact, both machine-gun killings and accidental killings of innocent bystanders in drug shootouts (at stoplights or anywhere else) were virtually nonexistent, even in Miami during the peak of its drug-related homicide problem. Perhaps the sort of incident Conroy described did occur once. However, *Newsweek* neither bothered to confirm it nor to question the claim that it was "almost common." Even in Miami less than 1 percent of homicides in 1980 involved machine guns, and none of these involved innocent bystanders being killed (Kleck 1991, chapter 3).

The article also contained a long series of half-truths and unsupported assertions similar to those repeated four years later in the CBS "48 Hours" documentary — for instance, that assault rifles are easily converted to fully automatic fire, so the distinction between these weapons and machine guns is an "increasingly tenuous" one (pp. 48–49); that they pose a major threat to police officers (p. 50); that they are unusually lethal (p. 51); and so on. And, as with the CBS documentary, not a single expert on guns and violence, either favoring or opposing the premises of the story, was quoted or cited. Because few experts in the field could have provided evidence supporting the main propositions of the story (Kleck 1991, chapter 3), the omission of expert commentary was perhaps understandable.

The Bernhard Goetz Case

Perhaps the most heavily publicized case of a purported defensive use of a gun in recent decades was an incident in which Bernhard Goetz shot four young men in a New York subway train on December 22, 1984. As the story was handled by the national press, the following were the salient facts of the incident. The four individuals who were shot by Goetz had "asked" for money, the stories hinting that they may have merely been panhandling rather than attempting to rob Goetz. The four were "youths" who were merely acting a bit rambunctious, rather than menacing.

Although the four had prior records of "brushes with the law," the offenses involved were "minor." After shooting two of the four, Goetz shot at least one, possibly two of them, in the back as they were attempting to flee. After turning himself in to police, Goetz confessed to shooting all four, then pausing, seeing one of them already wounded, and firing another shot into the helpless victim. Goetz was described as a "subway vigilante" and writers speculated that the incident would stimulate future criminal use of guns by citizens encouraged to carry guns as Goetz did. Goetz was acquitted of the most serious charges connected with the shootings, being convicted only of unlawful possession of a fire-arm. The press hinted that Goetz had been treated leniently by the court and reported speculations that the leniency was racially motivated, and was due to the fact that Goetz was white and the four victims were black (see, e.g., *Newsweek* 3-11-85, 4-1-85; *Time* 1-21-85).

The only problem with this account of the case was that nearly all of it was either false, misleading, or unsupported by the available facts. From the very beginning there had been no doubt that the incident began with an attempted robbery. Two of the four victims admitted to police and reporters that they had intended to rob Goetz. (Even 12 years after the incident, the *Los Angeles Times* was uncritically repeating the robbers' claim that "they were only panhandling" – see Goldman 1996.) Leaving aside its wisdom or morality, New York State law is clear that victims of robbery may use force, including deadly force, to resist robbery, regardless of whether the robbers are armed or whether the victim could safely retreat (Fletcher 1988, p. 25).

The victims were not ordinary, rambunctious children – all were 18 or 19 years old at the time, and all four had extensive criminal records. At the time of the incident, there were a total of nine convictions, many more arrests, plus 12 cases pending and 10 bench warrants for nonappearance in court against the four. Some later news reports conceded this, but others attempted to undercut it by only acknowledging the more minor offenses (e.g. *Newsweek* 4-1-85, p. 23). In fact, the charges included rape, armed robbery, and assault with a deadly weapon. At the time of the incident Darrell Cabey was awaiting trial on charges of armed robbery with a shotgun, and six months later James Ramseur was arrested for (and later convicted of) the rape and robbery of a pregnant woman, who required 40 stitches to close her wounds and had to be hospitalized for four days.

News accounts laid special emphasis on Goetz' videotaped confession in which he stated that, after wounding all four of the robbers, he paused, looked the fourth (Cabey) over, said "You don't look too bad, here's another," and shot the already-wounded man a second time (*Newsweek* 4-1-85, p. 23). Although Goetz did tell police something like this, the confession was contradicted by seven eyewitnesses, who agreed that the shots had all been fired in rapid succession without a pause. No one saw Goetz calmly shoot a helpless man after walking over to him and delivering a speech. Even the prosecutor expressed doubts about whether Goetz spoke, at the scene, the words he later confessed to, though he nonetheless insisted that Goetz had shot one of the men a second time without justification (Lesley 1988, pp. 193–214).

The press freely used the term "vigilante" to describe Goetz, but the use was inaccurate. The word derives from "vigilance committee" and traditionally refers to members of groups who seek to punish criminals where the legally constituted authorities are unable or unwilling to do so. Scholars have noted the existence of modern vigilantes, but these are always members of anti-crime groups (Brown 1969, pp. 187–93). The term "lone vigilante" is therefore an oxymoron, since vigilantism is by definition a group activity. More importantly, there was never any clear evidence Goetz set out to punish criminals or sought contact with either the four he shot or any other criminals (Lesley 1988, p. 317). Instead, whether morally justified or not, whether excessive or not, Goetz' act was believed by the jury to be an act of self-defense. Further, there is no evidence that this incident encouraged other people to commit illegal acts of self-defense. The only possible effect on criminal behavior documented so far was a pronounced decrease in subway robberies in the weeks and months following the incident (drops the New York authorities attributed to added transit police in the subways) (*New York Times* 3-22-85, p. B4; 4-18-85, p. B7).

Finally, there is no evidence Goetz was treated leniently by the court, for any reason. There was never any solid legal foundation for doubting that the four young men were attempting to rob Goetz, nor any ambiguity about whether New York State law permits use of force against robbers. Consequently, there was little legal basis for convicting Goetz for shooting the first three men, and only conflicting and inconsistent evidence sustaining the charges pertaining to the second wounding of the fourth man (Lesley 1988). Goetz was convicted of an unlawful weapons possession charge, a Class D Felony of which he was undoubtedly guilty. In 1989, of 2,308 people convicted in New York City for illegal gun possession, half received no jail time at all, including the four out of ten who received only probation (*New York Times* 1-29-90). Goetz was sentenced to one year in jail (and served over eight months), five years' probation, 280 hours of community service, a $5,000 fine or another year in jail, and was ordered to seek psychiatric help (Lesley 1988, p. 320). In short, Goetz was treated more harshly than most less-publicized defendants convicted of the same charge.

One might argue that the acquittal on the shooting-related charges was itself the product of racism. For example, Benjamin Hooks, head of the NAACP, was quoted in the press as asking: "If a white youth had been shot in similar circumstances by a black man, what would have been the outcome?" Oddly enough, a similar incident was in fact handled by the New York courts around the same time, with the races of the participants reversed. According to a newspaper account, a 23-year-old black man named Austin Weeks, while riding a New York City subway train, was accosted by two white teenagers who called him a racist name. Weeks shot and killed one of them with an unlicensed pistol. A Brooklyn grand jury refused to indict Weeks, he never had to face the prolonged trial Goetz faced, and consequently Weeks received no legal punishment of any kind (Kerrison 1987). Thus, in a shooting with a more legally questionable justification (no robbery was involved, but only a verbal provocation) and a fatal outcome, a black man accused of killing a white teenager was treated more leniently than a white man accused of nonfatally shooting four black teenagers. The Weeks case was ignored by the national press.

Is It Bias or Just Random Sloppiness?

It might be argued that these many specific examples only represent the inevitable imperfections of work done under a deadline and with limited resources. Reporters are human and make mistakes like everyone else. Although this is obviously true, it cannot account for the unbalanced, consistently pro-control character of the flaws. If these flaws were truly just innocent mistakes unrelated to biased views of guns and gun control, they would be randomly distributed and equally likely to be pro- or anti-control in their implications. They are not.

The prevalence and direction of bias was addressed directly in former reporter Tamryn Etten's (1991) content analysis of newspaper stories on gun issues. Etten examined a nationally representative sample of 117 gun stories published in 1989 and selected from Newsbank, a database covering virtually all large circulation, and many small-to-medium circulation, daily newspapers in the United States. Each story was coded for indications of bias in the content of the story, such as unrebutted statements favoring one side or the other, use of words tending to weaken or strengthen the impact of pro- or anti-control arguments (e.g., advocate Smith "claimed" versus "stated"), use of unattributed facts or opinions, and use of sarcasm directed at advocates or arguments on one side or the other. Using a "net bias" score that measured the excess of pro-control bias over anti-control bias, Etten's results indicated that 71 percent of the stories contained net bias in one direction or another, and that among stories with some net bias, 81 percent were biased in favor of gun control. Thus, stories biased in favor of the pro-control side outnumbered stories favoring the anti-control side by a margin of four to one (Etten 1991).

Perhaps the most telling evidence of the one-sided character of national news media coverage of the gun debate is the almost total absence of complaints about it from the pro-control side. Even though the gun press is filled with bitter complaints of anti-gun bias in the national media (e.g., Brown 1989; Blackman 1987), the writings of gun control advocates almost never even mention the issue. Either they see little national news coverage to object to, or they are remarkably forbearing in saying anything about it. One especially strong supporter of strict gun controls approvingly described early television news coverage of gun issues as "balanced" (Bakal 1966, p. 127). The Chairman of Handgun Control Inc., Pete Shields, all but acknowledged the nation's newspapers as an active ally in the gun control movement: "I would be remiss if I failed to mention the support that the handgun control movement has received from the editorial pages of papers across the nation. Some of these papers have supported the movement for its entire life. As a group, American editorial writers have done a great deal to keep the cause of handgun control before the American public" (Shields 1981, p. 89).

This sort of free media support provided more than just the intangible benefits of public goodwill and organizational legitimacy. Shields recalled the effects of interviews he gave in 1977 to *Parade* magazine and the top-rated "60 Minutes" news magazine program on CBS-TV, crediting them with providing a critical early boost to his organization's growth. "As a result of these two features, we were accorded what you might call 'instant credibility.' The phones (at Handgun Control Inc.) rang more than ever, and the mail thundered in. The huge number of contributions and letters of support showed us that . . . the American people favored some form of gun control" (1981, p. 134).

Discussion and Conclusions

Etten's content analysis results indicated that strong pro-control/anti-gun bias is not universal. Some major news sources have covered the gun issue in a competent and balanced fashion, notably PBS television (which produced what may be the best broadcast documentary on the issue, in its "Frontline" series), the *Wall Street Journal,* and *U.S. News and World Report.* And there are certainly many local newspapers that also cover gun control issues in a reasonably balanced way, though many of these are small-circulation outlets with strictly local impact. Nevertheless, even though the anti-gun bias is not universal among the major national news outlets, it is certainly widespread. Further, it is not balanced by important news sources with a pro-gun bias. No major national news source, broadcast or print, can reasonably be described as biased in a pro-gun or anti-gun control direction.

To be sure, biases in news coverage of gun control are not unique to that issue. The news industry's handling of drug issues is at least as distorted, and coverage of crime issues in general is superficial, sloppy, and uncritical of official views (Cohen and Young 1981). Nevertheless, the partiality and lack of skepticism toward one side in the dispute seem especially pronounced in connection with gun control.

Why should such bias exist? How can professional journalists, committed to an ethic of objectivity and fairness, nevertheless engage in such unbalanced coverage of an issue and apparently be so unaware of any bias? One possible explanation is that many news professionals do not believe there are two legitimate sides to the gun debate. Although there are obviously two parties to the dispute, only one is believed to have a legitimate case to make, one that goes beyond mere narrow self-interest. One possible consequence is that some members of influential news organizations set the gun issue apart, make it an exception, and do not feel bound by customary standards of objectivity and even-handedness where gun control is concerned. Consider the following unusually frank excerpt from a form letter sent from the editorial offices of *Time* magazine to a reader who had objected to one of their stories on guns:

> The July 17 (1989) cover story is the most recent in a growing number of attempts on the part of *Time* editors to keep the gun-availability issue resolutely in view. Such an editorial closing of ranks represents the exception rather than the rule in the history of the magazine, which has always endeavored to provide a variety of opinions and comment, in addition to straightforward news reporting, as a way of engaging readers in interpreting the significance of issues and events as they arise. *But the time for opinions on the dangers of gun availability is long since gone, replaced by overwhelming evidence that it represents a growing threat to public safety.* (Hammond 1989, emphasis added)

"The time for opinions . . . is long since gone." Were the issue any other one, would any respectable journalist fail to find such a sentiment disturbing? The guns–violence issue is evidently beyond debate in the editorial offices of *Time*. In sharp contrast to the debates among experts on the subject, there were no honestly differing views among the editors on "the dangers of gun availability" or the assertion that it was "a growing threat to public safety." This was not an issue with two sides, which *Time* was obliged to cover fairly, but rather was an issue with only one valid or respectable side. The only remaining issue was how best to convey to the readers of *Time* the indisputable truth that the editors saw so clearly.

The political implications of this imbalance are important.

Few would dispute that the mass media influence public opinion and lawmaking in a democracy. Consequently, the one-sided character of much of the news reporting on the gun issue is a serious matter, although clearly not one that has been widely acknowledged among opinion leaders. Media manipulation of information in general has certainly not gone unnoticed (see, e.g., Cohen and Young [1981], concerning media treatment of crime, deviance and social problems; Bagdikian [1987] on economic and political issues in general; and Herman and Chomsky [1988] on political, especially foreign policy, issues). However, the unequal character of the propaganda struggle over guns is not as well known or as frequently addressed by scholars.

Author Roger Caras commented in 1970 on the quality of the debate over guns: "Any careful observer of the battle must be distressed at the ignorance, ill will, and dishonesty apparent on both sides" (1970, p. 122). Caras' assessment was true as far as it went, but its bland evenhandedness obscured the extremely unequal impact of "the ignorance, ill will, and dishonesty" of each side. The purveyors of misinformation are not all equally influential or well-placed to disseminate their views. The indisputably biased publications of the National Rifle Association (NRA) and the rest of the gun press have a combined circulation probably well under ten million (about 5.5 million in 1982, for the four largest circulation gun and outdoor magazines, according to Standard Rate and Data Service 1983 figures [SRDS 1983]), whereas *Time* and *Newsweek* alone reach over 7 million households every week, and the commercial television networks reach many tens of millions of households every day. The biased views of gun control proponents find a sympathetic outlet in the major print and broadcast media, whereas the equally biased views of gun control opponents are largely confined to the pages of gun and hunting magazines, where they are read almost exclusively by a comparatively small audience of the already-converted faithful.

Regardless of how successful a political lobbying organization the NRA may or may not be (see Langbein and Lotwis 1990 for evidence that NRA influence is exaggerated), this power is greatly counterbalanced by the disproportionately pro-control slant of the nation's most influential providers of news. Whereas the NRA has to purchase (when media advertising departments permit it to do so) print and broadcast advertisements in order to reach a substantial share of the general public, pro-control forces are in effect given sympathetic media dissemination of their views free of charge.

When a California referendum to limit private possession of handguns was defeated in 1982 by a 63 percent to 37 percent margin, its supporters attributed its defeat to NRA spending, specifically $5.5 to $7 million spent on print and broadcast advertisements, compared to only $1.5 to $2.6 million spent by proponents (Bordua 1983). Did the NRA's much higher media spending "buy" it the referendum? The ads and air time it bought surely helped, but the issue of media impact can also be considered from a broader perspective. David Bordua (1983) noted that CBS broadcast a 15-minute, strongly anti-handgun segment on its highest rated program, "60 Minutes," just nine days before the referendum vote. Bordua also noted that the referendum was preceded by no fewer than nine pro-control editorials by the *Los Angeles Times*, not to mention similar ones from much of the rest of the state's newspapers. Proponents of the referendum did not have to buy this mass media help, but it was obviously to their benefit and was certainly intended to persuade voters. Bordua estimated that 15 minutes of CBS airtime during the "60 Minutes" program would cost about $6 million if it had been purchased as pro-referendum advertising rather than being granted as a free gift, as it were, by CBS. Even if one assesses the value of the segment simply by the costs of the commercial time usually purchased during a 15-minute period, the segment was worth about $800,000. Depending on a variety of assumptions about the value of various forms of free media exposure, and counting in the value of newspaper editorials and free air time on local TV and radio stations available to proponents under the Fairness Doctrine (still in effect back in 1982), Bordua's analysis indicated that supporters of the referendum may actually have received greater media exposure, paid and unpaid, than opponents.

The lesson is that it is unrealistic to view the gun lobby as the only powerful player in the political struggle over guns. The most important mass media news sources are powerful, and many of the more influential among them have taken sides on the gun issue. For the battle to be portrayed by these media sources as a pro-control David against an anti-control Goliath is not only inaccurate but also blatantly self-serving. It allows the news media to inaccurately portray themselves as neutral bystanders in a political struggle they merely report rather than one in which they play an active part. This is especially apparent in news coverage of the pro-control findings of public opinion surveys, which are reported as if public opinion was something that existed and evolved on its own and that the media merely reported, rather than something heavily shaped by the media themselves.

If the media were in fact neutral, the struggle would indeed be a very unequal one, for the NRA is undoubtedly a better funded lobbying organization than its opposite numbers on the pro-control side. However, the news establishment is not neutral on the gun issue, and so the struggle is considerably more equal than one would guess from news stories that narrowly focus on campaign spending and lobbying efforts by the advocacy groups and ignore the media's own crucial role (e.g., Kohn 1981; *New York Times* 4-12-86, p. A26; *Boston Globe* 4-3-89).

What are the effects of this slanted coverage of the gun issue? First, the public is poorly informed. With limited space and time, bad coverage drives out good coverage, and unbiased sources are drowned out by biased ones. Second, gun owners are made to feel like embattled victims of a disinformation campaign whose distortions can only be fought with further distortions in the opposite direction. Public debate gets deformed by pushing responsible moderates to the extremes and polarizing the issue. Discussion degenerates into exchanges of increasingly outrageous claims and insults (Kates 1984). Finally, the legislative process is warped by inducing lawmakers to focus on highly publicized but substantively trivial side-show issues, such as bans on "assault weapons," plastic guns, "cop killer" bullets, and "Saturday Night Specials," rather than addressing more serious, but perhaps less exciting, control measures like gun buyer background checks or improved enforcement of existing bans on criminal possession and unlawful carrying of guns. Because the news media affect public opinion, politicians can ill afford to ignore the implicit policy agenda set by the news industry when it focuses disproportionate attention on trivial or unproductive policies.

References

Askari, Emilia. 1989. Telephone conversation, October, 1989, between author and Emilia Askari, reporter for the *Los Angeles Herald Examiner*.

Bagdikian, Ben H. 1987. *The Media Monopoly*. 2nd ed. Boston: Beacon Press.

Bakal, Carl. 1966. *No Right to Bear Arms*. N.Y.: McGraw-Hill.

Blackman, Paul. 1987. "Mugged by the Media." *American Rifleman* 135: 34–36, 80–81 (June, 1987).

Bordua, David J. 1983. "Adversary Polling and the Construction of Social Meaning." *Law & Policy Quarterly* 5:345-66.

Brown, Marshall J. 1989. "Wound Ballistics Expert Exposes Media AK Fakery." *Gun Week*, May 5, 1989.

Brown, Richard Maxwell. 1969. "The American Vigilante Tradition." Pp. 144–218 in *Violence in America*, edited by Hugh Davis Graham and Ted Robert Gurr. N.Y.: Signet.

Caras, Roger. 1970. *Death as a Way of Life*. Boston: Little, Brown.

Cohen, Stanley, and Jock Young. 1981. *The Manufacture of News: Deviance, Social Problems and the Mass Media*. London: Constable.

DIALOG. 1990. Computer search of DIALOG database POLL file of public opinion survey results. Palo Alto, CA: DIALOG Information Services, Inc.

Etten, Tamryn. 1991. "Taking Sides: A Look at Media Bias and Gun Control." Unpublished master's thesis, School of Criminology. Tallahassee: Florida State University.

Fackler, Martin, J.A. Malinowski, S.W. Hoxie, and A. Jason. 1990. "Wounding Effects of the AK-47 Rifle Used by Patrick Purdy in the Stockton Schoolyard Shooting of 17 January 1989." *American Journal of Forensic Medicine and Pathology* 11:185-9.

Fletcher, George P. 1988. *A Crime of Self-Defense*. New York: The Free Press.

Goldman, John J. 1996. "Jury Awards Millions to Victim of Shooting by Subway Gunman." Los Angeles Times wire service story appearing in *Tallahassee Democrat*, April, 1996, p. 1A.

Hammond, Gloria. 1989. Form letter from Gloria Hammond, Editorial Offices of *Time*, dated August 1, 1989.

Hawaii. 1980. *Hawaii Revised Statutes*. Section 134-32. St. Paul: West Publishing.

Herman, Edward S., and Noam Chomsky. 1988. *Manufacturing Consent*.

Kates, Don B., Jr. 1984. "Conclusion." Pp. 523–37 in *Firearms and Violence*, edited by Don B. Kates, Jr. Cambridge: Ballinger.

Kennett, Lee, and James LaVerne Anderson. 1975. *The Gun in America*. Westport, Conn.: Greenwood Press.

Kerrison, Ray. 1987. "Here's Proof Goetz verdict Wasn't Racist." *New York Post*, June 23, 1987.

Kleck, Gary. 1991. *Point Blank: Guns and Violence in America*. Hawthorne, N.Y.: Aldine de Gruyter.

Kleck, Gary. 1996. Unpublished compilation of results of reports on assault weapons prevalence.

Kohn, Howard. 1981. "Inside the Gun Lobby." *Rolling Stone*, 5-14-81, pp. 1, 19–25, 70.

Langbein, Laura I., and Mark A. Lotwis. 1990. "The Political Efficacy of Lobbying and Money: Gun Control in the U.S. House, 1986." *Legislative Studies Quarterly* 15:414–40.

Lesley, Mark. 1988. *Subway Gunman*. Latham, N.Y.: British American Publishing.

Lewis, I. A., and William Schneider. 1982. "Is the Public Lying to the Pollsters?" *Public Opinion* 5:42–47.

Morganthau, Tom. 1985. "Machine Gun U.S.A." *Newsweek*, October 14, pp. 46–51.

National Rifle Association. 1987. "Legislative Status." Fact sheet on state gun laws. Washington, D.C.: National Rifle Association.

Owen, Ed. 1989. Telephone conversation with Ed Owen, chief of the Firearms Technology Branch of the Bureau of Alcohol, Tobacco, and Firearms.

Rand, Michael. 1994. *Guns and Crime*. Crime Data Brief. Bureau of Justice Statistics. Washington, D.C.: U.S. Government Printing Office.

Shields, Pete. 1981. *Guns Don't Die – People Do*. N.Y.: Arbor House.

Standard Rate and Data Service (SRDS). 1983. "Consumer Magazine and Farm Publications." *Rates and Data* 65.

U.S. Bureau of Alcohol, Tobacco and Firearms. 1988. *Federal Firearms Regulation 1988–89*. Washington, DC: U.S. Government Printing Office.

U.S. Congressional Research Service. 1992. *"Assault Weapons": Military-Style Semiautomatic Firearms Facts and Issues*. Report 92-434 GOV. Washington, DC: Congressional Research Service.

U.S. Federal Bureau of Investigation. 1990. *Uniform Crime Reports – 1989* (and earlier issues, covering 1974–1988). Washington, DC: U.S. Government Printing Office.

U.S. Senate. 1989. Committee on the Judiciary, Subcommittee on the
    Constitution. *Assault Weapons*. Hearings on S. 386 and S. 747. Feb.
    10 and May 5, 1989. Washington, DC: U.S. Government Printing
    Office.

Van Horn, Dwight. 1989. Telephone conversation with Deputy Sheriff
    Dwight Van Horn of the Los Angeles County Sheriff's Depart-
    ment, 9-12-89.

Webster, Daniel W., Howard R. Champion, Patricia S. Gainer, and
    Leon Sykes. 1992. "Epidemiological Changes in Gunshot
    Wounds in Washington, D.C., 1983–1990." *Archives of Surgery*
    127: 694–698.

Young, Jock. 1981. "Beyond the Consensual Paradigm." Pp. 393–421 in
    *The Manufacture of News: Deviance, Social Problems and the Mass
    Media,* edited by Stanley Cohen and Jock Young. Beverly Hills:
    Sage.

Warner, Ken. 1988. *Gun Digest – 1989/43rd Annual Edition*. Northbrook,
    Ill.: DBI Books.

Wright, James D. 1991a. Letter to the author, dated February 15, 1991.

Wright, James D. 1991b. "Guns and Crime." Pp. 441–57 in *Criminology:
    A Contemporary Handbook,* edited by Joseph H. Sheley. Belmont,
    Calif.: Wadsworth.

Chapter 4

Public Opinion: The Effects of Extremist Discourse on the Gun Debate*

Don B. Kates, Jr.[1]

Public Opinion on "Gun Control"

One of the most interesting things to me as a criminologist is that the general public seems intuitively to grasp principles that have taken us decades of research to formulate and verify. Most Americans are neither pro- nor anti-gun. I call them "pro-control." By that I mean that they recognize *both* that people have the right to firearms to defend their homes and families and that society should exercise reasonable control over such deadly instruments. The question for the great majority of us who are pro-control is only how to sensibly accommodate these two rights with each other. In fact, most Americans, *including most gun owners*, support

*This chapter is adapted from "A White Paper on Firearms and Crime," which comprised the author's presentation before the Select Committee of the Pennsylvania Legislature to Investigate the Use of Automatic and Semi-automatic Firearms, Harrisburg, September 20, 1994. Additional material is derived from "Bigotry, Symbolism and Ideology in the Battle Over Gun Control," a paper presented at the 1990 Annual Meeting of the Law and Society Association. A different version of this latter paper has appeared under the same title in the 1992 *Public Interest Law Review*.

more gun control of some types than we presently have in most jurisdictions, but far less severe measures than those that exist in the most restrictive areas. Oversimplifying, the public supports controls directed at disarming criminals while allowing the ordinary citizenry to possess firearms for their defense.[2]

At the same time the public seems to intuitively recognize the inherently very limited value gun controls of any type can have in controlling crime. In 1982 the Congressional Research Service summarized previous polls as showing that "very few people appear to see the gun control issue as an important problem facing this country."[3] This remains equally true today. In a 1994 poll 34 percent of respondents said "crime" was the gravest problem currently facing their area of the nation (making it far and away the problem most frequently listed), but only 3 percent mentioned guns per se as such a problem. Guns came in after nine other problems.[4] Over the years there has actually been a sharp reduction in the percentage of people who deem guns *per se* to constitute a major social problem.[5]

These results are particularly significant because they appear despite (or perhaps because of) a substantial increase in public concern about crime. Decades of polling have shown that the state of the economy has been the subject of most concern to the American public. Yet in an August 1994 *U.S. News* survey, crime was mentioned as the single most important problem more than four times as often as the economy. Similarly, a *National Law Journal* poll released in April 1994 found 62 percent of Americans describing themselves as "truly desperate" about crime — almost twice as many as felt that way five years earlier.[6] But,

> three out of four people say the police and the justice system alone cannot protect people adequately; citizens have to take more responsibility for safeguarding themselves. Instead of more law enforcement, 62 percent of Americans say that the need for guns for personal protection is increasing. Seventy-three percent of blacks, who consistently have the highest [crime] victimization rates, think so.[7]

(It is of interest to note the corresponding results from polls of police officers and administrators, which the National Association of Chiefs of Police have taken annually in over 15,000 departments nationwide since 1987. Year in and year out well over 90 percent of the respondents answer "Yes" to the question: "Do you feel that because of limited police manpower citizens should retain the right to own firearms for self-defense at home or business?"[8])

In sum, increase in public experience and fear of crime seems to have led to decreased confidence in the ability of police to protect the public. This, in turn, seems progressively to reduce public support for measures perceived as likely to disarm victims. In 1959 when crime was still very low, 59 percent of those Gallup sampled favored "outlaw[ing] handguns except for police use." (September 4, 1959, Gallup release.) Neither Gallup nor Harris seems to have asked a similar question until 1975 when crime was at an all-time high. At that point sentiment had reversed. The public opposed such legislation by a large margin: 55 to 41 percent in the Gallup poll; 57 to 37 percent in the Harris poll. Support had dropped to only 29 percent in 1989, 14 crime-filled years later.[9]

Although it was funded by the obviously highly partisan National Rifle Association, the June 10, 1993, Luntz-Weber poll release seems correct in asserting that "Americans Fear Crime— Not Guns" (noting that 78 percent or more oppose banning guns). Three other surveys confirm that 74 to 80 percent of respondents: (a) feel "ordinary Americans should be allowed to have guns in their homes"; and (b) oppose banning guns or any law that would greatly restrict the sale of guns. Indeed, for every respondent who supports banning guns, there is a respondent who believes that gun laws are too strict.[10]

Concomitantly, when asked, the great majority of Americans—including most of the relatively small minority who want to ban guns!—assert that no level of gun control, even prohibition, will disarm criminals or have any substantial effect on crime.[11] As detailed below, the impetus to banning firearms comes less from a belief that it will reduce crime than from a cultural and moral opposition to them. At bottom it replicates the view of many who opposed legalization of homosexual and other practices deemed "deviant" on moral grounds even while agreeing that laws will not eradicate such practices. In this view prohibition is desirable even though ineffective, because it brands the banned conduct (gun ownership, homosexual love, or whatever) as loathsome and immoral.

It is interesting to compare this (presumably more or less intuitive) recognition of the pragmatic limitations of law to the conclusion of the doyen of American gun control analysts, Professor Gary Kleck of the Florida State University School of Criminology:

> Fixating on guns seems to be, for many people, a fetish
> which allows them to ignore the more intransigent causes
> of American violence, including inequality, deteriorating
> family structure, and the all-pervasive economic and social
> consequences of a history of slavery and racism. And just as
> gun control serves this purpose for liberals, equally useless
> "get tough" proposals, like longer prison terms, mandatory
> sentencing, and more use of the death penalty serve the pur-
> pose for conservatives. All parties to the crime debate
> would do well to give more concentrated attention to more
> difficult, but far more relevant, issues like how to generate
> more good-paying jobs for the underclass which is at the
> heart of the violence problem.[12]

As we shall see. Kleck's is the dominant view among criminologists today.

Anti-Gun Bigotry Engenders
Fanatic Opposition to Gun Control

It is a truism that many gun owners hysterically oppose controls that are indistinguishable from those that they readily accept as applied to automobiles. Yet underlying this irony are crucial differences in the rationale and implications for actual implementation of even apparently identical control mechanisms to firearms rather than cars. Illustrative of the differences is the fact that car regulation is not premised on the basis that cars are evils from which any decent person would recoil in horror — that anyone wanting to possess such an excrescence is atavistic and warped sexually, intellectually, educationally, and ethically. Nor are driver licensing, car registration, and so forth proposed or implemented as ways to radically reduce the availability of cars to ordinary citizens or with the goal of ultimately denying cars to all but the military, police, and those special individuals whom the military or police select to receive permits.[13]

Yet those are the terms many prominent and highly articulate "gun control" (more correctly, gun prohibition) advocates insist on using in promoting any kind of control proposal — regardless of whether it might be defended in more moderate terms.[14] To these advocates, just owning a gun is analogous not to owning a car but to driving it while inebriated: "The mere possession of a gun is, in itself, an urge to kill, not only by design, but by accident, by madness, by fright, by bravado."[15]

Gun ownership being a per se illegitimate choice, banning it does not implicate any issue of freedom of choice. Nor are the interests and desires of those who own, or want to own, guns entitled to consideration: "The need that some homeowners and shopkeepers believe they have for weapons to defend themselves" is contemptuously dismissed as representing "the worst instincts in the human character."[16] As detailed further below, such assertions that self-defense is atavistic and morally abhorrent run like a *leit motif* in statements by anti-gun luminaries and activists, both great and minor.[17]

The theme of gun ownership as a morally illegitimate choice pervades the control literature: "gun lunatics silence [the] sounds of civilization," proclaims one columnist.[18] Distinguished cultural historian Garry Wills agrees. A nationally syndicated columnist, he regularly reviles "gun fetishists," "gun nuts" as "anti-citizens," "traitors, enemies of their own *patriae*," arming "against their own neighbors."[19]

An even more eminent historian, Richard Hofstadter, applied to gun owners D. H. Lawrence's phillipic against "'the essential American soul'" as "'hard, isolate and a killer.'"[20] Ramsey Clark decries gun ownership as an insult to the state (for "a state in which a citizen needs a gun to protect himself from crime has failed to perform its first purpose.") and a return to barbarism, "anarchy, not order under law — a jungle where each relies on himself for survival."[21]

An alternative ground of denying that the interests of gun owners deserve respect or consideration is that espoused by Arthur Schlessinger, Jr., Harriet Van Horne, Rep. Fortney Stark, Dr. Joyce Brothers, Harlan Ellison, and others. They assert that gun ownership involves no real choice; it is actually only a preconditioned manifestation of sexual inadequacy or perversion.[22] (An amusing side-note to this assertion is that, although purporting to rely on Freud, it reverses his actual view. That was that people who fear or loathe firearms, knives, and so forth are sexual hysterics — unconscious victims of a terror that causes them to hysterically confuse long objects or pointed weapons with the penis.[23])

The definitive pre-1990 analysis of American gun control literature was done for the National Institute of Justice by the Social and Demographic Research Institute (hereinafter referred to as NIJ Evaluation). It characterizes those I call "anti-gun" as seeing gun owners as "demented and blood-thirsty psychopaths whose concept of fun is to rain death on innocent creatures, both human and otherwise."[24] (As an aside, it is worth noting that this view of gun owners is just a currently respectable bigotry lacking any vestige of empirical support. See the discussion under the heading "The Character of Gun Owners" in Chapter 1 of this volume.)

It bears emphasis that the anti-gun view dominates the so-called gun control movement and fixes its political agenda. That agenda was succinctly enunciated by Michael Dukakis as Governor of Massachusetts: "I do not believe in people owning guns. Guns should be owned [or possessed] only [by the] police and military. I am going to do everything I can to disarm this state."[25]

Likewise, Sarah Brady, the Chairperson and dominant force in Handgun Control, Inc. (HCI) and her husband, James, advocate outlawing ownership of firearms for self-defense, believing that "the only reason for guns in civilian hands is for sporting purposes."[26] The mechanism for this would be a national licensing program under which self-defense would not be accepted as a ground for gun ownership. Only sportsmen would be allowed to own guns.[27]

The foregoing should not be misunderstood as suggesting: (a) that the anti-gun program enunciated by HCI, Gov. Dukakis, and others is either the only possible control scheme or a hidden agenda in more moderate ones; (b) that such programs and the anti-gun view(s) underlying them are supported by all gun control proponents; or (c) that anti-gun views represent the only policy basis for gun laws. The point is that anti-gun rhetoric plays into the hand of the gun lobby by convincing gun owners that propositions a, b, and c are true.

A Tripartite Debate

To understand the American gun debate requires seeing that it has three sides rather than just the two in which it is normally conceptualized. This is not to deny that the debate is monopolized and its agenda fixed by the conflict between the anti-gun view (defined above), which dominates the active gun control movement, and the pro-gun view (hysterical opposition to any additional control proposal, however moderate and reasonable). But the debate's virtual monopolization by these opposing high-decibel extremes obscures the paucity of their adherents. The fact is that even if those adherents were added together, their combined numbers would not represent more than a minority of the American public. The vast majority — including a majority of gun owners — espouse the markedly different view I call "pro-control."[28] It differs from the anti-gun view in that it recognizes the legitimacy of, and accords consideration to, the choice to own guns (particularly for self-defense). At the same time, unlike the pro-gun view, the "pro-control" view recognizes the need to accommodate the legitimate interests of gun owners to the social imperative to control a dangerous instrumentality.[29]

Poisoning the Well for Gun Control

Unfortunately the pro-control consensus has been undermined and frustrated as the American gun debate has been monopolized over the past quarter-century by extreme views that are inimical to compromise and accommodation. Guns are owned by approximately 50 percent of American households.[30] So all that the gun lobby needs to do to marshall massive opposition against gun control proposals is to capitalize on the terms of the debate established by anti-gun luminaries. As one analyst notes, exposure to this debate

> convinces America's handgun owners that they are a hated minority whose days are numbered by mortal enemies — enemies who hate *them* more than crime. With the die cast so, gun owners are made to think that *they have everything to lose* if those who loath them have any success at all. [Knowing this, the gun lobby actually] disseminate[s] the nastier

[anti-gun] cartoons and vituperative op-ed pieces in publications read by gun owners to fan the flames of incipient
paranoia.[31]

The last point is both remarkable in itself and telling in its implications: In reprinting anti-gun cartoons, the gun lobby is actually
paying anti-gun cartoonists royalties for penning those cartoons!
This money is well spent.

Essential to mobilizing gun owner opposition is that they be
convinced that every gun control proposal is bottomed on hatred
for them—that however moderate and reasonable a control may
seem, it is actually only a further step toward the hatemongers'
ultimate goal of banning and confiscating all guns. Only by thus
convincing gun owners can the gun lobby move them to hysterically oppose controls, many of which they themselves deem reasonable and sensible in the abstract. Indispensable to gun lobby
success is an anti-gun discourse that convinces gun owners that
"gun control" is not a criminological imperative but a matter of
culturally or ethically based hatred of them.

This brings me to a further disclaimer: the subject here is the
political dynamic, not courtesy. Gun owner response to anti-gun
vituperation is no less hateful. *Inter alia* such gun owner response
is notoriously counterproductive as political rhetoric. But, in the
long run, anti-gun hatefulness is even more counterproductive. In
a nation where more than 100 million potential voters live in
households with over 230 million guns, anti-gun advocates create
almost insurmountable opposition to controls by presenting them
in terms of hatred and contempt for gun owners. Moreover, what
anti-gun advocates do by heaping contempt on gun owners is
alienate those whose compliance is indispensable if gun laws are
to work. No doubt anti-gun crusaders find emotional satisfaction
in reviling those who oppose their views as sexually warped
"bulletbrains"[32] who engage in "simply beastly behavior,"[33] "gun
lunatics [who] silence [the] sounds of civilization," the "pusher's
best friend,"[34] "terrorists,"[35] "psychotics," "hunters who drink
beer, don't vote and lie to their wives about where they were all
weekend,"[36] or characterize the murder of children as "another
slaughter co-sponsored by the National Rifle Association,"[37] and
cartoons of gun owners as intellectually retarded, educationally
backward, and morally obtuse thugs, vigilantes, or Klansmen.[38]

But the emotional satisfaction of engaging in such vituperation must be weighed against the catastrophic effects it has for the cause of gun control.

In sum, the key to the gun lobby's ability to defeat new controls is the divisive effect of anti-gun discourse on a consensus that is only pro-control. As discussed here, this is not just a matter of alienating gun owners (although that would probably suffice to stalemate the debate in any event) but of the unacceptability to most Americans of the moral and social premises underlying the anti-gun view.

The "Gun Control Paradox"

The problem to which this chapter addresses itself has been called "the gun control paradox." Fifty years of nationwide polls have documented a virtually universal American consensus for some forms of "gun control."[39] Moreover, polls that isolate gun owners as an opinion group find a majority of them also favor controls, many of which are anathema to the gun lobby.[40] Thus, the "paradox" is the gun lobby's notorious ability, over the same half-century, to defeat nearly all legislative proposals embodying this consensus.

One may quibble with the "paradox" concept, because some of its proponents give credence to meaningless polls incompetently phrased in terms of public approval of "gun control" (undefined). This is meaningless because it is impossible to divine from an affirmative answer whether respondents are expressing support: (a) for the approximately 20,000 controls that already exist, (b) for stricter enforcement of these existing laws; or (c) for some undefined additional control — much less, (d) for any specific kind of new control. Amazingly, such incompetent phraseology persists to this day, as do also similarly defective questions seeking to elicit opinion about "stricter" gun laws.[41]

Indicative of the fatuousness of these undefined questions is that, where polls do focus on specific new control proposals, one of the most popular is a law *requiring* that judges give severe prison terms to anyone found guilty of a gun crime.[42] Despite its apparently uniform support across the spectrum of pro-gun, pro-control, and anti-gun respondents, this proposal is the "gun control program" of the National Rifle Association. Conversely, despite what proponents of the measure and anti-gun advocates deem to be the primary goal for an acceptable gun control policy, polls consistently show that most Americans reject banning defensive handgun ownership.[43]

Nevertheless, it remains true that large majorities of the American populace support a variety of other control proposals that are anathema to the gun lobby. Its ability to defeat these popular proposals has already been explained. The pro-control consensus is constantly undercut by the divisive goals and vituperative rhetoric of a gun "control" movement that is ardently anti-gun. The first seriously divisive issue is self-defense, which the majority of Americans see as the most compelling reason to have a gun but anti-advocates see as the most compelling reason to forbid them.[44] Then there is a fundamental conceptual dissonance: the pro-control concept rests on the idea *accommodating* the legitimate interests of gun owners to the social imperative of regulating deadly weapons—but equally basic to the anti-gun concept is that owning a gun is not a legitimate choice and that the interests of those who would make that abhorrent choice do not deserve consideration. (Guns are simply evil; those who choose to own guns are "gun lunatics who silence the sound of civilization," "anti-citizens" who represent "the worst instincts in the human character.") Third, pejorative anti-gun advocacy helps the gun lobby convert gun owners from a rational pro-control stance to one of rabid, reflexive opposition at the mere mention of the words "gun control."

I shall take up these points in another section of this chapter. But first we must consider an alternative explanation of the "gun control paradox." This alternate explanation emphasizes differential levels of commitment between gun control supporters and opponents. Pollster George Gallup has argued that the extreme commitment level of gun owners frightens legislators into seeing gun control as too politically hazardous to embrace. Although the great majority of Americans support gun control, few of them are fervent enough to vote against legislators who eschew it; whereas

> Citizens who oppose any kind of gun control laws, though constituting a minority of the public, feel so strongly about this issue that they will do anything they can do to defeat

such legislation. As a result they have succeeded in keeping strict gun laws from being adopted in most states and by the federal government.[45]

This thesis misanalyzes the tripartite division of views I have limned as if it were only a dichotomy of pro-gun versus anti-gun. The conceptual error results in empirical falsification. For instance, what does his phrase "strict gun laws" mean? At a very minimum, from the anti-gun position "strict gun laws" would include banning defensive handgun ownership. Yet, as discussed above, polls consistently show that only a minority of the American people support such a prohibition. So there is nothing paradoxical about its non-enactment. Gallup's thesis only becomes empirically sustainable when a third group is recognized — a pro-control majority that is less fanatic than either the pro- or anti-gun extremists.

Gun Control Plebiscites

More problematic yet is that Gallup's hypothesis is directly contradicted by the outcomes when gun issues have been submitted to plebiscite. Inherent in Gallup's hypothesis is that if "strict gun laws" were put to a plebiscite, the public would enact them. The problem, as Gallup sees it, is that majoritarian sentiment is frustrated because it has to be implemented by legislators who are personally too timorous to translate it into law.

Belying this thesis are the overwhelming rejections of sweeping anti-gun initiatives when put to the voters in Massachusetts and California in 1976 and 1982, respectively. Also over the past 30 years voters in 10 other states have amended their state constitutions to add guarantees that every responsible, law-abiding adult may possess a gun.[46] Obviously, actual tallies of the electorate provide much better evidence of the views of the electorate (in these states at least) than Gallup's polling of only 500 to 1,000 citizens who supposedly represent the views of upwards of 215 million potential voters.

The Massachusetts and California initiatives are especially significant because the gun control movement itself chose those states as the ideal places to go on the offensive. Massachusetts and California were chosen because they had exhibited the nation's most "liberal" electoral records and because polls supposedly showed that urban electorates supported outlawing or radically reducing handgun ownership. Of particular significance for my thesis here is the pattern of opinion change in both states as the campaign progressed.

Polls taken at the outset showed both initiatives winning by roughly the same 65 to 70 percent majorities by which they eventually lost. (Not coincidentally, at the outset the sponsors, particularly in California, sought to present the initiative as a handgun registration measure, downplaying its prohibition of new handgun sales.) Subsequent polls showed support steadily diminishing as the campaign went on. In other words, the more the proposals were debated — with concomitant exposition of their anti-gun premises — the more opposition they garnered, until the eventual "landslide" defeat.[47]

These results dovetail with findings from sophisticated in-depth polls sponsored by both pro- and anti-gun groups (though using different independent polling organizations). Unlike the short Gallup and Harris polls, which miss nuances because the number of questions asked are severely limited, the sponsored polls involve extensive questioning designed to reveal patterns and attitudes. The results are highly consistent, despite the differing wording and antagonistic sponsors. They show that most Americans support permissive controls on guns similar to those now applied to automobiles and driving: a permit system to disarm felons, juveniles, and the mentally unstable — but without denying ordinary, responsible adults the freedom to choose to own guns for family defense.[48]

This analysis — and my thesis — are further confirmed by the gun lobby's defeat in the 1988 Maryland referendum. The referendum's subject was a law passed by the Maryland legislature to prohibit future sales of "Saturday Night Specials." The law incorporated standards expressly defining the only handguns to be banned as being diminutive and too cheap and poorly made to be useful for self-defense or sport. The law created a commission to apply those standards, its membership including representatives of a gun company, pro- and anti-gun groups, and law enforcement.

Pro-gun extremists, believing the commission's powers would be abused to outlaw sale of most or all handguns, dragooned a reluctant National Rifle Association into mounting a referendum under Maryland's highly restricted referendum procedure. Far from offering a clear-cut referendum on guns (or just on handguns), the campaign revolved around the fact that the standards embodied in the new law expressly guaranteed every responsible, law-abiding adult's freedom to buy any handgun that would be useful for self-defense or sport.

This was confirmed by the denouement (after voters ratified the statute by a 57 to 43 percent margin). Fifteen months later, two anti-gun commission members were complaining bitterly that under the standards the commission had been compelled to approve almost 99 percent of handguns submitted to it (10 rejections out of almost 800 models submitted) and that the approved weapons included a 36-shot "assault pistol."[49]

Four weeks later, the approved list had grown to 930, including the Mac-10 and -11 "assault pistols." This was particularly ironic as one complaining commissioner, Baltimore Police Chief Cornelius Behan, had just displayed a Mac-11 in a *New York Times* ad (sponsored by Handgun Control, Inc.) calling for a federal ban on such guns. Behan explained that he and the other commissioners had had to approve the Mac-11 because "The Maryland law is designed to take out of circulation [only] highly concealable, poorly manufactured, low-caliber weapons. The Mac-10 and -11 unfortunately don't fit into that category."[50]

It typifies the mutually skewed perspectives of pro- and anti-gun advocates that both see the 1988 Maryland referendum as a great anti-gun victory. What the referendum really represented was a *pro-control* victory — at the expense of both extremes. Obviously, it was a defeat for the gun lobby's fanatic anti-regulatory stance. But for the anti-gun lobby it was a pyrrhic victory attainable only by implicitly conceding the unsalability of its core view to the American people.

The fruits of that victory were meager: About 1 percent of handgun models representing perhaps .001 percent of the handguns sold annually in the United States were disapproved for future sale in Maryland[51] (without affecting either handguns currently owned in Maryland or long guns at all). And the victory itself was attainable only by the ruinous means of embracing a law that expressly rejects both the anti-gun purpose of outlawing handguns and the premises underlying that purpose.

On the Morality
of Personal Self-Defense

One of those premises is great dubiety about, or even flat rejection of, the legitimacy of self-defense against violence. A half century ago Wechsler could still justify the legal right of deadly force self-defense in terms of the "*universal* judgment that there is no social interest in preserving the lives of the aggressors at the cost of those of their victims."[52] That is not a universal judgment today. As of 1985, 13 percent of respondents to a Gallup poll answered negatively to the question: "If the situation arose, would you use deadly force against another person in self-defense?" Presumably some respondents were expressing only their personal repugnance at killing rather than any moral imperative. That that is not the whole explanation is clear from responses to another Gallup question posed at the height of the Bernhard Goetz controversy in two different samplings taken a month apart. In one survey, 23 percent of the respondents said that self-defense was "never" justified; in the other, 17 percent gave that response.

No less telling is the language in which the Gallup poll put the question: "Do you feel that *taking the law into one's own hands, often called vigilantism* is justified by circumstances? [Emphasis added.]" The italicized phrase treats the legal right of self defense as morally, if not legally, wrong. This language is subject to criticism as being highly prejudicial; perhaps even prejudicial enough to impugn the poll's results. But the Gallup organization's considered use of it is itself evidence of a concept that is now quite widespread as is also shown by endemic misuse of the word "vigilantism." That word is constantly misused as if it applied only to private citizens and signified that it is somehow illegal or wrong for private citizens to defend their own and their families' lives. This is a solecism as such conduct is clearly legal, and the misusage does not so much broaden the historical meaning of vigilantism as contradict it.[53]

In contrast to the responses given above from the two 1985 Gallup surveys, 71 to 80 percent of the respondents therein answered that there are circumstances in which self-defense may be justified. Indeed, 3 to 8 percent of them *volunteered* the assertion that self-defense is always justified, despite Gallup's failure to offer that option. Such approval sharply differentiates the beliefs of the majority of Americans from the moral premises embraced by anti-gun advocates.

Disapprobation for self-defense—and a desire to make it pragmatically impossible, if not legally so—permeates the anti-gun movement, surfacing whenever gun issues are debated. However moderate, even innocuous, a new gun control proposal may be, its appearance sparks impassioned philippics to the effect that "the only purpose of a [gun, handgun, etc.] is to kill." The clear implication is that the use of potentially deadly weapon is *always* wrong—even when necessary to defend against violent felony—and that the purpose of gun control is to prevent victims from having the means of self-defense.[54]

Illustrative is an article condemning defensive gun ownership by the editor, Rev. Allen Brockway, in the magazine of the Board of Church and Society of the United Methodist Church. Recall that it has always been lawful for victims to use deadly force to repel robbers or rapists or other felons whose acts threaten great bodily harm, maiming, or death; indeed, the maxim "a man's home is his castle" arose in early English cases upholding the use of deadly force against burglars and arsonists.[55] Yet Rev. Brockway solemnly advises women that their Christian duty is to submit to rape rather than do anything that might imperil a rapist's life. Rhetorically posing the question "Is the Robber My Brother," Rev. Brockway answers affirmatively, for although the burglary victim or the

> woman accosted in the park by a rapist is [not] likely to consider the violator to be a neighbor whose safety is of immediate concern. . . . Criminals are members of the larger community no less than are others. As such they are our neighbors or, as Jesus put it, our brothers. . . . [Though violent criminals act wrongfully,] it is equally wrong for the victim to kill, save in those extremely rare circumstances when the unambiguous alternative is one own's death.[56]

Such views are neither unrepresentative of the anti-gun movement nor uninfluential therein.[57] Indeed, the senior national anti-gun group, the National Coalition to Ban Handguns (NCBH), was the creature of Rev. Brockway's organization, the Board of Church and Society of the United Methodist Church. NCBH's national office was in the Methodist Board's Washington building, and the

Board was NCBH's official fiscal agent until 1976 when gun lobby complaints to the Internal Revenue Service threatened the Church's tax exemption.[58] (The NCBH has recently changed its name to Coalition Against Gun Violence.)

Nor are Rev. Brockway's views some bizarre expression of male sexist extremism. Rather they just typify the profoundly anti-self-defense attitude underlying the anti-gun movement. Feminist Betty Friedan enthusiastically embraces these attitudes from her own purely secular viewpoint. In a 1994 interview she denounced "the trend of women buying guns [as] 'a horrifying, obscene perversion of feminism'"; Ms. Friedan believes "that lethal violence even in self-defense only engenders more violence and that gun control should override any personal need for safety."[59] (Anyone desiring a distinctively *feminist* approach to firearms issues must look not to anti-gun luminaries but to those who argue against banning guns.[60]) Likewise then-New York Gov. Mario Cuomo avowed that Bernhard Goetz was morally wrong in shooting *even if that was clearly necessary* to resist felonious attack: "If this man was defending himself against attack with reasonable force, he would be legally [justified, but] not morally."[61]

Rev. Brockway seems to concede that a woman may shoot a rapist if she knows to a certainty that he will kill her. But another NCBH affiliate, the Presbyterian Church USA, disagrees. Its official position is that the handgun should be banned because a victim may not take an attacker's life under any circumstance, even if she knows he will kill her after the rape. Testifying in support of banning handguns before a Congressional panel, Rev. Kathy Young, the Church's representative (director of its Criminal Justice Program) stated: "The General Assembly [of the Presbyterian Church USA] has declared in the context of handgun control and in many other contexts, that it is *opposed to 'the killing of anyone, anywhere, for any reason.'* (1972)."[62] Rev. Young emphasized that the Presbyterian position is moderate in that it seeks only to ban handguns, not hunting guns. Rifles and shotguns are not condemned because the Church sees them as owned "by sports people," unlike handguns whose purpose is self-defense.

Making no distinction between murderers and victims lawfully defending themselves, the Presbyterian Church USA proclaims: "There is no other reason to own a handgun (that we have envisioned, at least) than to kill someone with it." Other major

religious groups join the Presbyterians in denouncing gun ownership for self-defense as incipient vigilantism and categorically
condemning handguns as "weapons of death . . . that are designed
only for killing."[63]

The same general sentiments are embraced by HCI's Sarah
and James Brady, although in secular form and with concern to
preclude defensive possession of long guns as well as handguns.
Prof. Wills agrees, decrying "individual self-protection" as "anti-
social behavior," and calling for the confiscation of all handguns
(indeed, all firearms kept for self-defense):

> Every civilized society must disarm its citizens
> against each other. Those who do not trust their own peo-
> ple become predators upon their own people. The sick
> thing is that haters of fellow Americans often think of
> themselves as patriots.
> Give up your gun the gun nut says, and you give up
> your freedom. . . . *Trust no one but yourself to vindicate your
> cause. Not the law. Not your representatives. Not your fellow citi-
> zens.*
> Every handgun owned in America is an implicit decla-
> ration of war on one's neighbor. When the chips are down,
> its owner says, he will not trust any other arbiter but force
> personally wielded.[64]

Although the Bradys affirm that "the only reason for guns in
civilian hands is for sporting purposes,"[65] the *New York Times,* the
Detroit Daily Press, and many other anti-gun luminaries go further
yet. They seek to ban and have confiscated all firearms whatever,
asserting:

> No private citizen has any reason or need at any time
> to possess a gun. This applies to both honest citizens and
> criminals. We realize the Constitution guarantees the "right
> to bear arms" but this should be changed.[66]
> One way to discourage the gun culture is to remove
> the guns from the hands and shoulders of people who are
> not in the law enforcement business.[67]

To reiterate, despite differences over legislative strategy,
those who dominate the gun "control" movement are united in
their belief that self-defense is atavistic and morally abhorrent. The

natural outgrowth of this point of view is the law NCBH succeeded in having adopted by the District of Columbia City Council
in 1976: Householders may not buy handguns nor may guns of
any type be kept assembled or loaded for self-defense.[68] Handgun
Control, Inc. claims to be more moderate than NCBH, but it too
supports this as the ultimate gun control law. (Not only did HCI
file a brief supporting the law when it was challenged but in the
last several years HCI president Richard Aborn has urged adoption of the same law on cities around the country, as I heard him
do on a radio show in San Francisco.)

Gun control proposals presented in these terms are patently
unacceptable to the kind of people who own guns. Although those
peoples' attitudes and psychological profiles are not generally
distinguishable from the rest of the population,[69] one respect in
which they do differ is in being even more likely than nonowners
to approve the use of defensive force against violent felons.[70] This
approval seems to transcend political differences: Analysis of
another national poll reveals that, whereas liberals are less likely
to own guns than are the general populace, those liberals who do
own a gun are just as willing as other gun owners to use it if
necessary to repel a burglar.[71]

But it cannot be inferred that belief in the legitimacy of
self-defense is confined to gun owners. Although such belief is no
longer "universal," it was exhibited by 78 percent of the respondents in the 1985 Gallup poll who averred that, if the situation
arose, they would themselves use deadly force against an attacker.[72] Even if 50 of those 78 percentage points reside in the
roughly 50 percent of households that have guns, that leaves
another 28 percentage points (i.e., over half of the non-gun owners) who accept the legitimacy of deadly force self-defense. It is
little wonder that public enthusiasm for gun control proposals
fades as those associated with them express an attitude toward
self-defense that is disagreeable to a large majority of the public
and vehemently so to upwards of 50 percent of the public.

Conclusion

Why do those I describe as "anti-gun" insist that advocacy of
gun controls includes portraying gun owners as "lunatics," "anti-

citizens," "terrorists," and so forth? Although this may partially reflect mere cultural antagonism against gun owners,[73] it also involves genuine, ethically based abhorrence of self-defense and consequent abhorrence of the gun owners and the gun as symbols thereof. To reiterate some of the quotations given earlier:

> No private citizen has any reason at any time to possess a gun. . . . the need that some homeowners and shopkeepers believe they have for weapons to defend themselves [represents] the worst instincts in the human character. . . . I see no reason . . . why anyone in a democracy should own a weapon. . . . [W]eapons of death . . . designed only for killing. . . . There is no other reason to own a handgun (that we have envisioned, at least) than to kill someone with it. . . . The mere possession of a gun is an urge to kill.

Anti-gun insistence on this kind of discourse is indispensable to the gun lobby's success in defeating control proposals that, in principle, enjoy overwhelming support. Instead of dealing with the proposals' individual merits, the gun lobby is able to mobilize gun owners' opposition by portraying all "control" as a hate-inspired scheme designed to systematically multiply controls to the ultimate purpose of making gun ownership impossible. It is this discourse that convinces gun owners that "gun control" is not a criminological imperative but an expression of culturally or ethically based hatred of them.

Recognizing this, gun control groups often try to refrain from officially expressing anti-gun rationales. Unfortunately, that is not enough to counteract the chorus of (more or less) unofficial anti-gun champions hailing even the most moderate control proposals as steps toward the eventual banning of all guns. In principle, pro-control forces could defuse this by disavowing and vehemently denouncing overtly anti-gun rationales for moderate controls. But anti-gun advocates are so numerous and influential in the so-called gun control movement that it is impossible for less extreme forces to repudiate anti-gun ideology and disassociate their proposals from it. Yet the failure to repudiate anti-gun extremism makes it impossible to convince skeptical gun owners that a restriction championed by those who revile them does not really do or imply what those enemies claim.

Thus, one reason for the defeat of gun controls that seems to have almost universal support is that anti-gun discourse has made fanatic opponents out of gun owners who would otherwise have been supporters. The second (and related) obstacle to enactment of gun controls is that certain elements that underlie anti-gun discourse tend to alienate a substantial proportion of even non-gun owners who would otherwise support moderate controls. Although polls show that most Americans support "gun control" (undefined), what that means to them (and why they support it) is very different from what (and why) anti-gun activists support. Close analysis of recent state plebiscites demonstrates this and the baleful effect expression of anti-gun rationales has upon gun control efforts that otherwise would enjoy overwhelming support. The intense debate in these campaigns exposes how different the public's "pro-control" pragmatism is from the moralism of "anti-gun" groups.

It is not the innate strength of the gun lobby that defeats gun control proposals. Rather it is anti-gun zealots whose extreme proposals, and extremist arguments for even moderate controls, alienate a public that is open to rational ideas for control.

Notes

1. I wish to thank the following for assistance: Professors David Bordua (Sociology, U. of Illinois), Philip J. Cook (Public Policy Studies and Economics, Duke U.), Robert Cottrol (Law, Goerge Washington University), Jo Dixon (Sociology, NYU), F. Smith Fussner (History, Emeritus, Reed College), Ted Robert Gurr (Political Science, U. of Maryland), James Jacobs (Law, NYU), Gary Kleck (Criminology, Florida State U.) and James D. Wright (Sociology, Tulane), Ms. P. Kates, Tracy, Ca. Ms. E. Byrd, Berkeley, Ca., Ms. S. Byrd, Oakland, Ca. and Mr. C. Kates, San Rafael, Ca. Of course, for errors of fact or interpretation the responsibility is mine alone.

2. See generally, Gary Kleck, *Point Blank: Guns and Violence in America* (N.Y., Aldine, 1991), ch. 9; Bordua, "Adversary Polling and the Construction of Social Meaning" 5 *Law & Pol. Q.* 345 (1983); Congressional Research Service, "Attitudes Toward Gun Control: A Review" in *Federal Regulation of Firearms: A Report Prepared for the Use of the Committee on the Judiciary U.S. Senate (97th Cong. 2nd Sess.) by the Congressional Research Service, Library of Congress* (U.S. Gov't. Printing Office, 1982); Wright, "Public Opinion and Gun Control: A Comparison of Results from Two Recent Surveys," 455 *Annals Amer. Acad. Of Pol. & Soc. Sci.* 24 (1981); Schuman & Presser, "Attitude Measurement and the Gun Control Paradox," 41 *Pub. Opin Q.* 427 (1978); Erskine, "The Polls: Gun Control" 36 *Pub. Opin Q.* 455 (1972).

3. "Attitudes Toward Gun Control: A Survey," above, at 263–4; see generally *Point Blank*, above, at 370–71.

4. *U.S. News & World Report* Aug. 8, 1994 release of poll done jointly for *U.S. News & World Report* by Republican and Democratic polling organizations, pp. 2–3.

5. A 1975 national survey found 11 percent of respondents answering "gun control" when asked what should be done to reduce crime. 121 *Congressional Record* (Dec. 19, 1975) 1–10. In 1986 and 1990 polls only 1 and 2 percent, respectively, mentioned gun ownership as a problem or gun control as a solution to crime. *Point Blank*, supra at 364. Given the margin of error, these results are not significantly different from the 3 percent in the 1994 *U.S. News & World Report* poll.

6. "Crime's Toll on the U.S.: Fear, Despair and Guns," *National Law Journal*, Ap. 18, 1994.

7. *National Law Journal*, id.

8. Two other significant questions are: "Do you believe your police department is undermanned?" 89.1 percent said Yes. And "Would

you agree with the statement that because of a lack of police manpower you can no longer provide the type of service and crime prevention activities that you did ten years ago?" 72.3 percent said Yes.

Poll questions and results for each year are available from
the National Association of Chiefs of Police, 3801 Biscayne Blvd.,
Miami, FL 33137; (305) 573-0202.

9. *Point Blank,* supra at 359-60, reporting February, 1989 TIME-
    Yankelovich poll. In the fall of 1996, the National Opinion Re-
    search Center conducted a national poll for the strongly anti-gun
    Johns Hopkins Center for Gun Policy and Research, with a set of
    questions formulated by the latter. One question was whether
    "There should be a total ban on handgun ownership?" Only 16.1
    percent of respondents supported such a ban. But this question is
    so differently worded from those previously asked by Gallup, Har-
    ris, and Yankelovich that the answer may not be fully comparable
    to their results.

10. Compare *U.S. News* and *National Law Journal,* (Aug. and April,
    1994) supra, to Gallup Poll Monthly, Jan. 1994 (reporting 1993 poll
    results).

11. See polling discussed in *Point Blank,* supra, at 370ff and Gary
    Kleck, "Crime, Culture Conflict and the Sources of Support for
    Gun Control," 39 *American Behavioral Scientist* 387–404 (1996).

12. Gary Kleck, "Guns and Violence: An Interpretive Review of the
    Field," 1 *Social Pathology* 12 (1995).

13. As detailed below, there are differences and gradations in the anti-
    gun position and among anti-gun groups and advocates. The
    more moderate Handgun Control seeks only banning and confisca-
    tion of all firearms designed for self-defense, prohibition on keep-
    ing any firearm loaded or assembled for self-defense, and a
    national licensing program under which only sportsmen would be
    eligible, so as to outlaw gun ownership for self-defense. (Handgun
    Control, Inc. chairperson Sarah Brady quoted in Eckholm, "A Lit-
    tle Control, A Lot of Guns," *N.Y. Times,* Aug. 15, 1993 and Jackson,
    "Keeping the Battle Alive," *Tampa Tribune* Oct. 21, 1993.) The *Wash-
    ington Post* and *Los Angeles Times* agree. See *Los Angeles Times* Oct.
    22, 1993 editorial "Taming the Gun Monster: How Far to Go" and
    Washington Post Sept. 26, 1972 editorial: "Guns and the Civilizing
    Process" — both quoted below. This federal legislation would be
    supplemented by state and local laws HCI advocates nationwide,
    to be patterned after the one it supports in the District of Colum-
    bia. Under that law, except when used for target shooting or hunt-
    ing, guns must be kept unloaded and disassembled so that they
    cannot be used for self-defense.

    Though concurring in general, the Presbyterian Church, the

Board of Church and Society of the United Methodist Church, and the National Coalition to Ban Handguns (now renamed the Coalition Against Gun Violence National Coalition to Ban Handguns) seek the banning and confiscation of at least all handguns, whether or not specially adapted to self-defense. Many anti-gun advocates deny the legitimacy of civilian gun ownership for any purpose and under any circumstances and seek, ultimately, the banning and confiscation of all firearms. See discussion below.

14. See, e.g. Charles Krauthammer, "Disarm the Citizenry," *Washington Post* April 5, 1996 ("ultimately, a civilized society must disarm its citizenry. . . . [T]he assault weapon ban is a purely symbolic move [whose] real justification is not to reduce crime but to desensitize the public to the regulation of weapons in preparation for their ultimate confiscation."), Garry Wills ("Every civilized society must disarm its citizens against each other.") in "NRA is Complicit in the Deaths of Two Children," *Detroit Free Press,* September 6, 1994; see also Wills, "The Terrorists Who Pack an NRA Card," *Albany, N.Y. Times Union,* April 22, 1996 and other columns cited hereinafter. See also discussion and citations given in T. Markus Funk, "Is the True Meaning of the Second Amendment Really Such a Riddle," *Howard L. J.* v. 39: 411-36 at p. 412, fn. 4 (1995).

15. Harris, *Chicago Daily News,* Ap. 11, 1967.

16. *Washington Post* editorial, above.

17. E.g. James Brady, interviewed by *Parade* magazine: Q. "Aren't any handguns defensible?" A. "For target shooting, that's ok. Get a license and go to the range. [But not f]or defense of the home — that's why we have police departments." "In Step With: James Brady, *Parade,* June 26, 1994, p. 18; HCI vice president Jeanne Shield's description of NRA members as macho men who "don't understand the definition of a civilized society" (*Newsweek* interview, May 8, 1978); Robert Replogle, M.D., University of Chicago Professor and co-founder of the Medical Council on Handgun Abuse, testifying before a Congressional Committee, "The only legitimate use of a handgun that I can understand is for target shooting." Handgun Crime Control Hearings, 1975-6 Senate Judiciary Committee [Subcommittee re Juvenile Delinquency] Oversight of the 1968 Gun Control Act, v. II at 1974.); Rev. Kathy Young, testifying before another Congressional committe on behalf of the Presbyterian Church USA that it does not seek to ban rifles and shotguns because they are to be used for sport but only handguns, which are illegitimate because their purpose is personal defense — 1985-6 Hearings on Legislation to Modify the 1968 Gun Control Act, House Judiciary Committee, Subcommittee on Crime; v. I at 127 and 128; Prof. Morris Janowitz, quoted in "The Gun Under

Fire,",Time, June 21, 1968 at 17: "I see no reason . . . why anyone in a democracy should own a weapon."

18. Braucher, *Miami Herald,* July 19, 1982: "Gun Lunatics Silence Sounds of Civilization." See also Braucher, "Handgun Nuts are Just That—Really Nuts," *Miami Herald,* Oct. 29, 1981.

  Similar pronouncements may be cited ad infinitum, e.g. *Atlanta Constitution* editorial Aug. 20, 1993 p. A12 ("the crazy gun lobbyists . . . say guns don't kill people. No, guns are doing something worse—they are killing civilization."); and the characterization of defensive gun ownership as "simply beastly behavior" in "Gun Toting: A Fashion Needing Change," 93 *Science News* 613, 614 (1968). See generally Luedens, "Wretchedness Is a Warm Gun" 48 *Progressive* 50 (1984) and Ellison, "Fear Not Your Enemies," *Heavy Metal.* Mar., 1981.

19. In addition to his more recent columns cited above, see: Wills, "Handguns that Kill," *Washington Star,* Jan. 18, 1981, "John Lennon's War," *Chicago Sun Times,* Dec. 12, 1980 and "Or Worldwide Gun Control," *Philadelphia Inquirer,* May 17, 1981.

20. "America as a Gun Culture" in *American Heritage,* Oct. 1970 at 82.

21. R. Clark, *Crime In America* 88 (1971).

22. See, e.g. *U.S. Catholic* magazine editorial "Sex Education Belongs in the Gun Store," August, 1979; *N.Y. Post* magazine, June 21, 1976, p. 2; "Fear Not Your Enemies," *Heavy Metal,* March, 1981. See generally, Don B. Kates, Henry E. Schaffer, et al., "Guns and Public Health: Epidemic of Violence or Pandemic of Propaganda," 62 *Tenn. L. Rev.* 513–596 (1995) at 528–29.

23. Ibid.

24. J. Wright, P. Rossi, K. Daly, *Under The Gun: Weapons, Crime and Violence in the United States* (N.Y., Aldine: 1983) at p. 4. Unless otherwise expressly stated, all references to the NIJ Evaluation herein are to this, the commercially published version, rather than the NIJ version, J. Wright, P. Rossi & K. Daly, *Weapons, Crime and Violence in America: A Literature Review and Research Agenda* (Washington, D.C., Gov't. Print. Off.: 1981).

25. The statement was made on June 16, 1986, during a meeting with representatives of the principal Massachusetts gun lobby group, the Gun Owners Action League (GOAL). Predictably, during Gov. Dukakis' presidential campaign the statement was highlighted by the National Rifle Association, which devoted the entire cover of the October, 1988 *American Rifleman* (c. 3 million subscribers) to it.

26. Oct. 21, 1993 *Tampa Tribune* interview with Handgun Control, Inc. chairperson Sarah Brady, above, see note 13.

  Anti-gun advocates sometimes deny confiscatory objectives, often in rather exuberant terms. See, e.g. Andrew D. Herz, "Gun

Crazy: Constitutional False Consciousness and Dereliction of Dia-logic Responsibilities," 75 *Boston U. Law Rev.* 57, 89*ff.* (1995) ("Vir-tually no one in the gun control movement calls for confiscation.") The disingenuousness of this is revealed by the author's solemn as-sertion that although "Senator John H. Chaffee (R-R.I.) has called for a ban on handguns, [his bill] does not contemplate confisca-tion." Id. at 89 and footnote 126. This denial is assigned to a foot-note that fails to explain what the Chaffee bill actually requires. That is that the handgun owner either surrender the gun or keep it locked in a police station or other facility under police supervision. In other words, although the Chaffee bill does not propose to con-fiscate the property itself, it would preclude the sole or primary use many property owners have for it, which is to defend self, fam-ily, and home. One might as well deny that a law forbidding the driving of cars is confiscation because, after all, the owners still re-tain paper title and can still use the car for some purpose, e.g. standing on it to reach objects located high up in the garage.

27. Eckholm, "A Little Control, A Lot of Guns," *N.Y. Times,* Aug. 15, 1993, quoting Sarah Brady. See also her Sept. 21, 1993 speech to the Women's National Democratic Club: "In the future we would like to see needs-based licensing . . . where it would be much more difficult for *anybody* to be able to purchase handguns." (Emphasis hers.) Compare *Los Angeles Times* editorial "Taming the Monster: The Guns Among Us" Dec. 10, 1993: "Under our plan individuals could own sporting weapons only if they had submitted to a back-ground check and passed a firearms safety course. Other special, closely monitored exceptions could be made, such as for serious collectors." To the same effect see *Los Angeles Times* editorial "Tam-ing the Gun Monster: How Far to Go" Oct. 22, 1993, recommend-ing that federal law limit ordinary citizens to "ownership [only] of sporting and hunting weapons."

28. See sources cited at footnote 2 above.

29. Public opinion polls consistently show most Americans are skepti-cal that gun controls can do much about crime and are particularly dubious about the likelihood of disarming criminals through gun control (see note 11 above). The difference between the people I call pro-gun and those I call pro-control may be illustrated by their disparate reactions to the fact that most Americans still support gun controls, despite this skepticism. The pro-gun view would condemn this as contradictory and irrational—why support legis-lation that you see as of little or no use? A pro-control person would reply that that is the logic of oversimplification: of course it is not realistic to think that all or most criminals (i.e. people who are willing to violate laws) will obey gun laws. But a law is sensi-

ble if it causes even one criminal to disarm or allows his incarceration when he is found illegally in possession of a gun. Why would one not see at least a minimal social value in a law against felons having guns (unless one deems there to be some social value in their being armed)?

30. *Point Blank*, above, at 49–52. For more recent estimates of total and per capita gun ownership see Don B. Kates, Henry E. Schaffer, et al., "Guns and Public Health: Epidemic of Violence or Pandemic of Propaganda," 62 *Tenn. L. Rev.* 513–596 (1995) at 572 (table 3).

31. Stell "Guns, Politics and Reason," 9 *J. Am. Culture* 71, 73 (1986) (emphasis in original). See also Kates, "The Battle Over Gun Control" *The Public Interest*, Summer, 1986.

    Compare the observation by the author of a Ford Foundation study of gun control: "gun owners believe (rightly in my view) that the gun controllers would be willing to sacrifice their interests even if the crime control benefits were tiny." Moore, "The Bird in Hand: A Feasible Strategy for Gun Control" 2 *J. Policy An. & Mangmnt.* 185, 187-8 (1983).

32. Grizzard, "Bulletbrains and the Guns That Don't Kill," *Atlanta Constitution* Jan. 19, 1981.

33. "Gun Toting: A Fashion Needing Change" in 93 *Science News* 613, 614 (1968).

34. Guest editorial by Senator Edward Kennedy, "Pusher's Best Friend, the NRA," March 22, 1989, *New York Times.* See also P. Hamill, *New York Post,* "A Meeting of NRA's Harlem Branch," April 4, 1989, *Louisville Courier-journal Magazine,* Aug. 7, 1988, p. 6 ("The National Rifle Association, its propagandists and it supporters work day and night to make sure that every hood in the country can get his hands on a gun. They couldn't be more guilty if they stood there slipping pistols to the drug dealers and robbers. If justice were done, they would be in prison."). In fact (though it has often obtusely opposed even reasonable controls that affect law-abiding citizens), the NRA is the principal architect of laws barring gun ownership by anyone who has been convicted of a felony. Don B. Kates, "Handgun Prohibition and the Original Meaning of the Second Amendment," 82 *Mich. L. Rev.* 203-73 (1983) at 209-210 (citing state laws dating from the early 20th century and federal laws from the 1930s through the present day).

35. Garry Wills, "The Terrorists who Pack an NRA Card," nationally syndicated columns, see e.g., *Albany, N.Y. Times Union,* April 22, 1996.

36. A remark by N.Y. Governor Mario Cuomo who subsequently wrote the NRA to apologize because "it is unintelligent and unfair" to "disparage any large group." *Time,* May 27, 1985.

37. Editorial cartoon, *Milwaukee Journal,* Jan. 22, 1989, p. 12J.

38. Morin (Miami Herald) cartoon, *Arizona Republic,* March 21, 1989 (showing gun store with sign "drug dealers, gangs, welcome), Herblock cartoon, *Washington Post,* March 21, 1989 ("these guys who want to spray the streets with bullets"); *San Jose Mercury-News,* March 3, 1989 ("I.Q.-47"), *Los Angeles Herald Examiner,* January 31, 1989 (showing "Crips, Bloods and NRA" as "Three Citizen Groups Opposed to Outlawing Assault Rifles"), Interlandi cartoon, *Los Angeles Times,* Dec. 16, 1980.

39. Polls addressing specific kinds of controls show support for a permit system whose object is to disarm felons, juveniles, and the mentally unstable, but without denying ordinary responsible citizens the option to own a gun for family defense. This kind of scheme is at once far more stringent than the controls the least restrictive states now have, but far more lenient than the policy in the highly restrictive states (see note 2 supra).

40. In a late 1989 poll of gun owners only: 87 percent supported a waiting period/background check for handgun buyers; 73 percent supported registration of all "semi-automatic weapons"; 72 percent supported registration of all handguns; 54 percent supported registration of all rifles and 50 percent of all shotguns. *Time,* Jan. 29, 1990, p. 16. Two 1975 Gallup polls found registration of all guns and a permit requirement for possessing a gun outside the owner's own premises supported by 55 percent and 68 percent of all gun owners (respectively) and by 76 and 85 percent of all nonowners (respectively). Gallup releases for June 5, 1975 and Oct. 30, 1975. For discussion of prior polling to the same effect, see Erskine, supra at 455.

    The *Time* poll found that 67 percent of gun owners expressed general agreement with the NRA and 63 percent did not think strict controls would reduce violence. But this does not sharply differentiate gun owners from most Americans: polls show substantial dubiety that gun laws can reduce crime and general disbelief that they will reduce crime. See Congressional Research Service supra at 256ff. Wright, 455 *Annals* supra, harmonizes this result with the majority's support for various gun control laws on the theory that such laws are perceived as "sensible" even though their effectiveness will inherently or necessarily be limited.

41. See examples cited in *Point Blank* 361–63 and by the Congressional Research Service analysis supra at p. 247–8 with the comment: Absent "information about the level of knowledge [each respondent had] about current laws regulating the sale of handguns, the meaning of the results of such questions may be particularly difficult to determine. The analyst may be left asking the question 'more strict, relative to what' or 'keep which gun laws the same?'"

42. Congressional Research Service, table 7 at p. 249.
43. See note 9 above.
44. See discussion below under the heading "On the Morality of Personal Self-Defense."
45. G. Gallup, *The Sophisticated Poll Watcher's Guide* (1972) 105.
46. Idaho, Louisiana, New Hampshire, Nevada, West Virginia, Utah, Maine, Virginia, North Dakota, and Nebraska. (In addition, Delaware enacted such a constitutional provision by legislative action.) See discussion in Stephen P. Halbrook, *A Right to Bear Arms* 118*ff*. (Westport, CT, Greenwood Press: 1989) and Robert Dowlut, "Bearing Arms in State Bills of Rights, Judicial Interpretation, and Public Housing" 5 *St. Thomas Law Review* 203 (1992).
47. See generally, David Bordua, "Adversary Polling and the Construction of Social Meaning: Implications in Gun Control Elections in Massachusetts and California" 5 *Law & Pol. Q.* 345–66 (1983).
48. Wright, "Public Opinion and Gun Control: A Comparison of Results from Two Recent Surveys," 455 *Annals Amer. Acad. of Pol. & Soc. Sci.* 24 (1981), Bordua, above.
49. *Washington Post,* Jan. 9, 1990: "Md. Panel Approves More Guns for Sale."
50. *Baltimore Sun,* February 9, 1990: "No Way Out: Behan Has to Vote for Gun He Hates."
51. The commission approved every gun type submitted to it by every major domestic and foreign manufacturer. See last two footnotes and Don B. Kates, "Bigotry, Symbolism, and Ideology in the Battle Over Gun Control," 1992 *Public Interest Law Journal* 31.
52. Wechsler, "A Rationale of the Law of Homicide," 27 *Colum. L. Rev.* 701, 736 (1937) (emphasis added).
53. For discussion of the law see e.g. Kates & Engberg, "Deadly Force Self-Defense Against Rape" 15 *U.C.-Davis L. Rev.* 873, 877–80 (1982). As to "vigilantism," accurately used it does not distinguish between private citizens and police, it does not necessarily imply deadly force, and it would never apply to any *defensive* use of force, even excessive force. Vigilantism defines a highly specific kind of wrongdoing: It refers to anyone, whether civilian or police officer who takes the law into his own hands by imposing *punishment* on a supposed criminal without due process of law. The limitations of the concept may be illustrated by three alternative hypotheticals of the facts in the Goetz case: (a) if Goetz shot in reasonably necessary defense against robbers, the shooting was lawful and thus not vigilantism; (b) if Goetz actually but unreasonably feared that mere panhandlers were robbers, the shooting was illegal—but it was still not vigilantism; (c) the shooting was vigilantism only if Goetz used deadly force (or any force

at all) knowing it was unnecessary and for the purpose of arrogating to himself the judicial function of punishing.

In sum, vigilantism is always illegal, whether engaged in by private citizens or police. Conversely, it is oxymoronic to apply the term to lawful conduct either by private citizens or by police.

54. See testimony of the Presbyterian Church USA urging the banning and confiscation of all handguns, discussed below. Concomitantly, anti-gun authors label gun owners "violence prone" — based on survey data in which what gun owners actually approved was not illegal violence but the use of force necessary to stop crime or aid its victims. E.g. Williams and McGrath, "Why People Own Guns," 26 *Journal of Communication* 22 (1976). Compare Alan J. Lizotte & Jo Dixon, "Gun Ownership and the 'Southern Subculture of Violence'," 93 *American Journal of Sociology* 383 (1987) showing that gun owners approve defensive use of force (i.e., use to defend victims) but not offensive uses (e.g. police brutality or private force used to suppress dissent).

55. See 82 *Mich L. Rev.* at 205, fn. 5, and Kates & Engberg, above.

56. Brockway, "But the Bible Doesn't Mention Pistols", May, 1977 *Engage-Social Action Forum*. The language quoted in the text is from pp. 39-40 of this issue, which has been published as a separate pamphlet by the Methodist Board of Church and Society under the title *Handguns in the United States.*

57. See, e.g., footnotes 13, 14, 16, and 17, above, and accompanying text.

58. A. Gottlieb, *The Gun Grabbers*, ch. 2 (Bellevue, WA: Merril; 1986). NCBH has recently changed its name to Coalition Against Gun Violence to facilitate its current emphasis on banning rifles and shotguns as well as handguns. See discussion in Don B. Kates, Henry E. Schaffer, et al., "Guns and Public Health: Epidemic of Violence or Pandemic of Propaganda," 62 *Tenn. L. Rev.* 513–596 (1995) at 515–16.

59. Interview by A. Japenga *Health* magazine, March/April 1994, p. 54.

60. See, e.g. Inge Anna Larish, "Why Annie Can't Get Her Gun: A Feminist Perspective on the Second Amendment," 1996 *U. Ill. L. Rev.* 467-508; Laura Ingraham, "Why Feminists Should Be Trigger Happy," *Wall Street Journal,* May 13, 1996, p. A18; Mary Z. Stange, "Arms and the Woman: A Feminist Reappraisal" in David B. Kopel, *Guns: Who Should Have Them* (Buffalo, NY, Prometheus: 1995); Sayoko Blodgett-Ford, "Do Battered Women Have A Right to Bear Arms," 11 *Yale Law & Policy Rev.* 509–560 (1993); Margaret Howard, "Husband-Wife Homicide: An Essay from a Family Law Perspective," 49 *Law & Contemp. Prob.* 63–88 (1986).

61. *Newsweek,* Jan. 7, 1985.

62. 1985–6 Hearings on Legislation to Modify the 1968 Gun Control
    Act, House Judiciary Committee, Subcommittee on Crime; v. I at
    128 (emphasis added).
63. Ibid. For similar views from the Union of American Hebrew Con-
    gregations and the Board of Church and Society of the Methodist
    Church (condemning handgun ownership for self-defense as "vigi-
    lantism"), see id. at 121-5 and 141. See also June 19, 1975 Press
    Statement of the Young Christian Women's Association of the
    United States.
64. Garry Wills: "NRA is Complicit in the Deaths of Two Children,"
    Detroit Free Press, September 6, 1994; "Or Worldwide Gun Con-
    trol" *Philadelphia Inquirer,* May 17, 1981; "Handguns that Kill,"
    Washington Star, Jan. 18, 1981; and "John Lennon's War," *Chicago
    Sun-times,* Dec. 12, 1980 (emphasis added).
65. Eckholm, "A Little Control, A Lot of Guns," *N.Y. Times,* Aug. 15,
    1993 (quoting Sarah Brady).
66. *Detroit Daily Press* editorial, Jan. 22, 1968. Among the countless
    statements to the same effect see nationally syndicated columnists
    Molly Ivins, "Ban the Things. Ban Them All," *Washington Post,*
    March 16, 1993, and Charles Krauthammer (quoted above extol-
    ling the ban on assault weapons not for its crime-reductive poten-
    tial, which he concedes is negligible, but as a step that helps
    acclimatize the population to the confiscation of all firearms), "Dis-
    arm the Citizenry," *Washington Post* April 5, 1996.
67. *New York Times* editorial 9/24/1975.
68. D.C. Code §§ 6-2132(4) and 6–2372.
69. See section titled "The Character of Gun Owners" in Chapter 1
    and references cited therein.
70. Lizotte & Dixon, "Gun Ownership and the 'Southern Subculture
    of Violence'," 93 *American Journal Of Sociology* 383 (1987). This ap-
    proval of "defensive force" must be distinguished from generally
    "violent attitudes" (as defined by approval of violence against so-
    cial deviants or dissenters). Gun owners are no more likely to have
    generally violent attitudes than are nonowners. Id. Indeed, the
    holders of violent attitudes were less likely than the average gun
    owner to approve of defensive force (perhaps perceiving it would
    be directed against violent people like themselves).
71. Whitehead and Langworthy, "Gun Ownership: Another Look," 6
    Justice Quarterly 263 (1989).
72. Of the remaining respondents 9 percent did not know whether
    they would use deadly force and 13 percent would not.
73. Stell, supra, NIJ Evaluation, supra at 3234, Bruce-Briggs, "The
    Great American Gun War," 45 *The Public Interest* 37, 61 (1976).

Chapter 5

Sagecraft: Bias and Mendacity in the Public Health Literature on Gun Usage*

Don B Kates, Jr.
with John K. Lattimer and James Boen

The 1980s saw a flowering of unbiased academic research and analysis of firearms issues. This was at least in part a result of the influence of the National Institute of Justice Literature Evaluation.[1] Medical and public health literature discussing firearms represents, however, a marked exception to this salubrious trend. Medical and public health discussion of firearms issues have consistently exemplified "sagecraft" in the Znanieckian concept of partisan academic "sages" inventing, selecting, or misinterpreting data to validate preordained conclusions.[2]

*This chapter was presented in somewhat different form at the 1992 annual meeting of the American Society of Criminology. The same themes have been elaborated in a much different format in Don B. Kates, Henry E. Schaffer, et al., "Guns and Public Health: Epidemic of Violence or Pandemic of Propaganda," 62 *TENN. L. REV.* 513-596 (1995).

The CDC's Anti-Gun Campaign

The Centers for Disease Control (hereinafter CDC) is an arm of the U.S. Public Health Service, an agency that until the late 1970s was primarily devoted to study and reduction of infectious disease. But in 1979 the Public Health Service came to the conclusion that firearms, if not strictly an infectious disease, are a comparable evil to be gradually eliminated from American life.[3] The CDC seems to have been primarily invested with that mission through the Intentional Injuries Section of its National Center on Injury Prevention and Control (NCIPC). Concomitantly, the gun lobby has bitterly assailed the CDC for slanted and biased research, preordained anti-gun conclusions, and open and covert advocacy of firearms prohibition.[4]

It bears emphasis that when thus assailed CDC adamantly denies following a preordained objective of providing *post hoc* validation for its parent's objective of gradually eliminating gun ownership. When making such denials at least, the CDC is quick to profess a belief that extant empirical evidence is insufficient to determine whether firearms should be banned. So said Dr. Mark Rosenberg, the NCIPC's director, when a Los Angeles physician, Dr. David Stolinsky, taxed him, NCIPC, and CDC with having an anti-gun agenda. Not content with flatly denying that, Dr. Rosenberg explained that any such agenda would be premature as "our scientific understanding of the role that firearms play in violent events is rudimentary." In a subsequent letter Dr. Rosenberg elaborated, "there is a strong need for further scientific investigations of the relationships among firearms ownership, firearms regulations and the risk of firearm-related injury. *This is an area that has not been given adequate scrutiny.* Hopefully, by addressing these important and appropriate scientific issues we will *eventually* arrive at conclusions which support effective, preventive actions."[5]

As of mid-1996 Dr. Rosenberg was still denying (this time to a Congressional committee) that he, his NCIPC, or the CDC want to ban guns or are "working toward changing society's attitudes so that it becomes socially unacceptable to own handguns."[6] But his credibility has been undercut by such past indiscretions as his boast to the *Washington Post* two years before that his agenda was to create a public perception of firearms as "dirty, deadly—and banned";[7] and characterizing his agenda the year before that to *Rolling Stone* as one that "envisioned a long term campaign, similar to [the campaigns against] tobacco use and auto safety, to convince Americans that guns are, first and foremost, a public health menace."[8]

Concomitantly, Dr. Rosenberg is listed as a member of Cease-Fire's Advisory Panel in the same CeaseFire materials that list its objectives as "promot[ing] handgun-free homes." He and other CDC officials regularly teach at conferences of HELP (the Handgun Epidemic Lowering Plan), a group lobbying for gun bans whose conferences are officially limited to those who share those goals. All this is difficult to square with Dr. Rosenberg's denials — when under fire — of anti-gun views and activity and his professions to the press that "we [CDC and NCIPC] are trying to depoliticize the subject. . . . We're trying to transform it from politics into science."[9] Equally unconvincing are the denials of CDC Director David Satcher, M.D. and spokeswoman Mary Fenley that the CDC is "trying to eliminate guns."[10]

From the mid-1980s when Dr. Rosenberg was appointed to head NCIPC's predecessor division, his own and other CDC-sponsored or published publications have been proclaiming (for instance) that "8,600 homicides and 5,370 suicides [annually] could be avoided" by confiscating all firearms from "the general population."[11] Only in Alice in Wonderland would advocacy of banning and confiscating all firearms constitute "trying to depoliticize the subject" — or comport with Dr. Rosenberg's professions five to ten years later that he believes the facts needed to justify such laws have not been adequately scrutinized and that our understanding is insufficient to allow such conclusions to be drawn.

Unfortunately, what the CDC says under fire appears to be only inversely related to what it says and does in actual practice. It may be useful to review a long letter one of Dr. Rosenberg's subordinates at the NCIPC, Dr. Patrick O'Carroll, published in the July 1989 *Journal of the American Medical Association* (*JAMA*). Although mostly given over to limning the social harms with which gun ownership is associated, the ostensible purpose of the letter was to repudiate a prior *JAMA* article in which Dr. O'Carroll claimed he had been misquoted:

In [that] article, I am correctly described as saying that the

CDC will bring a sober, scientific approach to determining what effect the accessibility of firearms may have on the risk of violent injury. Unfortunately, the next paragraph misquotes me and indicates quite the opposite—that the CDC is trying "to systematically build a case that owning firearms causes deaths." Such an approach would be anathema to any unbiased scientific inquiry because it assumes the conclusion at the outset and then attempts to find evidence to support it.[12]

It may be seen that the approach anathematized by Dr. O'Carroll corresponds closely to the concept of "sagecraft" discussed above. Regrettably, Dr. O'Carroll's disclaimer is itself an example of particularly disingenuous sagecraft. Had that disclaimer been sincere, candor would have required that Dr. O'Carroll repudiate the anti-gun objectives adopted by CDC's parent organization (USPHS) in 1979. Instead, however, Dr. O'Carroll has himself endorsed handgun prohibition with no mention of the 1979 objective, much less any denunciation of it as "anathema to any unbiased scientific inquiry" because it assumed a conclusion in 1979 for which the evidence was not sufficient even as late as 1991 or 1996 (as Dr. Rosenberg himself then admitted).

Candor would also have forced Dr. O'Carroll not to deny, but rather to admit, that the CDC has actively endorsed the conclusion "that owning firearms causes deaths," by fostering research and articles designed "to systematically build a case" for that conclusion.[13] Indicative thereof is the devotion (shortly after Dr. O'Carroll's *JAMA* disclaimer) of an entire edition of the Injury Prevention Network *Newsletter* to the cause of handgun prohibition. The tone of this CDC-affiliated publication is typified by the editor's own contribution, "The NRA: The Myth of Protection, the Marketing of Fear." No less indicative of CDC dedication to "unbiased scientific inquiry" is a dishonest and disgraceful personal attack on two scholars of unimpeachable integrity who drew CDC ire by offering a less negative view of firearms owners than the CDC's.[14]

To avoid a libel suit, the *Newsletter* later abjectly retracted its attack on Prof. Alan Lizotte, of the School of Criminology, State University of New York-Albany, and Prof. David Bordua of the University of Illinois Department of Sociology. (It bears emphasis that, unlike the CDC, as honest scholars Bordua and Lizotte come to conclusions without regard to whether they favor or discomfit the gun lobby. Strangely, when their conclusions are adverse to the gun lobby—and thus favorable to the CDC's preordained position—Bordua and Lizotte suddenly become valid sources for citation by public health writers.)[15]

Problematic Statements and Citations

Some of the problems with the medical-public health literature may be attributed to sheer ignorance of firearms or of the relevant criminological literature. In many other cases, however, the problem seems to be outright mendacity: Anti-gun arguments in medical-public health articles are supported with statistical misrepresentations when accurate rendition would have undermined, or even negated, anti-gun conclusions. To validate the falsified statistics, falsified "references" are cited; the cited reference source either gives a different (sometimes opposite) statistic or turns out not to cover the subject matter at all. Articles or publications and eminent authorities are cited as holding positions that they do not support—or even positions with which they disagree.[16]

1. Comparison of firearms availability to homicide rates as a way "to systematically build a case that owning firearms causes deaths."

One major issue involving guns is their relationship to crime: Does acquiring a gun cause previously law-abiding people to go out and rape, rob, or murder? Or do high or rising rates of crime induce law-abiding people to buy guns, thereby producing the correlation observed in the era 1964 to 1974 between crime increases and increased gun sales? The criminological research available for that period, and for the American population and its sub-groups in general over the last three decades, strongly supports the latter hypothesis in preference to the former.[17] As Toch and Lizotte emphasize,

> if firearms stimulate aggression [i]t is hard to explain that
> where firearms are most dense, violent crime rates are low-

est, and where guns are least dense violent crime rates are
highest. . . . [T]he fact that national patterns show little violent crime where guns are most dense implies that guns do
not elicit aggression in any meaningful way.[18]

This conclusion is exemplified by trend data for the 20-year period
1973 to 1992, which saw a doubling of the number of handguns
coincide with a *decline* in homicide, gun homicide, and handgun
homicide.[19]

Despite the overwhelming evidence to the contrary, it is an
article of faith among medical-public health writers on firearms
issues that, in and of itself, the mere availability of firearms to
law-abiding, responsible adults "causes" them to murder one
another. To buttress this faith, a 1989 official CDC report to Congress claims: "Since the early 1970s the year-to-year fluctuations
in firearm availability has [sic] paralleled the numbers of homicides."[20] No supporting reference is given for this misstatement,
which diametrically reverses the actual trend data. Of course a
1989 report cannot be taxed with inconsistency to the 20-year data
given above that extends into the 1990s. But the same trend was
evident in the 15-year period 1974 to 1988. It saw a 69 percent
increase in the American handgun stock, accompanied by a 27
percent *decline* in handgun murders and a 47 percent increase in
guns of all kinds, accompanied by a 31 percent *decline* in gun
murder overall.[21] In sum, the falsehood in the CDC report to
Congress is so patently contradictory to the actual data that it is
virtually inexplicable except as a lie deliberately perpetrated to
buttress the CDC's opposition to handgun ownership. Nor can
CDC be excused by the fact that a similarly misleading statement
is perpetrated in other anti-gun medical-public health articles,
including one by Dr. Garen Wintemute, a very well-published
advocate among medical-public health researchers.[22]

Can the CDC be acquitted of mendacity on the theory that its
report just inadvertently happened to assert falsely something that
just happens to be crucial to the CDC desire "to systematically
build a case that owning firearms causes death"? Perhaps; but to
blame the error on mere incompetence rather than duplicity requires indulging either of two dubious assumptions in the CDC's
favor. They are: (a) that the authors were somehow unaware of the
15-year decline in handgun homicide — though the CDC had pub-

lished numerous homicide trend data, with special emphasis on firearms involvement,[23] and though the report itself contained a score of other references to firearms injury or death and devoted both a detailed table and a figure to firearms injury or death;[24] or (b) that the authors just didn't bother checking the assertion against the firearms homicide trend data because they were positive it would confirm their faith that "owning firearms causes deaths."[25]

Even indulging assumptions a and b in the CDC's favor, this report amply justifies the charge Dr. O'Carroll's denied—that, in the firearms area at least, the CDC employs procedures that are "anathema to any unbiased scientific inquiry." Indeed, even if assumptions a and b are indulged in the CDC's favor, the report meets the legal criteria for fraudulent nondisclosure and negligent fraud—misrepresentations made without checking the facts and without disclosing that the makers had no idea whether they were true or false.

2. Falsified comparisons to exaggerate handgun involvement in gun accidents.

Other instances of mendacity in the public health literature's championing of handgun prohibition are too clear cut to admit the excuse of mere incompetence. For at least two decades, anti-gun advocates have recognized the political desirability of presenting their goals initially as outlawing only handguns and even overtly eschewing the intent to eventually confiscate rifles and shotguns as well.[26] This gradualistic approach (epitomized by the 1979 USPHS goal of decreasing handgun ownership beginning with a 25 percent decline by the year 2000) is often endorsed in the medical-public health literature.[27] But, for the reasons set out below, an anti-handgun approach is inconsistent with another public health objective, minimizing death from gun accidents. (Accidental gun fatalities and suicides are of such deep concern to public health specialists that they routinely aggregate them with statistics of gun murder.[28] This simultaneously magnifies the social harms associated with firearms and conceals the lack of any increase in murder that accompanied the 110-plus percent increase in the handgun stock over the 20-year period 1973 to 1992.)

The problem that a strategy of banning only handguns ought to create for public health specialists is that it would radically increase the incidence of fatal gun accidents.[29] Given the fear of crime that impels citizens to buy handguns, it is obvious that any measure to make them unavailable would cause citizens to keep loaded long guns as substitute weapons. This is readily conceded by gun control advocates who are too ignorant of firearms to realize that such substitution might increase accidental death because long guns are much less safe as defensive weapons than are handguns.[30] For a host of technical reasons, long guns are both far more susceptible to accidental discharge than handguns and far more deadly when so discharged.

Current statistics suggest that long guns kept loaded in the home are involved in almost seven times as many fatal accidents as are similarly kept handguns. The trend data indicate the magnitude of the risks involved in a handgun-only ban that would encourage a return to people relying on loaded long guns for home defense: the "proliferation of handguns" since 1967 has resulted in the handgun largely displacing the long gun as the weapon kept loaded in the home for self-defense — as a result of which accidental firearm deaths *decreased* by almost 60 percent.[31] From the available data it may be estimated that if the 85.2 percent of loaded handguns in American homes in the year 1980 had been long guns instead, the number of fatal gun accidents would have more than quadrupled, from 1,244 to approximately 5,346. Or, to put it another way, an additional 4,100 lives per year would be lost in accidental shootings in the home if a handgun ban resulted in loaded long guns being kept for defense in the same numbers in which handguns are now kept loaded.[32]

Some medical-public health writers employ duplicity to avoid having to deal with the possibility that banning handguns would sharply increase accidental gun deaths: They misrepresent the statistical evidence as suggesting that handguns represent a greater danger of accidental death than long guns, wherefore it appears that the prohibition of handguns is an unalloyed good with no possible costs. For instance, Dr. Diane H. Shetky argues for banning handguns, but not "taking away all firearms," because, she claims, "Handguns account for only 20% of the nation's firearms yet account for 90% of all firearms [mis]use, both criminal and accidental."[33] Likewise, a CDC article solemnly asserts:

> Our recommendations for legislation and control are di-

rected primarily at handguns, not all guns. Handguns account for *only 20 percent of the firearms in use today, but they are involved in the majority of both criminal and unintentional firearm injuries.*[34] (Emphasis added)

Dr. Shetky supports her assertion by reference to what she calls "Federal Bureau of Investigation, Uniform Crime Reports, Annual Crime Surveys, 1963–73,"[35] and the CDC references "Crime in the United States, 1979: FBI Uniform Crime Reports."

Of course neither Dr. Shetky nor the CDC give page references for their citations—because both statistics and their allegedly supporting citations are patent fabrications. The Uniform Crime Reports do not include *any* figures for gun accidents or accidents in general. As its name suggests, the subject of the Uniform Crime Reports (hereinafter UCRs) is crime. They offer *no* figures on firearms ownership (much less do they compare handgun to long gun ownership). Indeed the ludicrous citation of the UCRs as covering these subjects raises questions about the contributions the medical-public health community so prides itself on making to the study of violence: Shetky and Smith and Falk are so ignorant of criminological research that they can't even produce a faked citation with minimal plausibility. They were so unacquainted with the UCR (the traditional mainstay of American criminal statistics) that they chose to miscite it, even though the citation would immediately incite the suspicion of any criminologist as it purports to address areas the UCR does not cover.

The citations being faked, the claim that "Handguns account for only 20% of the nation's firearms yet account for 90% of all firearms [mis]use, both criminal and accidental" is predictably false as well. Insofar as the issues are even relevant to the UCR, they are still not covered therein. The UCR does give figures on crime in general, but it provides no general figure for firearms crime, much less does it provide figures that allow for comparison of the frequency of handgun use in crime to long gun use.[36] Nor does the UCR give any figure for the subject on which Smith and Falk miscite it: "criminal . . . firearms injury."

Dr. Shetky's claim that 90 percent of "accidental" gun use involves handguns is also baseless as it would include incidents in which a gun accident occurred with no injury to anyone. Presumably there are many such incidents each year. But no regular accounting is made of total gun accidents, much less is there available a breakdown between handgun and long gun accidents. There are no data available to substantiate even what Smith and Falk claimed, that is, that handguns predominate in firearms accidents in which there is some injury. Partial data are available on injury accidents, but, again, there is no breakdown between long gun and handgun accidents.[37] This is another example of Shetky and Smith and Falk fabricating statistics to lend spurious weight to their opposition to handgun ownership.

It should be noted that since 1979 statistics for comparative handgun involvement in *fatal* gun accidents have been available from the National Safety Council. Shetky and Smith and Falk do not mention these data because, consistent with the general safety of handguns, they contradict Smith and Falk's claim that handguns are involved in most accidents (much less Shetky's that they are involved in 90 percent). In fact, handguns can be identified as the weapon involved in only about 13 percent of fatal gun accidents.

This 13 percent figure is misleading, however, as in more than half of the accidental gun fatalities the kind of firearm is not identified. Assuming the same proportion of handgun involvement in these fatalities as in those in which the kind of firearm can be identified, handguns were involved in about 41 percent of all accidental firearm fatalities from 1979 through 1991. This is, of course, less than half of Shetky's 90 percent figure and substantially less than Smith and Falk's "majority." The available statistics for the years 1979 to 1991 are set out in Table 5.1.

Finally the claim by Shetky and Smith and Falk that handguns represent only 20 percent of the American gun stock is almost 100 percent lower than the best data available when they wrote. Checking those data would have shown them authoritative estimates that even in 1968 handguns had constituted almost 27 percent of the total gun stock—and that handguns had risen to 37 percent by 1978.[38] In sum, to exaggerate the argument for banning handguns—and minimize problems therewith—Shetky and Smith and Falk each falsified figures:(a) for involvement of handguns in gun crimes; (b) for involvement of handguns in gun accidents-injuries; and (c) for the proportion handguns make up of the total gun stock.

Moreover, the latter issue was irrelevant to—and reverses the policy implications of—the relative involvement of handguns in

TABLE 5.1   NSC Gun Accident Statistics

	Total	Handgun	Shotgun	Rifle	Unspecified*	% Handgun**
1991	1441	255	163	94	929	50%
1990	1416	241	160	73	942	51%
1989	1489	231	175	86	997	47%
1988	1501	202	185	93	1021	42%
1987	1440	206	178	105	951	42%
1986	1452	183	190	108	971	37%
1985	1649	190	215	113	1131	37%
1984	1668	225	214	118	1111	40%
1983	1695	209	260	132	1094	35%
1982	1756	219	232	127	1178	38%
1981	1871	224	273	140	1234	35%
1980	1955	288	283	129	1255	41%
1979	2004	311	254	145	1294	44%
1979–91	21337	2984	2782	1463	14108	41%

*This category includes a small number of what are called "military rifle" fatalities. The rifle category is "hunting rifles"; the shotgun category includes "automatics."
**Percentages are rounded off.

fatal gun accidents. By definition, an *unloaded* firearm cannot be accidentally fired; therefore, the relevant issue is the proportion that loaded handguns bear to all firearms that are kept loaded. The available evidence indicates that now, with handguns readily available, they are "nearly all of the guns kept loaded" at any one time.[39] Less than 15 percent of the firearms kept loaded in the home are long guns. Yet in approximately 60 percent of fatal gun accidents, they are the firearm involved. That comparison suggests the safety dangers of a policy that would result in frightened people substituting loaded long guns for the handguns they presently keep for defense.

3. More falsified comparisons between handgun and long gun misuse.

Wintemute's erroneous claim that "since the 1970s" firearms availability and firearms murders have risen "in parallel" is noted above. The statement is highly misleading, and it is difficult to believe that this was not intended. Dr. Wintemute cannot possibly be unaware that from "the early 1970s" through the late 1980s gun

homicides *declined* almost as substantially as firearms availability
increased. Dr. Garen Wintemute and his frequent co-author Professor Stephen Teret are among the most prolific authors of anti-
gun medical-public health articles.[40] Other than duplicity, it is
difficult to explain either Dr. Wintemute's claim of parallelism or
his making the following assertion:

> While [handguns] account for only approximately 25% of
> the firearms in the United States, they are used in 70–75%
> of firearms homicides, approximately 70% of firearm sui-
> cides, and a like number of unintended firearms deaths.[41]

The least of the problems with this is that the best estimate (from
the NIJ Literature Evaluation, of which Dr. Wintemute was well
aware) was that handguns were approximately 37 percent of the
total gun stock,[42] not 25 percent as he claimed. Far more egregious
is his claim that handguns are responsible for approximately 70
percent of fatal gun accidents when, on their face, 1979 to 1988
National Safety Council figures showed 13.3 percent of such accidents involving handguns.[43]

Similar is Dr. Wintemute's misrepresentation of handgun
involvement in suicide. In a typical year (1980) there are well over
15,000 gun suicides—of which only about 2,100, or 13.7 percent,
can be identified as being by handgun. As with gun accidents, this
13.7 percent figure is under-inclusive because the kind of firearm
is not identified in roughly two-thirds of gun suicides. Presumably, some proportion of these are handgun suicides. Assuming,
however, that handguns account for the same percentage in unidentified suicides as in those in which the kind of firearm is
identified, handguns are involved in only 41 percent of gun suicides—not Professor Wintemute's claimed 70 percent. These particular calculations come from *Point Blank*, a source not published
when Dr. Wintemute wrote. But he is in no position to complain
about that. As a leading researcher in the area, he was just as able
as Kleck to make the same simple mathematical calculation involved. Or, if he didn't wish to go to the trouble, he could have
relied on the readily available NSC data showing that in only 13.3
percent of gun suicides in which the kind of gun was identified
was it a handgun. The issue here is not whether the 13.3 percent
figure is as comprehensive as Kleck's 41 percent. Clearly it is not.

The issue here is why did Wintemute choose, instead of either 41 or 13 percent, his 70 percent figure, which has no provenance and grossly exaggerates the number of handgun suicides?

Appendix
Calculation of Increase in Fatal Accidents that Would Result from Long Gun Substitution

The precise number of accidental fatalities that would result from a handgun ban can only be speculated because, *inter alia*, we cannot be sure what proportion of people who now keep handguns for protection in the home would switch to relying on loaded long guns instead. But there can be little doubt that fatal accidental shootings would greatly increase insofar as a handgun ban caused widespread substitution of the far more dangerous long gun in the home defense role.

Given the level of crime and fear, millions of Americans feel it prudent or necessary to keep a loaded firearm in their home for self-defense, a practice from which no amount of preachments seems able to dissuade them. Earlier in the century, when long guns were more commonly kept by families for hunting, and cost reasons reduced the availability of handguns, long guns were kept loaded for home defense.[44] Thus, it may confidently be assumed that if a ban made handguns less available, many Americans would substitute loaded long guns for handguns in the home defense role.[45]

Necessarily, the effect of such substitution on a large scale would be to greatly increase accidental fatalities. This is because a loaded long gun is much more problematic than a handgun kept for home defense: If kept loaded and ready for rapid defensive deployment, a long gun is much more difficult to secure and keep away from a child. Moreover, long guns are both more likely to accidentally discharge and deadlier when discharged than are handguns.[46]

We calculate that a long gun kept loaded in the home is almost seven times more likely to be involved in a fatal gun accident than a handgun. This calculation is based on the following, admittedly spotty, data: 1989 national survey data indicate that 31 percent of gun owners keep a loaded gun in the home at any one time.[47] Further survey data suggest that 85 to 90 percent of the guns kept loaded in the home are handguns, and 10 to 15 percent are long guns. If so, in 1980 approximately 9,923,480 households kept loaded handguns at any one time, whereas about

1,720,381 kept a loaded long gun.[48] In 1980 there were 1,244 fatal gun accidents in homes, of which 562 were with handguns and 682 were with long guns. (*Point Blank,* table 7.10 on p. 316.) This works out to 5.66 fatalities per 100,000 loaded handgun households and 39.64 per 100,000 loaded long gun households, that is, almost seven times more fatal home accidents with long guns than with handguns.[49]

It does not necessarily follow that a handgun ban would increase fatal home gun accidents by a factor of seven, of course. In the first place, many handgun owners would defy a ban. Among those who did comply, some might be dissuaded from substituting a loaded long gun by the greater danger of accident. Nonetheless, substitution of a long gun for a handgun would be easy and natural for those who deem it necessary to keep a loaded home defense gun. It would be particularly easy for those who already own one or more of the approximately 150 million American long guns.[50] Those who do not now own a long gun, or who wish to purchase one deemed particularly suitable for home defense, will find such long guns comparable in price to similarly suitable handguns.[51]

In sum, to the extent a handgun ban caused long gun substitution in home defense weaponry, the result would almost certainly be sharply increased accidental home fatalities. The following figure is illustrative: If the loaded handgun households in 1980 had experienced accidental fatalities at the long gun rate, they would have suffered 5,346 fatal gun accidents rather than only 562.

Notes

1. Originally published as J. Wright, P. Rossi & K. Daly, *Weapons, Crime and Violence in America: A Literature Review and Research Agenda* (Washington, D.C., Gov't. Print. Off.: 1981), the report was published in revised form, and is still available, as J. Wright, P. Rossi, K. Daly, *Under the Gun: Weapons, Crime and Violence in the United States* (N.Y., Aldine: 1983). Citations to it here are to this later, commercial publication.
2. For explication of the "sagecraft" concept, see Tonso, "Social Science and Sagecraft in the Debate Over Gun Control" 5 *Law & Policy Q*. 325 (1983). For an extended treatment of this literature by two of us, co-authored by two Harvard Medical School professors and a North Carolina State University biostatistician, see Don B. Kates, Henry E. Schaffer, et al., "Guns and Public Health: Epidemic of Violence or Pandemic of Propaganda," 62 *Tenn. L. Rev.* 513-596 (1995).
3. The 1979 objective to radically reduce handgun ownership, with an initial objective of a 25 percent reduction by the year 2000 is discussed in Fingerhut, L.A. and J.C. Kleinman, "Firearm Mortality Among Children and Youth." Advance Data #178. *NCHS* (Nov. 3, 1989) and "International and Interstate Comparisons of Homicides Among Young Males." *JAMA* 263 (1989): 3292-3295. Fingerhut and Kleinman add, significantly, "The data presented in this report underscore these concerns." Not coincidentally, no CDC publication in this area fails to underscore the anti-gun objectives adopted in 1979 by its parent agency, USPHS and reaffirmed on subsequent occasions. See, e.g. Public Health Service, *Healthy People* The Surgeon General's Report on Health Promotion and Disease Prevention. Washington, D.C. (1979) at 9-21 and USPHS, *Healthy People* The Surgeon General's Report on Health Promotion and Disease Prevention: Background Papers. Washington, D.C. (1979) at 18, 64–7, 465, USPHS (1986) Surgeon General's Workshop on Violence and Public Health: Report, 1985. Rockville, Md. at 53 (necessity to ban private possession of handguns), National Committee for Injury Prevention and Control, "Injury Prevention: Meeting the Challenge," *American Journal of Preventive Medicine* (Supp. 1989) at p. 3 (same).
4. See, e.g. Lori Montgomery, "CDC Research Wilts Under NRA Attack," *Detroit Free Press*, May 1, 1996, and other articles cited in the text below.
   Using a disease model to address firearms, public health writers generally describe them as disease "vectors," "toxins," or

causes of an epidemic. See, e.g. Colburn, "Gunshots as an Epidemic: Some Doctors Call Firearms a 'Toxin' in the Environment," *Washington Post Health*, Nov. 1, 1988, and "Epidemiologists Aim at New Target: Health Risk of Handgun Proliferation," Feb. 3, 1989, *JAMA*, v. 261 at 675-676 (quoting, *inter alia*, the president of the American College of Epidemiology that "Homicide is not a disease, but it is a public health condition whose primary cause is possession of guns"). See also Arthur L. Kellermann, "Obstacles to Firearm and Violence Research," 12 *Health Affairs* 142, 150-151 (1993) and James A. Mercy & Mark Rosenberg, et al., "Public Health Policy for Preventing Violence," 12 *Health Affairs* 7 (1993).

5. Feb. 7, 1991 and March 19, 1991 letters from Dr. Rosenberg to Dr. Stolinsky; our emphasis.

6. Jeff Nesmith, "CDC and Guns," *Atlanta Journal & Constitution*, May 2, 1996, p. 5A.

7. William Rasberry, "Sick People With Guns," *Washington Post*, Oct. 19, 1994, p. A23.

8. Frank Wilkinson, "Gunning for Guns," *Rolling Stone*, Dec. 9, 1993, at p. 36.

9. Quoted by Doug Levy in *USA Today*, Aug. 25, 1995, "Doctors, NRA Take Aim at CDC's Anti-Violence Program."

10. Elizabeth Schwinn, "Gun Lobbyists Blast Research," *New Orleans Times-Picayune*, July 7, 1996, p. A3 (quoting Fenley); Satcher OpEd, Nov. 5, 1995 *Washington Post.*

11. Rosenberg, et al. "Violence: Homicide, Assault, and Suicide," pp. 164-178 in Health Policy Consultation, eds. *Closing the Gap*. New York: Oxford, at 175-76 (1987); see also Rice, D.P. et al. (1989) Cost of Injury in the United States: A Report to Congress. Atlanta: CDC, at 127 (estimating thousands of lives to be saved by gun control) and Rosenberg, Stark & Zahn, "Interpersonal Violence: Homicide and Spouse Abuse," pp. 1399-1426 in J.M. Last, ed. *Public Health and Preventive Medicine*, 12th Edition. Norwalk, Conn: Appleton-Century-Crofts.

12. O'Carroll, P.W. (1989) "Correspondence: CDC's Approach to Firearms Injuries." *JAMA* 262 (July 21): 348-349 at 349.

13. In addition to the Fingerhut & Kleinman and other CDC works cited in footnote 3 above, and those by Rosenberg cited above, see, e.g. Rice, et al., above; Smith and Falk "Unintentional Injuries," pp. 143-163 in Health Policy Consultation, eds., *Closing the Gap*. New York: Oxford at p. 157 (1987) ("Our recommendations for legislation and control are directed primarily at handguns."); Sloan, et al. (1988) "Handgun Regulations, Crime, Assaults, and Homicide: A Tale of Two Cities." *NEJM* 319 (Nov. 10): 1256-1262; Gulaid, et al. (1988) "Differences in Death Rates Due to Injury Among

Blacks and Whites, 1984." *MMWR* 37 (SS-3): 25-31; Mercy and Saltzman "Fatal Violence Among Spouses in the United States, 1976–85." *American Journal of Public Health* 79: 595–599 (1989). See also Meredith, "The Murder Epidemic." *Science* 84: 42–48 (1984) and Forsyth "Epidemic of Killing." *Washington Post/Health* (Feb. 20):9–10 (1985).

14. Eisen, "Guns: In Whose Hands?: A portrait of Gunowners and Their Culture," Injury Prevention Network *Newsletter*, Winter, 1989-90 at p. 9 assailed as "racist" a finding in Lizotte and Bordua, "Patterns of Legal Firearms Ownership: A Cultural and Situational Analysis of Illinois Counties," *Law and Policy Quarterly* 1:147-75 (1979); see also Lizotte and Bordua, "Firearms Ownership for Sport and Protection: Two Divergent Models." *American Sociological Review* 45:229-44 (1980). The finding in question was that, statistically, women who live in or near crime areas, or areas with large black populations, are much more likely to own firearms than women living elsewhere. Although this might reflect racism on the part of the gun owners, Eisen does not explain what is — or could be — "racist" about Lizotte and Bordua stating a *statistical fact* upon which they offer no comment.

15. See, e.g., National Committee for Injury Prevention and Control, Injury Prevention: Meeting the Challenge. *American Journal of Preventive Medicine* (Supp. 1989) at 265, citing Gary Kleck and David Bordua, "The Factual Foundation for Certain Key Assumptions of Gun Control," 5 *Law & Policy Q.* 271, 281 (1983) for favorable comments on background checks for prospective gun purchasers; and Kassirer, "Editor's Reply," 326 *NEJM* 1161 (1992) citing McDowall, Lizotte and Wiersema, "General Deterrence Through Civilian Gun Ownership: An Evaluation of the Quasi-Experimental Evidence," 29 *Criminology* 541 (1989).

16. See discussion below and the 62 *Tenn L. Rev.* article cited above.

17. See, e.g., Gary Kleck & Britt Patterson, "The Impact of Gun Control and Gun Ownership Levels on City Violence Rates," 9 *J. Quant. Crimin.* 249-87 (1993); David J. Bordua, "Firearms Ownership and Violent Crime: A Comparison of Illinois Counties," in J. Byrne and R. Sampson (ed.) *The Social Ecology of Crime* (1986); Chris Eskridge, "Zero-Order Inverse Correlations between Crimes of Violence and Hunting Licenses in the United States," 71 *Sociology & Social Research* 55 (1986); David McDowall, "Gun Availability and Robbery Rates: A Panel Study of Large U.S. Cities, 1974-1978," 8 *Law & Policy Q.* 135 (1986); Kleck, "The Relationship between Gun Ownership Levels and Rates of Violence in the United States," in D. Kates (ed.) *Firearms and Violence* (1984); Lizotte and Bordua, "Firearms Ownership for Sport and Protection:

Two Divergent Models," 45 *Am. Soc. Rev.* (1980); Lizotte, Bordua and White, "Firearms Ownership for Sport and Protection: Two Not So Divergent Models," 46 *Am. Soc. Rev.* 499, 503 (1981);David J. Bordua & Alan J. Lizotte, "Patterns of Legal Firearms Ownership: A Situational and Cultural Analysis of Illinois Counties," 2 *Law & Policy Q.* 147 (1979); Douglas Murray, "Handguns, Gun Control Law and Firearm Violence," 23 *Social Problems* 81 (1975).

18. Toch & Lizotte, "Research & Policy: The Case of Gun Control" in P. Suedfeld & P. Tetlock, *Psychology and Social Advocacy* (NY Hemisphere Press, 1990).

   Ceteris paribus, if gun ownership did fuel violent crime, it should be the case that areas with high gun ownership should have higher violent crime rates than areas with lower ownership. Thus, it is noteworthy that numerous studies trying to link gun ownership to violence rates find either no relationship or a negative one, that is, cities and counties with high gun ownership suffer less violence than demographically comparable areas with lower gun ownership. See Lizotte and Bordua, op. cit.; McDowall, "Gun Availability and Robbery Rates: A Panel Study of Large U.S. Cities, 1974-1978," 8 *Law & Policy Q.* 135 (1986); Bordua, "Firearms Ownership and Violent Crime: A Comparison of Illinois Counties"; Kleck & Patterson, supra.

19. See 62 *Tenn. L. Rev.,* above, at table 3 and 572-74. See also Don B. Kates, "Firearms and Violence: Old Premises and Current Evidence" in T. Gurr (ed.) *Violence in America* (1989) at p. 201: "England's foremost gun control analyst, Colin Greenwood, jocularly asks: Since America so greatly exceeds England not just in the rate of gun crime but in that with knives, should we assume that butcher knives are illegal in England? And if more guns explain the much higher U.S. gun crime rates, what explains the much higher rates of unarmed Americans robbing or beating each other to death: do Americans 'have more hands and feet than' Britons?

   "Claiming that in any society the number of guns always suffices to arm the few who want to obtain and use them illegally, Greenwood feels the issue is simply one of the relative size of that group: Why is it that perhaps 1 in 300 Americans is inclined toward violent crime while the comparable figure for Japanese and Europeans (including the well-armed Swiss) may be 1 in 30,000? He attributes American crime 'not to the availability of any particular class of weapon' but to socio-economic and cultural factors which dictate that American criminals are more willing to use extreme violence[; quoting a report of the British Office of Health Economics:] 'One reason often given for the high numbers of murders and manslaughters in the United States is the easy availability of firearms. . . . But the strong correlation with racial and linked socio-economic factors suggests that the underlying determinants of the homicide rate relate to particular cultural factors.'"

20. D.P. Rice, et al. "Cost of Injury in the United States: A Report to Congress "(CDC, 1989) at 23.

21. *Point Blank,* table 2.1, showing: (a) that, on the average, 2 million new handguns per year were purchased by Americans between 1974 and 1988; (b) that in the same period approximately 5 million new guns of all guns types were purchased per year; (c) that the accumulated handgun stock increased from 39 million to 65.8 million in that period and the total gun stock from 134.5 million to 198.3 million, an increase from 187.9 to 270.6 in handguns per 1000 Americans and from 627.0 to 815.5 in all guns per 1000 Americans. In contrast, handgun homicide declined 27 percent: in 1974, when the total U.S. population was 211 million, handguns were involved in approximately 11,125 murders (54 percent of all murders), but by 1988 the total U.S. population was 245 million and handguns were involved in approximately 8,278 murders (45 percent of all murders). Homicide by all means also declined, though at a lesser rate (almost 10 percent).

22. Wintemute, "Firearms as a Cause of Death in the United States." 27 *J. of Trauma* 532, 534 (1987). ("Since the early 1970s year-to-year changes in new firearm availability and firearms homicide have often occurred in parallel.") For what it is worth, Professor Wintemute's formulation is slightly less mendacious than the CDC's.

23. See, e.g.: CDC, "Firearms-Associated Homicides Among Family Members, Relatives, or Friends—Ohio." *MMWR* 38 (April 21, 1989): 253-256; Fingerhut, L.A. and J.C. Kleinman, "Firearm Mortality Among Children and Youth." Advance Data #178. NCHS (Nov. 3, 1989) and "International and Interstate Comparisons of Homicides Among Young Males." *JAMA* 263 (1989): 3292-3295, CDC, "Premature Mortality Due to Homicides—United States, 1968-1985." *MMWR* 35 (Sept. 9, 1988d): 543-545; CDC, "Homicide Surveillance: High-Risk Racial and Ethical Groups—Blacks and Hispanics 1970 to 1983." Atlanta (1986); CDC, "Premature Mortality Due to Suicide and Homicide—United States, 1984." *MMWR* 36 (Aug. 21, 1987): 531-34; CDC, "Homicide Surveillance: High-Risk Racial and Ethnic Groups—Blacks and Hispanics, 1970-1983." *MMWR* 38 (Oct. 2, 1987): 634-636; CDC, "Progress Toward Achieving the National 1990 Objectives for Injury Prevention and Control." *MMWR* 37 (March 11, 1988): 138-149; CDC, "Impact of Homicide on Years of Potential Life Lost in Michigan's Black Population." *MMWR* 38 (Jan. 13, 1989): 4-11.

24. See *Cost of Injury,* op. cit., pp. xxvii, 11, 14, 21, 22, 24, 35, 43, 46, 47, 48, 62, 83, 129, 130, 141, 143, 163, 191, 210, 251.

25. On reading this manuscript in preparing the book, Gary Kleck offered a partially exculpatory hypothesis that, in fairness, we quote *in haec verba:* [The] [p]eriod [the CDC] referred to could be 1970 to 1985 [rather than 1974 to 1988], since CDC relies largely on [V]ital [S]tatistics data, and the latest available as of 1989 would have been 1985. Also since [the CDC] statement vaguely alludes to 'firearm availability,' it is arguable that CDC had in mind survey measures of household gun prevalence, esp[escially] handgun prevalence. Likewise, maybe 'numbers of homicides' was a sloppy reference to *handgun* homicides. Nevertheless, I can't see *any* sense in which the CDC 1989 claim could be accurate, other than the increase from 1970 to 1974 in homicides (total gun or handgun), paralleled by increases in gun/handgun stock over the same period." [Emphasis by Prof. Kleck.]

26. See, e.g. R. Clark, *Crime in America* (Simon & Schuster, 1970) 93, N. Morris and G. Hawkins, *The Honest Politician's Guide to Crime Control* (U. Chi. Press, 1969) 70; see also Fields, "Handgun Prohibition and Social Necessity," 23 *St.L.U.L.J.* 35, 36 (1979).

27. See e.g. Rosenberg, Stark & Zahn, "Interpersonal Violence: Homicide and Spouse Abuse," pp. 1399-1426 in J.M. Last, ed. *Public Health and Preventive Medicine,* 12th Edition. Norwalk, Conn: Appleton-Century-Crofts, at p. 1422 (1986); "Epidemiologists Aim at New Target: Health Risk of Handgun Proliferation," Feb. 3, 1989, *JAMA,* v. 261 at 675-676; Baker, "Without Guns Do People Kill People?" 75 *Am. J. Pub. Health* 587 (1985); *Washington Post/Health,* Nov. 1, 1988: "Gunshots as An Epidemic"; Shetky, "Children and Handguns: A Public Health Concern," 139 *American Journal of Diseases of Children* 229 (1985) and reply to a critical letter to the editor printed in *The Pediatric Forum* section of the Journal's Jan. 1986 issue.

28. See, e.g., Stephen Teret & Garen Wintemute, "Handgun Injuries: The Epidemiologic Evidence for Assessing Legal Responsibility," 6 *Hamline L. Rev.* 341 (1983); Susan B. Baker, et al., *The Injury Fact Book* 90-91 (1984), Susan B. Baker, "Without Guns Do People Kill People?" 75 *Am. J. Pub. Health* 587 (1985); Rosenberg, Stark & Zahn, op. cit., Teret, "Litigating for the Public's Health," 76 *Am. J. Pub. Health* 1027, 1028 (1986); "Epidemiologists Aim at New Target," supra.

29. In general we have consigned the references for this and the following paragraph to the Appendix, which provides a comprehensive discussion of the dangers of fatal gun accident from

handguns and long guns, respectively, kept loaded for defense in the home.

30. See an article by the then-principal spokesman for the National Coalition to Ban Handguns claiming that a handgun ban would reduce accidental deaths because "law-abiding citizens would then turn to *safer* long guns [i.e. rifles and shotguns] for self-protection." Fields, "Handgun Prohibition and Social Necessity," 23 *ST.L.U.L.J.* 23, 51 (1979) (emphasis added).

31. G. Kleck, *Point Blank: Guns and Violence in America* (Aldine, 1991) 275, 280–1 and 304. Compare table 2.1, showing a 173 percent increase in handgun ownership in the 20-year period 1967 to 1986 (i.e., a 106 percent increase per capita) to table 7.1, showing a decrease in fatal gun accidents from 1.47 per 100,000 population to .59 in the same period. This decrease has not continued past 1986, but since then the rate of fatal gun accidents has held steady at the same low figure.

32. That is to say, fatal accidental shootings would increase from the present almost 1,450 per year to between 3,170 and 4,865 per year. The Appendix hereto details the empirical bases underlying these estimates and the substantial problems therewith.

33. See Shetky, "Children and Handguns: A Public Health Concern," 139 *American Journal of Diseases of Children* 229 (1985) and her reply to a letter to the editor printed in *The Pediatric Forum* section of the Journal's Jan. 1986 issue. For similar erroneous assertions see Baker, "Without Guns Do People Kill People?" 75 *Am. J. Pub. Health* 587 (1985), Teret & Wintemute, "Handgun Injuries: The Epidemiologic Evidence for Assessing Legal Responsibility," 6 *Hamline L. Rev.* 341, 349-50 (1983).

34. Smith, G.S. and H. Falk (1987) "Unintentional Injuries," pp. 143-163 in Health Policy Consultation, eds. *Closing the Gap*. New York: Oxford, at p. 157.

35. Shetky, Jan. 1986 letter, above. A minor problem is that Dr. Shetky's reference does not exist as cited. Giving her the benefit of the doubt, we may assume that her locution is an inept reference not to a single volume covering the 11-year period 1963 to 1973, but to the *FBI, Uniform Crime Reports* for each of those years separately.

36. The only handgun and long gun figures the UCR gives are for murders. Significantly, those figures do not support Shetky's claim that 90 percent are by handgun. From the UCR figures an anti-gun writer has calculated handguns "are used in 70-75% of firearm homicides." Wintemute, "Closing the Gap Between Research and Policy: Firearms," *Injury Prevention Network Newsletter*, Winter, 1989–90, at p. 20.

37. The NIJ Literature Evaluation (the most authoritative source available when Shetky and Smith and Falk wrote) notes that estimates of the numbers of accidental firearms injuries are widely divergent, the best having only a 67 percent confidence level; *Under the Gun*, pp. 169-70 (citing estimates of approximately 20,000, 100,000, 155,000 and 183,000 for different years). The latest available estimate is 23,910 accidental woundings for the year 1986 from *Point Blank*, table 2.8. Its author himself reposes minimal confidence in it.

38. G. Newton & F. Zimring, *Firearms and Violence in the United States* (U.S. Gov't. Print. Off., 1969), ch. 1 (estimating 24 million handguns out of a total gun stock of 90 million), NIJ Literature Evaluation Table 2-5 (estimating 50 million handguns out of a total gun stock of 135 million). The authors take the table from other sources and are dubious about its totals — but note that the relative proportions it shows of handguns to other guns is supported by all available evidence.

39. *Point Blank* at 117. Again, for detailed discussion of the facts on which we rely, see the Appendix hereto.

40. See, e.g. Wintemute, "Closing the Gap Between Research and Policy: Firearms," *Injury Prevention Network Newsletter*, Winter, 1989–90; Wintemute, The Choice of Weapons in Suicide," *Am. J. of Public Health* 78: 824-826 (1988); Wintemute, "Firearms as a Cause of Death in the United States," *J. of Trauma* 27: 532-536. (1987); Wintemute, et al. "The Epidemiology of Firearm Death Among Residents of California," 146 *Western J. of Medicine* 374-377 (1987); Wintemute, Teret, Kraus, Wright, Bradfield. "When Children Shoot Children: 88 Unintended Deaths in California," *JAMA* 257: 3107-3109 (1987); Teret & Wintemute, "Handgun Injuries: The Epidemiologic Evidence for Assessing Legal Responsibility," 6 *Hamline L. Rev.* 341, 349-50 (1983). See also Webster, Chaulk, Teret & Wintemute, "Reducing Firearms Injuries," *Issues in Science and Technology*, Spring, 1991: 73–9.

41. Wintemute, "Closing the Gap Between Research and Policy: Firearm," *Injury Prevention Network Newsletter*, Winter, 1989–90, at p. 20.

42. NIJ Literature Evaluation Table 2-5.

43. See discussion at Table and accompanying text, supra. We reiterate that this 13.3 percent figure is under-inclusive because in more than half of the accidental gun fatalities the kind of firearm is not identified. Even assuming, however, the same percentage of handgun involvement in the unidentified fatalities as in those in which the kind of firearm can be identified, handguns are involved not in 70 percent but in about 41 percent of all accidental firearm fatalities.

44. In the 1920s and 1930s handgun ownership was estimated at 5 to 10 million, with a 7:1 ratio of long guns to handguns. Benenson,

"A Controlled Look at Gun Controls," 14 *N.Y.L. For.* 718, 720
(1968) (citing 1937 guesstimate by the U.S. Attorney General). According to available figures for domestic firearms production
(1899-1945) and imports (1917-45), by 1945 the total gun stock was
46.9 million, of which handguns were 12.7 million. *Point Blank,* table 2.1. By 1987, the total gun stock had quadrupled to 198 million
and handguns had quintupled to 65.8 million. *Id.*

　　Early in the century when income was much lower, and gun
costs much higher, families had to make a hunting weapon do
double duty as a defense weapon. The increased popularity of the
handgun, the defensive weapon *par excellence* is attributable to a
combination of factors: the growth in relative wealth, the decline
in economic dependence on hunting, and the consequent increase
in the relative importance of defensive gun ownership. See discussion in n. 1 to Bruce-Briggs, "The Great American Gun War," Fall
1976, *The Public Interest* [reprinted in L. Nisbet (ed.), *The Gun Control Debate* (Buffalo, Prometheus, 1990)].

45. This is readily conceded by gun control advocates who are too ignorant of firearms to realize that such substitution might increase
accidental death because long guns are much less safe as defensive
weapons than handguns. See, e.g. Fields, supra 23 *St.L.U.L.J.* at 51.

46. See discussion in Kates, "Handgun Prohibition and the Original
Meaning of the Second Amendment," 82 *Mich. L. Rev.* 203, 261-4
(1983). *Inter alia,* the dangers are particularly great for small children; toddlers cannot operate a handgun but can easily discharge
a long gun if their parents irresponsibly keep it loaded and readily
available to children in the home. *Id.*

47. *Point Blank,* p. 117: A total of 31 percent answered that they had a
loaded gun in their home at that time; 24 percent said that they
kept a gun loaded at all times.

48. This may be the appropriate point to note that although gun ownership surveys are numerous they present a host of problems: for
example, if the questions were about individual gun ownership
they do not necessarily comprehend the entire household's ownership; if the questions were limited to household ownership, they
may have been directed to a nonowner who answered based on assumption or guess rather than on personal knowledge as to how
many guns are owned, of what types, and for what reasons—or
whether any are kept loaded.

　　Strangely, only one national survey (the 1989 Time/CNN)
seems to have asked whether the household gun(s) is kept loaded,
and it failed to ask which kinds are kept loaded. Illinois survey
data indicate that a loaded gun is kept in 35.4 percent of handgun
owning households, in 31.9 percent of households that have both

handgun(s) and long gun(s), but in only 1.6 percent of households that have only a long gun. *Point Blank*, p. 117. As the data do not reveal what kinds of guns were loaded in the households having both handgun and long gun, they are discarded. Combining the data samples from the other two sets of households yields the conclusion that 15 percent of the guns kept loaded were long guns and 85 percent were handguns. These Illinois data are consistent with (and even more conservative than) the only other samples of which we are aware. First, based on a 1990 survey of 5,233 families with children conducted in 29 pediatric practices in Chicago, New Jersey, Houston, Utah, Georgia, Iowa, and South Carolina, of those keeping firearms loaded in their homes 89 percent kept handguns, whereas only 11 percent kept long guns. Yvonne D. Senturia, et al., "Children's Household Exposure to Guns: A Pediatric Pratice-Based Survey," 93 *Pediatrics* 469-475 (1994). Second, "Of North Carolina households with children less than 20 years of age surveyed, 35% had handguns and 40% of these kept their guns loaded." Webster, Wilson, Duggan and Pakula, "Parents' Beliefs About Preventing Gun Injuries to Children," 89 *Pediatrics* 908 (1992) AT 908, citing J.M. Bowling, *Unintentional Childhood Injury in North Carolina*, SCHS Studies, Raleigh, NC: State Center for Health Statistics, Division of Health Services, NC Department of Human Resources.

49. We have given 1980 figures because those are the most recent ones on which we have a handgun/long gun breakdown for fatal gun accidents in the home. As Table 5.1 shows, the rate of fatal gun accidents continued to decline from 1980 to 1986. Since then the rate has stayed virtually flat. As the rate decreased, the number of fatal gun accidents involving handguns increased, yet another indication that the handgun has replaced the long gun as the weapon kept loaded in the home for self-defense.

50. This figure is calculated from the figures for 1994 gun ownership in 62 *Tenn. L. Rev.* above at table 3.

51. The basic defense handgun is a revolver in .38 special or larger caliber. Cheap foreign manufactured revolvers of this type like the Armscor, Llama, Rossi, or Taurus retail from $200 or slightly above to $339. The standard American-made cheap .38 specials retail from $333 (S&W Model-10) through $435 (Colt King Cobra). K. Warner, *Gun Digest* (1992) 289-98. In comparison, Armscor 12 gauge pump-action riot guns start at $194, and standard cheap American-made riot guns retail for $276 to $407 (Mossberg 500 Security to Ithaca 87). *Id.* at 366 and 388.

PART III

GUNS
&
SELF-DEFENSE

Chapter 6

The Frequency of Defensive Gun Use*

Gary Kleck[1]

The ownership and use of guns for defense should have been of considerable interest to scholars in many areas, but until recently it has largely been ignored. For example, the prevalence of guns in America holds great significance for the "routine activities" approach to crime, which conceptualizes criminal incidents as the convergence in time and space of "likely offenders and suitable targets in the absence of capable guardians" (Cohen and Felson 1979, p. 590). The primary, ultimate source of "capability" is the appearance of being able and willing to use force, or to mobilize the forceful capabilities of others. Given the fact that at least half of all U.S. households and a quarter of retail businesses keep firearms (Crocker 1982; U.S. Small Business Administration 1969), gun ownership must surely be considered a very routine aspect of American life and one of obvious relevance to the activities of criminals.

Some scholars feel that shooting or threatening to shoot another person, even in self-defense, is so morally repugnant and utterly barbaric that it is preferable not to address the subject at all

*References for this chapter appear on pages 258–268.

(Goode 1972; see also Tonso 1984 re. scholars' attitudes toward firearms). It could even be argued that to study the matter seriously might imply some endorsement and encourage the indiscriminate spread of the behavior.

Yet, ignoring this issue can have serious costs. For example, a rational assessment of the impact of the more restrictive types of gun control laws requires an understanding of the consequences of disarming large segments of the civilian population. If civilian gun possession deters crime or otherwise prevents injury or property loss, reductions in general civilian gun ownership would amount to a reduction in a source of crime control as well as reduction of a possible cause of crime. Very different sorts of gun control would be called for under these circumstances than would be the case if one could assume that gun ownership has no desirable impact on crime rates.

These considerations may have been ignored until recently because students of violence thought they already knew everything they needed to know about whether guns can be effectively used by victims for self-defense. As far back as 1932, a noted homicide scholar stated that "the possession of firearms gives a false sense of security and encourages recklessness and arrogance. Those most experienced in such matters generally agree that it is almost suicidal for the average householder to attempt to use a firearm against a professional burglar or robber" (Brearley 1932, p. 76). These views have been echoed almost without modification in subsequent decades by scholars and gun control advocates (e.g. Newton and Zimring 1969, pp. 66–68; Yeager et al. 1976; Shields 1981, pp. 48–53, 125).

The Nature of Defensive Gun Use

Gun ownership for self-protection, and defensive gun use, must be distinguished from other forms of forceful activity directed at criminals, such as vigilantism, or activities of the criminal justice system (CJS) such as police making arrests. All of these can be coercive and all may be done by armed persons. However, vigilantism and CJS activity share a purpose that self-defensive actions do not—retribution. The CJS and the vigilante both seek to punish wrong-doers, the first lawfully, the second unlawfully, but the defensive gun user seeks to protect the bodily safety and property of himself and others. Antagonism may be mixed with the concern for self-preservation, but retribution is not an essential or defining part of self-defense. Vigilante action is unlawful per se, whereas self-defensive action may or may not be lawful, legality not being one of its defining attributes. Vigilantes act collectively, in concert with like-minded individuals, whereas defenders ordinarily act alone (Brown 1969). It therefore is an oxymoron to refer to a defensive gun user as a "lone vigilante." Both the goals and the actions of defensive gun users are more individualistic and less social than those of vigilantes.

Gun ownership, like defensive gun use, is individualistic and requires little pre-existing social organization, unlike either vigilantism or lawful collective activities like neighborhood watch or patrol activities. So gun ownership can flourish in socially disorganized areas where collective crime control strategies would flounder. Further, gun ownership is largely passive self-protection: Once a gun is acquired, the owner rarely does anything with it. Defensive owners only rarely make actual use of their guns for self-protection; the rest of the time they just keep the gun where it is available for use should the need arise. This contrasts sharply with neighborhood crime control strategies, which may require considerable investment of time and effort from each participant.

Gun ownership for self-defense is low-visibility protection. Unlike the activities of either police officers in marked patrol cars or of neighborhood patrol members, gun ownership by any one prospective crime victim is generally invisible to criminals. Although the occasional home or business might bear a sign saying "These premises protected by Smith and Wesson," with the image of a gun displayed, most armed premises would be externally indistinguishable from unarmed premises. This has two important implications. First, although owners bear the costs of gun ownership, their unarmed neighbors share in any deterrent benefits. (However, only gun owners will be able to actually use a gun to disrupt a criminal attempt made against them.) Second, criminals usually cannot avoid the risk of running into an armed occupant merely by carefully choosing which home or store to victimize. They are forced to treat this risk as a real possibility for *any* occupied premises. This sets defensive gun ownership apart from other, more visible, self-protective measures because it makes displacement of criminals from protected to unprotected targets less likely. Criminals can shift from heavily patrolled neighborhoods to less heavily patrolled ones, but they cannot so easily shift from victims they believe to be armed to those they can be confident are unarmed.

Gun ownership costs more money than simple measures like locking doors, having neighbors watch one's house, or avoidance behaviors like not going out at night, but it costs less (or involves less inconvenience) than buying and maintaining a dog, paying a security guard, or buying a burglar alarm system. Consequently, it is a self-protection measure available to many low-income people who cannot afford more expensive alternatives. Gun ownership is not a replacement or substitute for these other measures but rather is more accurately thought of as a complement to them.

Frequency of Defensive Use of Guns

Findings from Earlier Surveys

In any one year the fraction of the population victimized by serious violent crime or burglary is actually rather low. For example, even if minor violent crimes, such as assaults without injuries, are considered together with serious ones, only an estimated 3 percent of the U.S. population was the victim of a violent crime in 1982 (U.S. Bureau of Justice Statistics 1985b, p. 3). Consequently, the fraction of the population that has any reason to use a gun against a criminal in any one year is correspondingly low. Further, most crimes occur away from the victim's home or place of employment, that is, in places where even gun-owning victims will not have access to their weapons unless they carry them on their person.

At least 14 national or statewide surveys have asked probability samples of the general adult population about defensive gun use (DGU). The results and other noteworthy features of 13 of these surveys are summarized in Table 6.1; the 14th will be discussed in detail later. The surveys differ in many important respects. Some asked about uses of all types of guns, whereas others were confined to handguns. Some covered a specific time period, asking if the respondent (R) used a gun, for example, in

TABLE 6.1 Frequency of Defensive Gun Use in Previous Surveys

Survey:	Field	Bordua	Cambridge Reports	DMIa	DMIb	Hart	Ohio	Time/CNN	Mauser	Gallup	Gallup	L.A. Times	Tarrance
Area:	CA	IL	U.S.	U.S.	U.S.	U.S.	OH	U.S.	U.S.	U.S.	U.S.	U.S.	U.S.
Year of Interviews:	1976	1977	1978	1978	1978	1981	1982	1989	1990	1991	1993	1994	1994
Population covered:	Non-inst. adults	Non-inst. adults	Non-inst. adults	Reg. voters	Reg. voters	Reg. voters	Residents	"Firearm owners"	Residents	Non-inst. adults	Non-inst. adults	Non-inst. adults	Non-inst. adults
Gun Type Covered:	Hguns	All guns	Hguns	All guns	All guns	Hguns	Hguns	All guns	All guns	All guns	All guns	All guns	All guns
Recall Period:	Ever/ 1,2 yrs.	Ever	Ever	Ever	Ever	5 years	Ever	Ever	5 years	Ever	Ever	Ever	5 years
Excluded Uses Against Animals?	No	No	No	No	Yes	Yes	No	No	Yes	No	No	No	Yes
Excluded Military, Police Uses?	Yes	No	No	Yes	Yes	Yes	No	Yes	Yes	No	Yes	Yes	Yes
Defensive question asked of:	All Rs	All Rs	Protection hgun owners	All Rs	All Rs	All Rs	Rs in hgun hshlds	Gun owners	All Rs	Rs in hgun hshlds	Gun owners	All Rs	All Rs

TABLE 6.1 Frequency of Defensive Gun Use in Previous Surveys (*continued*)

Survey:	Field	Bordua	Cambridge Reports	DMIa	DMIb	Hart	Ohio	Time/CNN	Mauser Gallup	Gallup	L.A. Times	Tarrance
Defensive question refers to:	Resp.	Resp.	Resp.	Hshld	Hshld	Hshld	Resp.	Resp.	Hshld	Resp.	Resp.	Resp./Hshld
% Who Used	1.4/3/8.6[a]	5.0	18	15	7	4	6.5	n.a.	3.79	8	11	8[d]	1/2[e]
% Who Fired Gun	2.9	n.a.	12	6	n.a.	n.a.	2.6	9-16[c]	n.a.	n.a.	n.a.	n.a.
Implied number of def. gun uses[b]	3,052,717	1,414,544	n.a.	2,141,512	1,098,409	1,797,461	771,043	n.a.	1,487,342	777,153	1,621,377	3,609,682	764,036

Notes: [a] 1.4% in past year, 3% in past two years, 8.6% ever. [b] Estimated annual number of defensive uses of guns of all types against humans, excluding uses connected with military or police duties, after any necessary adjustments were made, for U.S., 1993. Adjustments are explained in detail in Appendix. [c] 9% fired gun for self-protection, 7% used gun "to scare someone." An unknown share of the latter could be defensive uses not overlapping with the former. [d] Covered only uses outside the home. [e] 1% of respondents, 2% of households.

R = respondent, Hshld = household, Hguns = handguns, Noninst. = noninstitutional, n.a. = not available.

the past five years, whereas others asked whether the R had ever used a gun defensively at any time in the past. Given the widely varying ages of Rs and the differing spans of time guns were owned, the former method of asking the question is clearly more informative. Some of the survey questions asked about "self-defense." This may narrowly suggest defense of one's own bodily safety. Others asked more broadly about "protection," which could include protection of other people and of property. Some questions asked only about the R's personal experiences, whereas others asked about defensive uses by anyone in the R's household. Most surveys asked the defensive uses questions of all Rs, but three of them "prescreened" Rs through question funneling, asking the question only of those who reported currently having a handgun or gun in the household. Most surveys specifically excluded guns used while in the military or as part of police duties, but some did not. Only some of the surveys distinguished defensive uses against animals from uses against human threats. Kleck and Gertz (1995) found that 9 percent of the Rs who reported a gun use for protection had used guns only against animals.

I rely principally on the surveys that covered a national population, asked about defensive uses during a specific limited time period, asked the question of all respondents, distinguished civilian use from other uses, and distinguished uses against humans from uses against animals. The results of the Hart survey as reported here were first published in Kleck (1988); they were obtained privately from Hart Research Associates, Inc. (Garin 1986). In this survey, 6 percent of the adults interviewed replied "yes" to the question: "Within the past five years, have you yourself or another member of your household used a handgun, even if it was not fired, for self-protection or for the protection of property at home, work, or elsewhere, excluding military service or police work?" Those who replied "yes" were then asked: "Was this to protect against an animal or a person?" Of the total sample, 2 percent replied "animal," 3 percent "person," and 1 percent "both." Therefore, 4 percent of the sample reported gun use against a person by someone in their household.

These and most of the rest of the percentages reported in Table 6.1 are percentages who reported defensive use, as a share of the entire sample. If the figures are calculated as a percentage of gun owners, they are much higher. For example, in the Cambridge Reports survey, 17 percent of the total sample reported personally owning a handgun for protection or self-defense. Only these persons were asked about defensive use of handguns. The original source indicates that 3 percent of the *total* sample reported personally using a handgun for defensive purposes at some time in the past. Thus, about 18 percent (3/17) of protective handgun owners had actually used their guns at least once for defensive purposes. Among all handgun owners, irrespective of reasons for ownership, the fraction is somewhat smaller. In the Hart survey, among Rs reporting an operable handgun in their household, 10 percent reported a household member using a handgun defensively against a person in the previous five years. Finally, the Luntz Weber national survey in June of 1993 found that 54 percent of households with a gun had "ever actually handled a gun, even if it wasn't fired, for self-protection" excluding uses in military or law enforcement service (DIALOG 1995). That is, the members of *most* gun-owning households claimed to have used a gun for self-protection at some time in their lives.

Like the crime victimization figures, the DGU percentages concerning short recall periods such as five years are small. However, when translated into absolute numbers, as crime figures are commonly reported, the percentages imply large numbers of defensive uses. In 1980 there were 80,622,000 U.S. households (U.S. Bureau of the Census 1982). Applying the 4 percent figure from the Hart survey yields in an estimate of 3,224,880 households with at least one person who used a handgun defensively at least once during the period 1976 to 1981. Conservatively assuming only one use per household over the entire five-year period, there were at least 644,976 defensive uses of handguns against persons per year, excluding police or military uses. There is considerable room for sampling error associated with the point estimates. The 95 percent confidence interval estimate of the proportion of household handguns used defensively against a person over the past five-year period is .029 to .051, implying from 468,000 to 822,000 uses per year.

The Hart survey asked only about handgun use, ignoring defensive uses of the far more numerous long guns (rifles and shotguns). The Hart handgun-only estimates were, however, confirmed by a more recent national survey that asked about all gun types. Mauser (1990) found that 3.79 percent reported a defensive use of a gun of any kind, a figure within the all-guns 95 percent interval estimate derived from extrapolating the Hart survey to all guns. Mauser's lower percentage of reported defensive use, therefore, could be due solely to random sampling error; it could also reflect genuinely declining defensive uses of guns between 1976 to 1981 and 1985 to 1990, paralleling the decline in criminal uses of guns (U.S. BJS 1992 and earlier annual issues).

Confidence in the estimates derived from the Hart and Mauser surveys is increased by the consistency of these results with those of the other 11 surveys summarized in Table 6.1, which shows alternative estimates of the number of defensive uses. There are now at least 14 surveys, with an aggregate sample size of over 20,000 cases, and all of the surveys indicate at least 700,000 DGUs. In addition to the estimates derived from the Hart and Mauser surveys, which require little adjustment, it was also possible to develop estimates, using reasonable adjustments, based on 11 other surveys.[2]

Two surveys (Cambridge Reports; Time/CNN) cannot yield comparable estimates because the DGU questions were not asked of all Rs and it is impossible to know the DGU prevalence among those not asked. This is important because a substantial share of DGUs are by persons in households that do not currently own (or at least do not report) guns (Kleck and Gertz 1995, pp. 177, 187), either because there was previously a gun in the household or because the user employed a gun belonging to someone else. Surveys that ask the DGU question only of current gun owners will therefore substantially underestimate the frequency of DGUs.

The Appendix explains how the adjusted estimates of DGUs for the 13 prior surveys were computed. All of the alternative surveys yield estimates of annual DUs in excess of 700,000.[3] Therefore, one cannot attribute the large estimates of DGUs to technical peculiarities of the Hart and Mauser surveys, and it would be inaccurate to claim that they depend on just one or two surveys.

By 1994 there were at least 14 surveys (hereinafter referred to as the "gun use surveys") that all indicated large numbers (700,000 or more) of DGUs each year, but only one that indicated a small number: the National Crime Victimization Survey (NCVS). The gun use surveys were quite diverse in how the key items were worded, sample size, which Rs were asked the questions, how the universe was defined, and when the surveys were fielded, spanning the period from 1976 to 1994, yet all yield estimates at least eight times the 80–82,000 annual DGUs implied by the NCVS (Cook 1991, p. 56; Rand 1994).

Of the 13 surveys, 11 can be adjusted to produce estimates that can be meaningfully compared with each other because these surveys asked the defensive use questions of all Rs. They imply between 760,000 and 3.6 million annual defensive uses of guns of all types against humans, excluding uses in law enforcement or the military. In contrast, the NCVS implies only about 80,000 annual DGUs against predatory criminals during the period 1979 to 1987 (Cook 1991, p. 56), or 65,000 per year from 1987 to 1990 (McDowall and Wiersema 1994), less than a tenth of the lowest estimate from any other survey (764,036 per year, based on the Tarrance survey covering 1989 to 1994).

Problems with the Surveys

It should be emphasized that these surveys do not permit an assessment of the legal or moral character of the DGUs reported, and one necessarily relies on the honesty of Rs as to the defensive character of the acts referred to. This is important because of the character of much violence. Wright and Rossi (1985, pp. 27, 29) have pointed out that predatory criminals frequently victimize other criminals much like themselves. In any given incident, who one concludes was "defending" himself may depend on which party one asks. Thus, the gun use surveys may count some incidents as DGUs that in legal terms were criminal assaults by the R.

The opposite problem applies to the victim surveys used to estimate the total number of crimes committed with guns. Strictly speaking, victim surveys do not even attempt to determine who is the victim and who the aggressor in an assault. The relevant survey questions simply ask whether the R was "knifed, shot at, or attacked" in the previous six months (Gove et al. 1985, p. 458; U.S. Bureau of Justice Statistics 1994, p. 122). Thus, if an R had criminally attacked or tried to rob (without a gun) someone who defended himself with a gun, the R could honestly report that he had been shot at or threatened with a gun. He would therefore be counted as a victim of a gun assault, even though he was not the victim of any gun crime but rather was the target of a defensive gun use.

In short, the incidents described as defensive uses in gun user surveys and as gun crimes in victim surveys overlap. Even if just one party uses a gun, the same incident may be describable as either a gun assault or a defensive use of a gun, depending on which party to the event happens to be questioned. Some instances of mutual combat could accurately be regarded as involving both aggressive and defensive uses of guns. Incidents can be misreported in either direction in both kinds of surveys. It is not clear how, or even whether, these problems affect comparisons between the number of gun crimes and the number of DGUs.

There is a problem, however, affecting all surveys that could consistently contribute to a net undercount of both defensive and criminal gun uses. It has often been recognized that criminals will be among the persons least likely to be interviewed in general population surveys, because of their low income, high mobility, time spent incarcerated, and reluctance to be interviewed even if successfully contacted (e.g. Cook 1985). Because it is criminals who are in most frequent contact with other criminals, it is they who are potentially most at risk. Relative to their share of the population, criminals may claim a disproportionate share of both DGUs and gun crime victimizations. Therefore, victimization and gun use surveys share a sampling bias that contributes to underestimating both criminal and defensive gun uses.

As to the comparison between numbers of DGUs and criminal gun uses, it is possible that there are biases that lead to more undercounting of defensive uses than criminal uses. The results of both victimization and gun use surveys, like all survey results, can be affected by recall failure and telescoping. Despite the highly dramatic nature of crime incidents, victims nevertheless frequently fail to recall them in survey interviews, even when questioned as little as six months after the events (U.S. LEAA 1972). The main difference between the two survey types discussed herein is that the recall period is only six months for the national victim surveys, whereas it was five years in the Hart and Mauser gun use surveys, and was the R's lifetime in most of the rest of the surveys. This suggests there is more recall failure in the gun use surveys.

Police, security guards, and armed forces personnel are especially likely to use weapons for defensive purposes, due to the violence-related nature of their occupations and the fact that they are commonly armed with a gun during the work hours. Because such people are eligible for inclusion in the victim and gun use surveys, one would expect them to account for a disproportionate share of the DGUs. Recall that the Hart and Mauser surveys excluded police and military uses of guns but not off-duty uses of guns by police officers and military personnel. The size of the share of defensive uses attributable to these sorts of users is relevant to assessing NCVS information used later to evaluate the effectiveness of DGUs, as that information is derived from questions that did not exclude any uses by persons with these violence-related occupations. Although the gun use surveys did not obtain sufficiently detailed occupational detail to assess this, the NCVS did. In the 1979 to 1985 sample, members of these occupations accounted for 15.4 percent of self-protection gun uses. They do therefore account for a disproportionate share of the NCVS-counted gun uses, but still a relatively small fraction. Again, it should be stressed that on-duty uses by such persons were explicitly excluded from the surveys used herein to estimate the number of DGUs.

The NCVS yields a DGU estimate that is less than one ninth of the smallest estimate derived from any of the gun use surveys. Given no known flaws in the 13 gun use surveys that could exaggerate DGUs by a factor of ten, one would think the likeliest inference would be that there are flaws in the one deviant survey that cause it to grossly underestimate this parameter. This is not, however, the inference drawn by critics who insist, virtually all evidence to the contrary notwithstanding, that "self-defense firearm use is infrequent" (McDowall and Wiersema 1994). Only the NCVS supports their position, and they have been forced to speculate about possible flaws in the gun use surveys that could lead to an enormous overestimation (Cook 1991; McDowall and Wiersema 1994; Reiss and Roth 1993). Their efforts are all conspicuously one-sided in that they systematically ignore obvious flaws in both the gun use surveys and the NCVS that would lead to an *underestimate* of DGUs.

For these speculated flaws to account for the discrepancy between the NCVS and all other known surveys on the subject, the flaws must be of such enormous magnitude that they could account for a 9:1 or greater difference in results. None of the critics have provided any evidence of flaws of the gun use surveys that could cause errors even remotely of this magnitude. For example, Cook (1991) speculated that one of the gun use surveys (the Hart survey) was subject to "telescoping": respondents remembered incidents as occurring within the five-year reference period used in that survey that actually occurred more than five years earlier. Cook is almost certainly correct that some telescoping occurred among Rs reporting DGUs in this survey as well as the other gun use surveys. The problem with his criticism, however, is that it is so one-sided and so vague as to the magnitude of error that telescoping could produce. Telescoping could only lead to a net overestimate of gun uses if its impact was greater than that of other flaws contributing to *underestimation*, in particular memory failure and intentional concealing. Indeed, the very Census Bureau technical reports Cook used to support his telescoping speculation routinely addressed memory failure in tandem with telescoping (e.g. see Skogan 1981, pp. 17 and 19 and the sources cited therein). Census Bureau evaluations of victim survey techniques indicate that even for short reference periods of six months or one year, the magnitude of overreporting of criminal victimizations due to telescoping is roughly matched by underreporting due to memory failure and other failures to report incidents that actually did occur in the reference period (see Skogan 1981 and technical reports cited therein: Dodge 1981; Murphy and Dodge 1981; Turner 1981 [U.S. LEAA 1972]).

Further, past survey research has indicated that as the length of the reference period increases the relative error caused by memory failure increases, whereas that caused by telescoping decreases (Woltman et al. 1981, p. 91). Thus, if the relative magnitude of telescoping and memory failure are already of roughly equal magnitude with a 12-month reference period, then with a five-year reference period the relative error due to memory failure will exceed that of telescoping. Therefore, the logical inference is that Rs in the gun use surveys almost certainly are forgetting more uses that occurred in the five-year (or longer) reference periods than they were telescoping in from earlier periods. Consequently, other things being equal, the gun use surveys probably understate the number of incidents involving what the Rs considered to be DGUs.

It is worth considering the potential magnitude of recall failure in the gun use surveys. Studies of the NCVS indicate that even with just a one-year reference period, Rs failed to report to interviewers 52 percent of known assault incidents that had been reported to police, and failed to report 78 percent of them when the offender was a relative (Turner 1981). If the reference period were lengthened by a factor of five or more, the degree of memory failure would increase. Consequently, it would be reasonable to expect that DGUs in assaults would actually be at least twice as frequent as survey results suggest, and probably considerably larger than this in surveys with five-year reference periods, as-suming memory failure was the only flaw in the surveys. There are, of course, additional flaws, which will be addressed later.

Memory failure is likely to be especially common with inci-dents that involved a DGU, because a larger-than-average share of such incidents involve neither injury nor property loss (Kleck and DeLone 1993). NCVS results consistently indicate that crime incidents without injury or property loss are less likely to be reported to the police, but the same is also likely to be true about underreporting incidents to NCVS interviewers: Rs will be espe-cially likely to forget incidents in which they were neither hurt nor lost property or to regard them as insufficiently serious to qualify for reporting.

The gun use surveys, however, almost certainly have other flaws beside memory failure. Perhaps because the telescoping speculation obviously cannot account for much (if any) of the 9:1 discrepancy between the NCVS and all other surveys, defenders of the NCVS-based estimate have developed a second speculation about the gun use surveys. They have conjectured that a huge fraction of the Rs who reported a DGU in these surveys grossly misunderstood the relevant question and, instead of reporting actual defensive *uses* of guns, were actually reporting merely owning or carrying a gun for self-protection (McDowall et al. 1992).

These critics provide neither evidence that this misunder-standing occurred often enough to produce huge errors in the estimates, nor even plausible reasoning as how 90 percent or more of these Rs could have been so inattentive, inarticulate or unintel-ligent as to misunderstand a question explicitly asking whether the R had "used" a gun for "self-protection." Although a few Rs may well have been so inattentive as to make an error this extreme, 90 percent or more of the Rs reporting a DGU would have had to have made this mistake, in the set of 13 surveys, for this alleged flaw to account for the gun use surveys yielding estimates nine or more times larger than the NCVS estimates.

Another variation on this speculation is the suspicion that some of the incidents recalled by the gun use Rs were not genuine instances of self-defense in response to a criminal victimization (Reiss and Roth 1993, pp. 264–266). Although totally speculative and unsupported by empirical evidence, this criticism nonetheless has some merit, although there is no reason to believe that misreports of this type would be enough to counterbalance the substantial underreporting that is to be expected in surveys asking about controversial or illegal behaviors and using reference periods of five years or more.

It has also been suggested that even if the incidents reported in the gun use surveys really were defensive in some sense, a large share of them were trivial, such as a man investigating a suspicious noise in his backyard while carrying a gun. This is a perfectly plausible suggestion, in light of the fact that most of what occurs in life is fairly trivial. Even most criminal victimizations in general are apparently insufficiently important or memorable for victims to remember and report them as crimes to interviewers even as little as six months later (Skogan 1981). No doubt many of both those incidents forgotten and those recalled by survey Rs are minor. However, this insight applies just as well to criminal uses of guns as it does to defensive uses. Findings from the NCVS indicate that only 3 percent of handgun victimizations involve a victim being wounded and only 16.6 percent involve the gun being fired at a victim (Rand 1994). Even if all of the remaining 83 percent of the cases really did involve a gun being used in a threat, many of these incidents would be relatively minor.

It is worth considering how the comparison of defensive and criminal gun uses would look if one responded to the critics' implied suggestion that one focus only on really serious cases. The only category of "serious" gun-related events for which comparable estimates can be produced is events that involved the gun being fired. NCVS data indicate that only 16.6 percent of "handgun crimes" involve the victim being shot at, and an average of 699,917 violent "gun crime" incidents per year over the period 1987 to 1992 (Rand 1994); this implies only 116,186 annual violent gun crime incidents in which the victim was actually shot at.

Some critics of the various gun use survey estimates have claimed that those estimates relied on dubious or strong assumptions, or required questionable adjustments (McDowall et al. 1992; Reiss and Roth 1993, pp. 264–266). This claim has only a kernel of truth and is extremely misleading. *Some* survey estimates require adjustments to make them useful for *some* purposes. For example, an estimate from a survey that asked only about handgun uses would have to be adjusted to yield an estimate of uses of guns of all types.

What these critics did not reveal to their readers, however, is that there are national survey estimates of defensive uses of both handguns and of all guns that require no adjustment whatsoever, and thus rely on no "strong" or "dubious" assumptions concerning adjustments. The 1990 Mauser survey provided a direct national estimate of defensive uses of guns of all types, without adjustment of any kind, whereas the 1981 Hart survey provided a direct national estimate of defensive uses of just handguns, again without requiring adjustments of any kind. Because these were the only surveys used to generate estimates on which previous conclusions about the frequency of DGUs were based (Kleck 1988; 1991), it is hard to discern the motives of critics who raised the issue of adjustments. The only assumption made in obtaining average annual estimates from either of these surveys was an extremely simple and conservative one: It was assumed that each R reporting a DGU experienced only one use in the five-year reference period and that this R was the only person in the household who had such an experience. Given the reality of repeat victimization and clustering of victimizations, at least a few Rs experienced more than one DGU, and at least a few households contained more than one person who experienced a DGU, so this assumption necessarily could contribute only to *underestimating* DGUs.

The claim that high estimates of DGUs rely on strong or dubious assumptions or adjustments is therefore simply wrong. For critics to treat flaws of the weakest surveys as if they applied to the strongest ones, especially when conclusions relied only on the stronger surveys, is unscrupulous and unconscionable. A particularly outrageous example is one where critics argued that estimates from the gun use surveys could have been too high because the "respondents in some surveys could well have been concerned about animal rather than human attackers" (Reiss and

Roth 1993, p. 265). The sources these authors cited (Kleck 1988; 1991) pointedly noted that both the Mauser and Hart surveys explicitly asked Rs whether the reported DGUs were against animals or humans, and that estimates derived from these surveys excluded the uses against animals. Because these were the only surveys used to generate numerical estimates on which conclusions concerning the frequency of DGUs were based, criticisms applying exclusively to the weaker surveys were irrelevant to the validity of those estimates.

Explaining the Deviant NCVS Results.   What is one to make of the extraordinarily deviant estimates produced by the NCVS? Some have assumed that the NCVS *must* somehow yield at least approximately reasonable estimates because so much money and technical expertise has gone into it. Cook (1991, p. 55), for example, has accurately, if not very relevantly, noted that "the National Crime Survey is a much larger and more sophisticated effort [than the gun use surveys such as that of Hart], based on questionnaires that have been devised and refined through a program of extensive testing." The reason this observation is not very relevant is that none of this considerable technical refinement was aimed specifically at yielding accurate estimates of defensive uses of guns, or even of other forceful self-protective actions. Further, none of the "extensive testing" has even addressed whether the NCVS accurately estimates the frequency of these behaviors. External evidence from 13 independent surveys strongly suggests that it does not.

The NCVS was designed to produce national estimates of criminal victimizations; estimates of forceful self-protection actions are merely an incidental by-product of the considerable effort devoted to achieving this central goal. The task of estimating forceful defensive actions is so fundamentally different from that of estimating criminal victimizations in general that the undoubted virtues of the NCVS for the latter task have no necessary bearing on the former. Ironically, many of the features of the NCVS that are advantageous for achieving its central purpose of producing crime estimates are handicaps for estimating DGUs. This, of course, does not imply any blame on the part of the designers of the NCVS, as they did not design the survey to produce DGU estimates.

Nevertheless, Cook appealed to common sense, asking whether the NCVS could really be so far off (1991, p. 55). How, he implicitly asked, could such an expensive and generally well-designed, large-scale survey be so inaccurate? No technical tests of the NCVS have focused on this particular issue, so we cannot know for certain. However, some characteristics of the NCVS have obvious and serious disadvantages for estimating DGUs.

Before assessing the NCVS, it is necessary to closely consider the nature of the task when estimating DGUs. Any forceful act of self-protection, whether or not it involves a gun, is a violent act. That is, by definition it involves either an attack or a threat on another human being. Even when the victim/defender is confident that the act was morally justified, he or she usually cannot be confident about how an interviewer would morally assess those actions, and many Rs do care what interviewers think. More important, regardless of whether the act was in fact lawful, few Rs could be certain this was so. The law of self-defense is extremely complex, and even legal experts are frequently uncertain whether a given forceful act was lawful (Gillespie 1989). Therefore, uncertainty among defensive actors themselves should also be widespread.

When an incident has involved defensive force, the NCVS interviewer is in effect asking the R to confess to an act of violence that the R committed, an act that may itself be criminal, and that in any case the R may think the interviewer will disapprove of. Thus, in connection with forceful self-protection, the NCVS becomes a "self-report" survey covering arguably deviant and possibly illegal acts committed by the R rather than merely being a survey of criminal acts committed against the R. The goals of a survey of self-reported deviance are fundamentally different from those of a victimization survey and call for fundamentally different technical features.

In a number of respects, the NCVS is, through no fault of its designers, the worst possible survey for estimating DGUs. First, the survey is conducted by one federal government agency (the U.S. Census Bureau) on behalf of another federal agency (the U.S. Justice Department). Government sponsorship and conduct of the survey is prominently mentioned to every NCVS respondent, in both an introductory letter and orally at the beginning of each interview (U.S. Bureau of the Census 1986, p. D2–11). Generally, this is an advantage for a survey, because it helps ensure higher rates of cooperation and interview completion. However, if one is attempting to get people to confess to violent acts of debatable legal character, government sponsorship is the last thing one wants.

Second, the NCVS is a nonanonymous household survey, with the R's address and telephone number known to the interviewer in a way that is apparent to the R. Thus, the R knows that his or her identity is known to the federal government agency conducting the survey. Although the interviewer promises confidentiality, the R has no way of being assured that this promise will be kept in light of the survey's nonanonymous character. In combination with government sponsorship, this must strongly discourage Rs from confessing to any violent acts, whether or not the Rs considered them self-protective. In sharp contrast, the gun use surveys were mostly anonymous telephone surveys using randomly generated telephone numbers.

Third, the sequencing of the NCVS incident report questions is such that the interviewer knows where the crime occurred, and specifically whether it occurred in a public place, before the questions about self-protection are asked. This means that an R who had used a gun for self-protection in a public place knows, by the time the self-protection questions are asked, that he has already revealed where he was when the crime occurred. Normally, getting additional detail about a crime would be a good idea, but in this context, using this sequence of questions, it is a very bad one. The vast majority of the U.S. population, and thus the NCVS sample, live in places where it is either completely forbidden for any civilian to possess a gun in public places or it is forbidden to all but the handful who possess a rarely granted carry permit (Blackman 1985). The crime of unlawful carrying is generally defined as a felony, frequently results in arrest, and is even subject to mandatory minimum prison sentences of one year or more in at least ten states (Kleck, 1991, Chapter 8; Ronhovde and Sugars 1982, pp. 204–205). Thus, if a victim had used a gun in self-protection in connection with a crime that occurred in a public place, it would usually be impossible for the victim to report the act of armed self-protection without also confessing to having committed a serious crime. It is unrealistic to think that all, or even most, respondents would admit such a crime in a nonanonymous government survey.

The seriousness of this problem can be appreciated when one

considers NCVS evidence for 1990 that indicates that only 13.1 percent of violent crime incidents occurred "at or in respondent's home" (U.S. BJS 1992, p. 75) The other 86.9 percent occurred in some location where, in order to possess their gun during the incident, the victim would have had to have carried the gun through public spaces. In contrast, the gun use surveys did not ask, before the DGU questions, for *any* details about the incident in which guns were used defensively. The lack of detail acquired before the DGU question was asked, which would ordinarily be problematic, is a strong advantage in encouraging Rs to report their own violent actions, which they would be reluctant to report if they knew they would be providing details about the actions to an interviewer.

Fourth, leaving aside the issue of locations where guns were possessed, many Rs could only possess guns in violation of the law, no matter where they were. This would apply with special force to the subset of the population most likely to be criminally victimized—criminals. Persons with prior criminal records are prohibited under federal law and most states' laws from possessing guns anywhere, and a common condition of probation or parole is to not possess weapons (Kleck 1991, chapter 8). In addition, millions of otherwise noncriminal persons possess guns illegally because they lack a permit or license legally required under local or state law. In two Illinois surveys of the general population, Bordua and his colleagues found that even among Rs willing to report gun ownership, 28 percent did not have the license required of all Illinois gun owners (1979, p. 160). For all such persons, to admit use of a gun for self-protection or for any other purpose would be tantamount to confessing to unlawful possession of a gun. Again, in the context of a nonanonymous government survey, it would seem highly unlikely that very many people would be willing to make such a confession. In light of these first four problems, perhaps what is so remarkable about NCVS results is not that so few Rs report self-protective gun use but rather that *any* of them do so. In contrast, because the gun use surveys were privately conducted and anonymous, these considerations are of less importance.

In general, then, Rs are likely to regard reporting a DGU in the NCVS as extremely risky. However, even if none of them felt this way, NCVS estimates of DGUs would still be far too low.

Given the way the NCVS orders questions, no Rs are even asked the self-protection questions unless they are first willing to report a criminal incident and provide some details about it. Thus, any tendency of Rs to underreport violent incidents would necessarily also contribute to an underreporting of self-protective actions involving guns. Cook (1985) has documented that the NCVS radically underestimates the number of criminal incidents involving gunshot woundings. Based on his best estimate of the number of gunshot woundings reported to police, Cook's data indicated that the NCVS was capturing only about one-third of the gunshot wound incidents (p. 96). Because all of his proposed explanations for this problem would apply at least as well to other forms of violence, there is no reason not to suppose that victims also radically underreport violent incidents in general. As many such cases would not be reported to either the police or NCVS interviewers, the fraction of all such incidents reported was probably even lower than 33 percent. Less serious incidents may be underreported still more because memory failure is greater with less serious offenses (Skogan 1981). If this applies to the violent incidents in which victims use guns for self-protection, it implies that one would have to multiply NCVS estimates by a factor of at least three just to correct for this one known flaw.

In his discussion of NCVS estimates of DGUs, Cook (1991) cites his own research on NCVS underestimation of gunshot woundings but minimizes its relevance, arguing "there is no reason to believe that the Hart poll would do any better in this respect." On the contrary, there is every reason to believe that both the Hart poll and most of the other gun surveys would do better in this respect, for in the latter surveys, it is unnecessary to report a violent victimization to be asked the self-protection questions. In most of these surveys, all Rs or all gun-owning Rs were simply asked the DGU question, without any preliminary questions being used to filter anyone out. Because the Rs were not asked, before the DGU question, any questions about any victimizations they might have been unwilling to talk about, they were all given the opportunity to report DGUs and were more likely to feel free to mention them without risk. Further, the Hart and other gun use surveys were not handicapped by either the nonanonymity or government conduct and sponsorship that afflicted the NCVS.

Cook's (1985) earlier assessment of the adequacy of the NCVS for estimating violent incidents is worth closer study. When faced with a conflict between low NCVS estimates of the number of criminal gunshot woundings and far higher estimates implied by four other small samples (all but one local in character), Cook concluded that the NCVS radically underestimated gunshot woundings and that the true figure could be three times larger than the NCVS-based estimate. His reasoning was that the four small-scale bodies of data could not all be radically wrong, so it must be that the NCVS was wrong. In sharp contrast, when faced with precisely the same conflict between NCVS estimates of *defensive* uses of guns and no less than 13 other bodies of data, Cook concluded that all the other bodies of evidence were indeed radically wrong, that it was the NCVS that was likely to be most correct, and that it was unlikely that the NCVS could be as seriously inaccurate as the conflicting bodies of data indicated (Cook 1991, pp. 54–56). The most obvious difference between the two situations, of course, is that in the first instance the NCVS was indicating a low estimate of one of the costs of gun availability, whereas in the second case the NCVS was indicating a low estimate of one of its benefits.

Finally, the NCVS also undercounts DGUs because its Rs radically underreport acts of domestic violence in the home. Some alternative national estimates indicate that the actual number of incidents of domestic violence may be 12 times as large the NCVS indicates (Loftin and MacKenzie 1990, pp. 22–23). If this is so, then the actual number of assault-related DGUs in the home would presumably be at least 12 times larger than the NCVS indicates, assuming this were the only flaw in the NCVS. Of course it is not, so one cannot get a meaningful estimate merely by correcting the NCVS estimate of domestic violence-linked DGUs by multiplying it by 12.[4]

To summarize, there are many obvious and profound flaws in the NCVS that almost certainly produce huge undercounts of DGUs. Indeed, it would not be an overstatement to assert that it is highly unlikely a given DGU would be reported to NCVS interviewers. The NCVS simply cannot be considered a useful way of estimating the incidence of DGUs. Consequently, efforts to adjust the NCVS estimates for one or two flaws, based on dubious assumptions about the size of errors produced by those flaws, are ill-considered, amounting to hopeless attempts to make a silk purse out of a sow's ear (see, e.g., McDowall et al. 1992). In contrast, the most consequential known flaw in the 13 gun use surveys is their use of long reference periods, a problem whose dominant effect is to contribute to an underestimation of DGUs. As previously noted (Kleck 1991, pp. 108–110), both the NCVS and the gun use surveys probably greatly underestimate DGUs, but the NCVS does it to far greater degree than the gun use surveys.

NCVS Exaggeration of Gun Crime.   Some Rs undoubtedly characterize incidents in which they were the aggressors or otherwise at fault as incidents in which they were the victims, thereby presenting aggressive uses of guns as defensive ones. The problem with the critics' discussion of this flaw is that, once again, the discussion is so one-sided. The DGU estimate has no meaning in isolation from other numbers; one cannot judge it as large or small without comparison to other numbers. The number with which it has been compared is the largest available estimate of the number of times guns are used for criminal purposes, based on the NCVS. One cannot tell how this comparison is affected by flaws in the evidence unless one considers flaws in the sources of both estimates.

Some problems in the NCVS contribute to an underestimation of victimization, but other problems can contribute to an overestimation. Although some Rs in the gun use surveys misreported aggressive gun uses as defensive uses, the NCVS almost certainly also mischaracterizes some DGUs of others against the R as criminal or aggressive uses. The NCVS does not clearly establish that Rs were the victims in crime incidents that they report. Rs are never directly asked whether they even considered themselves to be the victims in incidents in which they were attacked or threatened. Some attacks or threats involving guns could have been defensive actions taken by another person in response to aggressive, criminal actions initiated by the NCVS respondent. The set of actual criminal gun uses covered by the NCVS is thus some smaller subset, of unknown size, of those incidents indiscriminately labeled as "gun crimes" in NCVS publications.

Quite apart from the issue of whether NCVS "gun crime" victims were actually victims rather than criminals confronted by armed victims, the NCVS has other definitional problems that contribute to an exaggeration of the number of reported gun crimes. Of all incidents labeled "handgun victimizations" by the Bureau of Justice Statistics, only 3 percent involve the victim being shot, and only 16.6 percent involve the victim even being shot at (Rand 1994). Of course, a gun does not have to be fired at the victim for the incident to be a genuine gun crime—threatening a person with a gun certainly may be a criminal assault. The problem is that neither the current nor past versions of the NCVS interview schedule clearly establish, in the remaining 87 percent of incidents labeled "gun crimes," whether a threat with a gun actually occurred, as opposed to the offender merely possessing a gun during an incident in which he made a threat not involving the gun.

Further, the NCVS does not definitively establish that the offender actually had a gun. NCVS interviewers ask Rs whether the offender had a weapon but do not establish how or why the R thought the offender was armed. The R might have based this perception on statements by an offender who was bluffing about a gun he did not actually have. Or the R might have misinterpreted a bulge in the offender's clothing as a gun when in fact it was a wallet. Because Rs are never asked whether they *saw* a weapon in the offender's possession, the NCVS does not clearly establish, in cases where the gun was not actually used in an attack, that the offender even possessed a gun.

Also, in incidents where the gun was not actually fired, the NCVS cannot establish that the gun was used to threaten the R. The key question (Item 14 in the Incident Report) asks: "How were you threatened? Any other way?" There is one response category that the interviewer could mark if the incident involved a gun threat. Unfortunately, that category lumps together instances of a weapon being used to threaten and instances where the weapon was merely present (that is, instances where the R *thought* the offender had a weapon). Response number 4 for this item is: "Weapon present or threatened with weapon" (U.S. BJS 1992, p. 126; see also response 3 in item 7d of Incident Report used for the 1979–1985 period, e.g. U.S. BJS, 1984, p. 84). Even with the use of the R's responses to all other related questions, it is impossible for analysts to tell how many of the incidents where this response was checked involved the offender in any way threatening the R with a gun. For all anyone can tell, most of these involved nothing more than an offender whom the R thought, accurately or not, possessed a gun, which was never pointed at the R or any other victim, or even verbally referred to in a threatening manner (for example, "I've got a gun, and I'm going to use it.").

The implication of these observations is not trivial. Up to 83 percent of the incidents labeled violent "gun crimes" in NCVS publications may not have involved any gun use of any kind. If one reduced the criminal gun use estimates by 83 percent, or even half this, then even without adjusting the DGU estimates from the gun use surveys for memory failure, the DGU estimates would be many times larger than the criminal gun use estimates.

Based on the previous gun use surveys, the tentative conclusion must remain that defensive gun uses are at least as common as criminal gun uses, and probably more common.

The National Self-Defense Survey

The National Self-Defense Survey (Kleck and Gertz 1995), conducted in the spring of 1993, was the first survey ever devoted to the subject of armed self-defense. It was carefully designed to correct all of the known correctable or avoidable flaws of previous surveys that critics had identified. We used the most anonymous possible national survey format, that of the anonymous random digit-dialed telephone survey. We did not know the identities of those who were interviewed, and made this fact clear to the Rs. We interviewed a large (n = 4,977 completed interviews), nationally representative sample covering all adults (age 18 and over) in the lower 48 states and living in households with telephones. We asked DGU questions of all Rs in our sample, asking them separately about both their own DGU experiences and those of other members of their households. We used both a five-year recall period and a one-year recall period. We inquired about uses of both handguns and other types of guns and excluded occupational uses of guns and uses against animals. Finally, we asked a long series of detailed questions designed to establish exactly what Rs did with their guns, that they were confronting other humans, and what crime or crimes each DGU was connected with.

We consulted with North America's most experienced experts on gun-related surveys, David Bordua, James Wright, and Gary Mauser, along with survey expert Seymour Sudman, to craft a state-of-the-art survey instrument designed specifically to establish the frequency and nature of defensive gun uses (see, for example, Bordua et al. 1979; Lizotte and Bordua 1980; Wright and Rossi 1986; Mauser 1990; 1993; Mauser and Kopel 1992; Sudman and Bradburn 1974). A professional telephone polling firm, Research Network, of Tallahassee, Florida, carried out the sampling and interviewing. Only the firm's most experienced interviewers were used on the project. Interviews were monitored at random by survey supervisors. All interviews in which an alleged DGU was reported by the R were validated by supervisors with call-backs, along with a 20 percent random sample of all other interviews. Of all eligible residential telephone numbers called where a person (rather than an answering machine) answered, 61 percent resulted in a completed interview. Interviewing was carried out from February through April of 1993.

The quality of sampling procedures was likewise well above the level common in national surveys. Our sample was not only large and nationally representative but was also stratified by state. That is, 48 independent samples of residential telephone numbers were drawn, one from each of the lower 48 states, providing 48 independent, albeit often small, state samples. Given the nature of randomly generated samples of telephone numbers, there was no clustering of cases or multistage sampling, as there is in the NCVS (U.S. Bureau of Justice Statistics 1994, pp. 141–142), and thus no inflation of sampling error due to such procedures. To gain a larger raw number of sample DGU cases, we oversampled in the South and West regions where previous surveys have indicated gun ownership is higher (Kleck 1991, p. 57). We also oversampled within contacted households for males, who are both more likely to own guns and to be victims of crimes in which victims might use guns defensively (p. 56). Data were later weighted to adjust for oversampling.

Each interview began with a few general "throat-clearing" questions about problems facing the R's community and crime. The interviewers then asked the following question: "Within the past *five years*, have you yourself or another member of your household *used* a gun, even if it was not fired, for self-protection or for the protection of property at home, work, or elsewhere? Please do *not* include military service, police work, or work as a security guard." Rs who answered "yes" were then asked: "Was this to protect against an animal or a person?" Rs who reported a DGU against a person were then asked: "How many incidents involving defensive uses of guns against persons happened to members of your household in the past five years?" and then: "Did this incident [any of these incidents] happen in the *past 12 months*?" At this point, Rs were asked: "Was it *you* who used a gun defensively, or did someone else in your household do this?"

All Rs reporting a DGU were then asked a long, detailed series of questions establishing exactly what happened in the DGU incident. Rs who reported having experienced more than one DGU in the previous five years were asked about their most recent experience. When the original R was the one who had used a gun defensively, as was usually the case, interviewers obtained their firsthand account of the event. When the original R indicated that some other member of their household was the one who had the experience, interviewers made every effort to speak directly to the involved person, either speaking to them immediately, or obtaining times and dates to call them back. Up to three call-backs were made in attempting to directly contact the DGU-involved person.

We anticipated that it would sometimes prove impossible to make later contact with these persons, so interviewers were instructed to always obtain a proxy account of the DGU from the original R, on the assumption that a proxy account would be better than none at all. It was rarely necessary to rely on these proxy accounts—only six sample cases of DGU were reported only through proxies out of a total of 222 sample cases.

Although all Rs reporting a DGU were given the full interview, only a one-third random sample of Rs not reporting a DGU were interviewed. The rest were simply skipped to the end and thanked for their help. This procedure helped keep interviewing costs down. In the end, there were 222 completed interviews with Rs reporting DGUs, another 1,610 Rs not reporting a DGU but going through the full interview (other than the questions pertaining to details of the DGUs), for a total of 1,832 cases with the full interview, and 3,145 Rs who answered only enough questions to establish that no one in their household had experienced a DGU against a human in the previous five years (unweighted totals). These procedures effectively undersampled for non-DGU Rs or, equivalently, oversampled for DGU-involved Rs. Data were also weighted to account for this oversampling.

Questions about the details of DGU incidents permitted us to establish whether a given DGU met all of the following qualifications for an incident to be treated as a genuine DGU: (1) The incident involved defensive action against a human rather than an animal, but not in connection with police, military, or security guard duties; (2) the incident involved actual contact with a person, rather than merely investigating suspicious circumstances, and so forth; (3) the defender could state a specific crime that they thought was being committed at the time of the incident; (4) the gun was actually used in some way — at minimum it had to be used as part of a threat against a person, either by verbally referring to the gun (for example, "get away — I've got a gun") or by pointing it at an adversary. We made no effort to assess either the lawfulness or morality of the R's defensive actions.

An additional step was taken to minimize the possibility of DGU frequency being overstated. The senior author went through interview sheets on every one of the interviews in which a DGU was reported, looking for any indication that the incident might not be genuine. A case would be coded as questionable if even just one of four problems appeared to characterize it: (1) it was not clear whether the R actually confronted any adversaries they saw; (2) the R was a police officer, member of the military, or a security guard, and thus might have been reporting, despite instructions not to do so, an incident that occurred as part of his or her occupational duties; (3) the interviewer did not properly record exactly what the R had done with the gun, so it was possible that he or she had not used it in any meaningful way; or (4) the R did not state, or the interviewer did not record, a specific crime that the R thought was being committed against him or her at the time of the incident. There were a total of 26 cases where at least one of these problematic indications was present. It should be emphasized that we do not know that these cases were *not* genuine DGUs; we only mean to indicate that we do not have as high a degree of confidence on the matter as with the rest of the cases designated as DGUs. Estimates using all of the DGU cases are labeled herein as "A" estimates, whereas the more conservative estimates based only on cases devoid of any problematic indications are labeled "B" estimates.

Survey Results

Table 6.2 displays a large number of estimates of how often guns are used defensively. These estimates are not inconsistent with each other; rather, they each measure different things in different ways. Some estimates are based only on incidents that Rs reported as occurring in the 12 months preceding the interview, whereas others are based on incidents reported for the preceding five years. Both telescoping and recall failure should be lower with a one-year recall period, so estimates derived using it should be superior to those based on the longer recall period.

Some estimates are based only on incidents that Rs reported as involving themselves (person-based estimates), whereas others were based on all incidents that Rs reported as involving anyone in their household (household-based estimates). Because of its greater firsthand character, the person-based estimates should be better. Finally, some of the figures pertain only to DGUs involving use of handguns, whereas others pertain to DGUs involving any type of gun.

The methods used to compute the Table 6.2 estimates are very simple and straightforward. Prevalence ("% Used") figures were computed by dividing the weighted sample frequencies (in the top two rows of numbers) by the total weighted sample size of 4,977. The estimated number of persons or households who experienced a defensive gun use (DGU) (in the third and fourth rows) was then computed by multiplying these prevalence figures by the appropriate U.S. population base—population age 18 and over for person-based estimates, and the total number of households for household-based estimates.

Finally, the estimated number of defensive uses was computed by multiplying the number of DGU-involved persons or households by the following estimates of the number of all-guns DGU incidents per DGU-involved person or household, using a past-five-years recall period: person-based, A– 1.478; person-based, B–1.472; household-based, A–1.531; household-based, B–1.535. We did not establish how many DGUs occurred in the past year, and, for past-five-years DGUs, we did not separately establish how many of the DGUs involved handguns and how many involved other types of guns. Therefore, for all past-year estimates, and for past-five-years handgun estimates, it was necessary

TABLE 6.2 Prevalence and Incidence of Civilian Defensive Gun Use, United States, 1988–1993[a]

Recall Period: Base: Gun Types:		Past Year				Past Five Years			
		Person		Household		Person		Household	
		All Guns	Handguns	All Guns	Handguns	All Guns	Handguns	All Guns	Handguns
Weighted Sample Cases	A:[c]	66	49	79	55	165	132	194	148
	B:[c]	56	40	68	46	148	115	172	129
% Used[b]	A:	1.326	0.985	1.587	1.105	3.315	2.652	3.898	2.974
	B:	1.125	0.804	1.366	0.924	2.974	2.311	3.456	2.592
Persons/ Households	A:	2,549,862	1,893,079	1,540,405	1,072,434	637,465	55,099,724	3,782,767	2,885,822
	B:	2,163,519	1,545,371	1,325,918	896,945	571,787	24,442,941	3,353,794	2,515,345
Annual Uses	A:	2,549,862	1,893,079	1,540,405	1,072,434	1,884,348	1,442,941	1,158,283	515,345
	B:	2,163,519	1,545,371	1,325,918	896,945	1,683,342	888,588	1,029,615	505,069

Population Bases: Estimated resident population, age 18 and over, U.S., April, 1993: 190,538,000; estimated households (assuming the 1992–1993 percentage increase was the same as the 1991–1992 increase): 97,045,525 (U.S. Bureau of the Census 1993, pp. 17, 55).

Notes: [a] Defensive uses of guns against humans by civilians (i.e. excluding uses by police officers, security guards, or military personnel). All figures are based on weighted data (see text). [b] Percent of persons (households) with at least one defensive gun use during the five years (one year) preceding the interview. [c] A estimates are based on all reported defensive gun uses reported in the survey. B estimates are based on only cases with no indications that the case might not be a genuine defensive gun use.

to conservatively assume that there was only one DGU per DGU-involved person or household.

The most technically sound estimates presented in Table 6.2 are those based on the shorter one-year recall period and that rely on Rs' firsthand accounts of their own experiences (person-based estimates). These estimates appear in the first two columns. They indicate that each year in the United States there are about 2.2 to 2.5 million defensive uses of guns of all types by civilians against humans, with about 1.5 to 1.9 million of the incidents involving use of handguns.

These estimates are larger than those derived from the best previous surveys, indicating that technical improvements in the measurement procedures have, contrary to the expectations of Cook (1991), Reiss and Roth (1993), and McDowall and Wiersema (1994), *increased* rather than decreased estimates of the frequency with which DGUs occur. Defensive gun use is thus just another specific example of a commonplace pattern in criminological survey work (victimization surveys, self-report surveys of delinquency, surveys of illicit drug use, and so forth): the better the measurement procedures, the higher the estimates of controversial behaviors (for example, Hindelang, Hirschi and Weis 1981).

The present estimates are higher than earlier ones, due primarily to three significant improvements in the present survey: (1) a shorter recall period, (2) reliance on person-based information rather than just household-based information, and (3) information on how many household DGUs had been experienced in the recall period by those Rs reporting any such experiences.

Using a shorter recall period undoubtedly reduced the effects of memory loss, thereby reducing the artificial shrinkage to which earlier estimates were subject. Although telescoping was also undoubtedly reduced, and this would, by itself, tend to reduce estimates, the impact of reducing telescoping was apparently smaller than the impact of reducing case loss due to forgetting. Evidence internal to this survey directly indicates that a one-year recall period yields larger per-year estimates than a five-year recall period (compare figures in the right half of Table 6.2 with their counterparts in the left half).

This phenomenon, where less behavior is reported for a longer recall period than would be expected based on results obtained when using a shorter period, has also been observed in surveys of self-reported use of illicit drugs (Bachman and O'Malley 1981).

Further, basing estimates on what Rs report about DGUs in which they were personally involved also increases the estimates. One of the surprises of this survey was how few Rs were willing to report a DGU that involved some other member of their household. Nearly all (85 percent) of the reports of DGUs we obtained involved the original R, that is, the person with whom the interviewer first spoke. Given that most households contain more than one adult who was eligible to be interviewed, it was surprising that, when we contacted a DGU-involved household, the person who answered the phone would consistently turn out to also be the individual who had been involved in the DGU. Our strong suspicion is that many Rs feel that it is not their place to tell total strangers that some other member of their household has used a gun for self-protection. Some of them are willing to tell strangers about an incident in which they were themselves involved, but apparently few are willing to "inform" on others in their household. Still others may not have been aware of DGUs involving other household members. Evidence internal to the present survey supports this speculation (person-based estimates are 66 to 77 percent higher than household-based estimates), suggesting that there was much more complete reporting of DGUs involving the original respondent than of those involving other household members (Table 6.2). Consequently, those previous surveys that yielded only household-based estimates (four of the eleven gun surveys yielding usable annual estimates, and half of those that were national in scope) probably substantially underestimated DGUs for this reason as well.

We also had information on the number of times that DGU-involved households had experienced DGUs during the five-year recall period. It was necessary in computing previous estimates to conservatively assume that each DGU-involved person or household had experienced only one DGU, but our evidence indicates that repeat experiences were not uncommon, with 29.5 percent of DGU-involved households reporting more than one DGU within the previous five years. The average number of DGUs in this time span was 1.5 per DGU-involved household. Therefore, this information alone could account for a roughly 50 percent increase in DGU incidence estimates based on the five-year recall period.

Finally, our survey was superior to the NCVS in two additional ways: It was free of the taint of being conducted by, and on behalf of, employees of the federal government, and it was completely anonymous.

It would be incorrect to say that the present estimates are inconsistent with those derived from the earlier gun surveys. Avoiding apples-and-oranges comparisons, one should compare figures from Table 6.2 that can be meaningfully compared with earlier results summarized in Table 6.1. If one considers the household prevalence figures from the two previous national surveys that used a DGU question most similar to the one used in the present survey, the Hart and Mauser surveys, they indicate that 3.8 percent of households reported, in 1990, a DGU involving a gun of any kind in the previous five years (Mauser survey) and that 4 percent reported, in 1981, a DGU involving a handgun in the previous five years (Hart survey). Examining the past-five-years, household-based "% used" figures in Table 6.2, we find 3.9 percent for all guns and 3 percent for handguns. Thus, the present results are, where directly comparable, within sampling error of those of the best two previous surveys. Indeed, the consistency is remarkable given the substantial differences among the surveys and the 12-year time difference between the Hart survey and the current one. Further, the only prior survey with person-based estimates and a *one* year recall period, the 1976 Field poll in California, yielded a 1.4 percent prevalence figure for handguns (Table 6.1, note a), compared to 1 percent in the present survey (Table 6.2, 2nd column).

With a sample size of 4,977, random sampling error of the estimates is small. For example, the all-guns prevalence (% used) "A" estimates (95 percent confidence interval) are plus or minus 0.32 percent for past year, person; 0.35 percent for past year, household; 0.50 percent for past five years, person; and 0.54 percent for past five years, household. Given how small these are already, even increasing samples to the size of the enormous ones in the NCVS could produce only slight further reductions in sampling error.

Are these estimates plausible? Could it really be true that Americans use guns for self-protection as often as 2.1 to 2.5 million times a year? The estimate may seem remarkable in comparison to expectations based on conventional wisdom, but it is not implausibly large in comparison to various gun-related phenomena. There are probably over 230 million guns in private hands in the United States (extrapolation up to 1994 from 1987 data in Kleck 1991, p. 50), implying that only about 1 percent of them are used for defensive purposes in any one year, hardly an impossibly high fraction. In a December 1993 Gallup survey, 49 percent of U.S. households reported a gun, and 31 percent of adults reported personally owning one (Moore and Newport 1994, p. 18). These figures imply about 47.6 million households with a gun, with perhaps 93 million (49 percent of the adult U.S. population) adults living in households with guns, and about 59.1 million adults personally owning a gun. Again, it hardly seems implausible that 3 percent (2.5 million/93 million) of the people with immediate access to a gun could have used one defensively in a given year.

Huge numbers of Americans not only have access to guns but the overwhelming majority of gun owners are, if one can believe their own statements, willing to use a gun defensively. In a December 1989 national survey, 78 percent of American gun owners stated that they would not only be willing to use a gun defensively in some way but would be willing to *shoot* a burglar (Quinley 1990). The percentage willing to use a gun defensively in *some* way, though not necessarily by shooting someone, would presumably be even higher than this.

Nevertheless, having access to a gun and being willing to use it against criminals is not the same as actually doing so. The latter requires experiencing a crime under circumstances in which the victim can get to, or already possesses, a gun. We do not know how many such opportunities for crime victims to use guns defensively occur each year. It would be useful to know how large a fraction of crimes with direct offender-victim contact result in a DGU. Unfortunately, a large share of the incidents covered by our survey are probably outside the scope of incidents that are realistically likely to be reported to either the NCVS or police. If the DGU incidents reported in the present survey are not entirely a subset within the pool of cases covered by the NCVS, one cannot meaningfully use NCVS data to estimate the share of crime incidents that result in a DGU. Nevertheless, in a ten-state sample of incarcerated felons interviewed in 1982, 34 percent reported having been "scared off, shot at, wounded or captured by an armed victim" (Wright and Rossi 1986, p. 155). From the criminals' stand-point, this experience was not rare.

How could such a serious thing happen so often without it having become common knowledge? This phenomenon, regard-less of how widespread it really is, is largely an invisible one as far as governmental statistics are concerned. Neither the de-fender/victim nor the criminal ordinarily has much incentive to report this sort of event to the police, and either or both often have strong reasons not to do so. Consequently, many of these incidents never come to the attention of the police, whereas others may be reported, but with victims leaving out any mention of their own use of a gun. Even when a DGU is reported, it would rarely be recorded by the police, who ordinarily do not keep statistics on such matters (other than DGUs resulting in a death); police record-keeping is largely confined to information helpful in apprehend-ing perpetrators and making a legal case for convicting them. Such statistics are not kept, so we cannot even be certain that a large number of DGUs are *not* reported to the police.

The health system cannot shed much light on this phenome-non either, as very few of these incidents involve anyone, defender or criminal, being injured (Table 8.1, Panels A, E). In the rare cases where anyone is hurt, it is usually the criminal, who is unlikely to seek medical attention for any but the most life-threatening gun-shot wounds as this would ordinarily result in a police interroga-tion. As of 1989, physicians in at least 40 states were required by law to report treatment of gunshot wounds to the police (Lee et al. 1991, p. 519), making it necessary for medically treated criminals to explain to police how they received their wounds.

Finally, it is now clear that virtually none of the victims who use guns defensively tell interviewers about it in the NCVS. Our estimates imply that only about 3 percent of DGUs among NCVS Rs are reported to interviewers (the 85,000 DGUs estimated from the NCVS, divided by the 2.5 million estimate derived from the presented survey equals .03). Based on other comparisons of alternative survey estimates of violent events with NCVS esti-mates, this high level of underreporting is eminently plausible. Loftin and Mackenzie (1990, pp. 22–23) reported that rapes might be 33 times as frequent as NCVS estimates indicate, and spousal violence could easily be 12 times as high.

What is the significance of these figures? There is no inherent value to knowing the exact number of defensive uses of guns any more than there is any value to knowing the exact number of crimes that are committed each year. The estimates in Table 6.2 are at best only rough approximations, which are all probably too low. It is sufficient to conclude from these numbers that defensive gun use is very common, far more common than has been recognized to date by criminologists or policy makers, and certainly far more common than one would think based on any official sources of information.

Appendix

Adjusting Previous Survey
Estimates of Defensive Gun Use

The results of previous gun use surveys were adjusted to make them more comparable with one another and with the National Self-Defense Survey (Kleck and Gertz 1995). The basic idea was to estimate the annual, national estimate of defensive gun uses (DGUs) that each survey would have yielded if it had resembled the NSDS, that is, if it was a 1993 national survey of noninstitutionalized adults (age 18+) that covered uses involving any gun type, excluded uses against animals or uses connected with military, police, or security guard work, had a one-year recall period, and asked the DGU question of all respondents (Rs), not just gun or handgun owners. There was no attempt to adjust for differences in crime or gun ownership levels in different years or locales. Further, for all estimates it was conservatively assumed that there was only one DGU per DGU-involved person or household. (See Table 6A for a summary of adjustments applied to surveys.)

Adjustments

Adjustment A was applied to surveys inquiring only about uses of handguns, to produce an estimate pertaining to all gun types. The NSDS indicated that 79.7 percent of DGUs involved handguns (Table 8.1, Panel H), so the adjustment consists of multiplying a handgun-only estimate by 1.2547 (1/0.797).

Adjustment B was applied to surveys inquiring about an indefinite period of time ("have you ever . . ."), to produce an estimate pertaining to a one year recall period. The Field poll indicated that the same survey yielded a 1.4 percent prevalence figure for a one-year recall period and an 8.6 percent figure for the unlimited period (Table 6.1, Note a), so the adjustment consists of multiplying an "ever used" estimate by 0.16279 (1.4 percent/8.6 percent).

Adjustment C was applied to surveys inquiring about a five-year

TABLE 6A   Adjustments Applied to Surveys

Survey	Population Base Used	Adjustments Applied	Other Information Used
Field	Persons	A,D	Used the 1.4% past-year figure
Bordua	Persons	B,D	
DMIa	Households	B,D	
DMIb	Households	B	
Hart	Households	A,C3	
Ohio	Persons	A,B,D	26.4% of U.S. households had handguns in 1993 (average of 5 national surveys)
Mauser	Households	C2	
Gallup 91	Persons	A,B,D	46% of households reported a gun; 47% of these reported a handgun
Gallup 93	Persons	B,D,E	31% of Rs personally owned gun
L.A. Times	Persons	B,D,G	
Tarrance	Persons	C1	Used "1% of Rs" figure

recall period, to produce an estimate pertaining to a one-year recall period. The NSDS (Table 6.2) yielded the following ratios of one-year prevalence over five-year prevalence:

- ♦ C1 All guns, person-based: 1.326/3.315=0.40000
- ♦ C2 All guns, household-based: 1.587/3.898=0.40713
- ♦ C3 Handguns, household-based: 1.105/2.974=0.37155

Adjustment D was applied to surveys that failed to exclude uses of guns against animals, to produce an estimate pertaining only to uses against humans. The NSDS indicated that of 244 Rs initially reporting DGUs, 22 had used guns only against animals, so the adjustment consists of multiplying a humans-plus-animals estimate by 0.90984 (222/244).

Adjustment E was applied to surveys that asked the DGU question only of Rs who reported personally owning a gun or handgun, to produce an estimate pertaining to the entire population and thus reflecting uses among those who do not report current ownership of a gun. The NSDS indicated that only 59.5 percent of Rs reporting DGUs reported current personal ownership of a gun, so the adjustment consists of multiplying a gun-owners-only estimate by 1.68067 (1/0.595).

Adjustment F was applied to surveys that asked the DGU question only of Rs who lived in households reporting a gun, to produce an estimate pertaining to the entire population and thus reflecting uses among those who do not live in a household reporting current ownership of a gun. The NSDS indicated that only 79 percent of Rs reporting DGUs reported current household ownership of a gun, so the adjustment consists of multiplying a gun-owners-only estimate by 1.26582 (1/0.790).

Adjustment G was applied to surveys that inquired only about DGUs that occurred outside the R's home, to produce an estimate pertaining to all DGUs, regardless of location. The NSDS indicated that 62.7 percent of DGUs occurred outside the R's home, so the adjustment consists of multiplying an outside-the-home-only estimate by 1.59490 (1/0.627).

Population Bases Used

Persons: Estimated resident population, age 18 or older, as of March, 1993: 191,008,961 (U.S. Bureau of the Census, *Statistical Abstract of the U.S.*, p. 22: 1992 population projected to 1993 by assuming that the 1992–1993 percentage increase equalled the 1991–1992 percentage increase.)

Households: Estimated U.S. households as of March, 1993: 96,391,000 (U.S. Bureau of the Census, *Statistical Abstract of the U.S.*, p. 58).

Computational Procedures

Typically, the prevalence figure reported for the survey (for example, the proportion of adults who had used a gun for protection) was multiplied times the appropriate population base (for example, number of U.S. resident adults) and then times each of the necessary adjustment factors. In cases where the prevalence figure applied only to gun owners (or some subset thereof), the number of gun owners had to be computed first, using the gun owner prevalence figures generated in the same survey, or, in one case, figures generated in other national surveys conducted in the same year.

Illustrative Example

The 1993 Gallup poll estimate required considerable adjusting, so it serves as a useful example. In that survey, among persons reporting that they personally owned a gun (who constituted 31 percent of the entire sample), 11 percent reported that they had ever used a gun for protection. The survey did not exclude uses against animals. The estimate of DGUs was therefore computed as follows:

191,008,961 x 0.31		x 0.11	x 0.16278	x 0.90984	x 1.68067= 1,621,377
Population			B	D	E
# Adults	% of pop. that owns guns	% of owners w. DGU	1 year vs."ever"	Humans only	Entire pop. vs. only gun owners	Est. DGUs

Of an estimated 191,008,961 adults resident in the United States in 1993, 31 percent of them, or about 59,212,778 personally own a gun. Of these, 11 percent, or 6,513,406 would report "ever" using a gun for protection. An estimated 0.16278 of these, or 1,060,322, would report doing so in the previous one-year period. An estimated 0.90984 of them, or 964,719, used a gun against a human rather than an animal. The number of defensive gun users in the entire population (gun owners *and* nonowners) is 1.68067 times the number of users who currently personally own a gun, which implies 1,621,377 users in the entire population, including those who do not report current personal gun ownership. Conservatively assuming just one use per user, the estimated number of DGUs would therefore also be 1,621,377.

Notes

1. Portions of this chapter have been adapted from Kleck (1988), Chapter 4 of Kleck (1991), and Kleck and Gertz (1995).
2. The Cambridge Reports survey, sponsored by a pro-control organization (the Center for the Study and Prevention of Handgun Violence), stands out as the deviant case among the surveys listed in Table 6.1. It shows far smaller estimates of the proportion of the population that has used a gun defensively. This may be due to several technical peculiarities of the survey. First, the relevant question was asked only of persons who personally owned a handgun at the time of the survey, thereby excluding former owners and nonowners who had used guns defensively. Second, the question was only asked of that subset of handgun owners who owned specifically for defensive reasons, excluding those who owned exclusively for nondefensive reasons but nevertheless used the gun defensively. Third, the relevant question was oddly worded, asking whether the respondent had "ever *had* to use" their handgun defensively (my emphasis). This further restricted affirmative answers as some may have used guns defensively without being certain that they "had to" in the sense of having no other alternative.
3. Readers should note that the Hart and Mauser estimates in the last row of Table 6.1 are not the same as the estimates published elsewhere (Kleck 1991, p. 107) as they have been subjected to a more extensive series of adjustments (compare the Appendix in this chapter with Kleck 1991, pp. 106–107).
4. McDowall et al. (1992) tried to show how much the NCVS estimate of DGUs would be changed by adjusting for the underreporting of domestic violence. The problem with this effort is that it assumes that the underreporting of DGUs linked with domestic violence is due solely to the more general problem of the underreporting of domestic violence incidents of any kind. As noted here, this is clearly incorrect. In an abrupt *volte face,* McDowall et al. first admitted that their "'corrected' estimates are of limited value" because the "correction factors are arbitrary" (p. 8), yet they then turned around and concluded that "there is *strong* evidence that firearms are used to resist crime less frequently than is often believed" (p. 12, my emphasis).

Chapter 7

Keeping, Carrying, and Shooting Guns for Self-Protection*

Gary Kleck

Self-Defense Killings

Most uses of guns for either criminal or defensive purposes are much less dramatic or consequential than one might think. Only a tiny fraction of criminal gun assaults involve anyone actually being wounded, even nonfatally, and the same is true of defensive gun use (DGUs). More commonly, a gun is merely pointed at another person, or perhaps only referred to ("I've got a gun") or displayed, and this is sufficient to accomplish the ends of the user, whether criminal or noncriminal. Nevertheless, most gun owners questioned in surveys assert that they would be willing to shoot criminals under the right circumstances. The 1989 Time/CNN survey found that 80 percent of gun owners thought they would get their guns if they believed someone was breaking into their homes, and 78 percent said they would shoot a burglar if they felt threatened by that person (Quinley 1990, p. 9).

Despite this stated willingness of gun owners to shoot under

*References for this chapter appear on pages 258–268.

certain circumstances, most defensive uses of guns do not in fact involve shooting anyone. Although the surveys listed in Table 6.1 did not delve into much detail about the circumstances in which guns were used defensively, or the manner in which they were used, some did ask whether the gun was fired. The results of earlier gun use surveys generally indicate that the gun was fired in less than half of the defensive uses, and the National Self-Defense survey indicated that the gun was fired in only 24 percent of the incidents. The rest of the time, the gun was merely displayed or referred to in order to threaten or frighten away a criminal.

The rarest but most serious form of self-defense with a gun is a defensive killing. Although shootings of criminals represent a small fraction of defensive uses of guns, Americans nevertheless shoot criminals with a frequency that must be regarded as remark-able by any standard. The FBI does not publish statistics on all self-defense killings, but it does publish counts of civilian justifi-able homicides (CJH) gathered through their Supplementary Homicides Reports (SHR) program. For a variety of reasons the FBI SHR totals for CJHs represent only a minority of all civilian legal defensive homicides (CLDHs). First, some cases that even local police label as CJHs are not reported as such to the FBI. Wilbanks (1984, p. 3) reports that police in Dade County were unwilling to spend much time properly recording homicides where prosecution of the killer was not to be pursued. Although Dade County police and medical examiner records indicated 72 civilian justifiable homicides in the county in 1980 (p. 190), county law enforcement agencies reported only 24 to the FBI's SHR program (analysis of ICPSR 1984).

Second, many homicides ultimately ruled noncriminal by prosecutors or judges are reported to the FBI as criminal homicides because that is how the initial police investigation treated them. Homicides are classified, for FBI Uniform Crime Reporting pur-poses, solely on the basis of the initial police investigation (U.S. FBI 1980).

Third, and perhaps most significant, in jurisdictions that follow legal distinctions between justifiable and excusable homi-cides fairly closely, many CLDHs will be recorded as excusable rather than justifiable, and thus are not eligible to be counted by the FBI, as it does not count excusable homicides. The magnitude of this last problem is suggested by findings concerning Detroit homicides. Over the period from 1969 to 1980, 344 cases of civilian homicides were labeled justifiable, but another 741 were labeled excusable (Dietz 1983, p. 203). Excusable homicides can include some accidental deaths. But accidental vehicular homicides were excluded from these excusable totals, and it is known that there were only 123 accidental deaths from guns in Detroit over this period.[1] About half of fatal gun accidents are self-inflicted (Kleck 1991, Chapter 7), so only about 62 of the accidental gun deaths were accidental homicides (that is, one person killing another), and many of these would be labeled negligent manslaughters rather than excusable homicides. Thus, few of the 741 Detroit excusable homicides were accidental deaths. Likewise, homicides by police officers are almost invariably labeled justifiable (Wolfgang 1958; Wilbanks 1984), so they are unlikely to claim any significant share of the excusable homicides. Instead, most of these excusable homicides appear to be CLDHs, and thus are not counted by the FBI as CJHs. (See Appendix 5 in Kleck 1991 for an explanation of the various categories of noncriminal homicides and the FBI classification scheme).

Because no national data exist distinguishing between the different types of CLDHs, data from single legal jurisdictions like cities and counties must be relied on to judge the relative frequency of each homicide type. Table 7.1 summarizes information from six unusually detailed local homicide studies. Although the actual character of homicide may differ somewhat from city to city, the results nevertheless suggest that there are sharp differences from place to place in the willingness of authorities to classify homicides as noncriminal. Row 12 of the table indicates that the fraction of intentional civilian homicides labeled as CLDHs varied from 1.6 to 19.5 percent over the six jurisdictions.

The Detroit and Dade County results yielded middle-range values on this fraction, came from two regionally distinct parts of the country, and are also the most recent. Thus, they seem to be most likely to be representative of the contemporary United States as a whole. Therefore these results will be used, in combination with the national SHR counts of civilian justifiable homicides, to roughly estimate national totals for CLDHs. One way to do this (Estimation Method I) is to assume that self-defense homicides grow out of criminal threats to life, as indexed by murders and

TABLE 7.1 Civilian Legal Defensive Homicides in Six Local Studies

Study	Bensing and Schroeder (1960)	Wolfgang (1958)	Rushforth, et al. (1977)	Lundsgaarde (1977)	Dietz (1983)	Wilbanks (1984)
Location	Cuyahoga County (Cleveland)	Philadelphia	Cuyahoga County (Cleveland)	Houston	Detroit	Dade County (Miami)
Period Studied	1947–1953	1948–1952	1958–1974	1969	1980	1980
	Row					
Total sample homicides	(1) 662	625	3371	c.312	583	569
Criminal homicides	(2) 505	588	?	282	493	478
Murders, nonnegligent manslaughters	(3) 505	est. 502[a]	?	281	487	478
Estimated unintentional excusable homicides	(4) ?	23	?	up to 12	c.4	5
Involuntary/negligent manslaughters	(5) ?	est. 86[a]	?	1	6	0
Justifiable police homicides	(6) 35	14	c. 110	10	13	14
Estimated intentional civilian homicides[b]	(7) 627	502	c.3261	c. 289	560	550
Justifiable civilian homicides (CJH)	(8) 122	8	c. 329	19	16	7
CJH reported on SHRs	(9) n.a.	n.a.	n.a.	n.a.	12	24

TABLE 7.1 Civilian Legal Defensive Homicides in Six Local Studies *(continued)*

Study Location Period Studied		Bensing and Schroeder (1960) Cuyahoga County (Cleveland) 1947–1953	Wolfgang (1958) Philadelphia 1948–1952	Rushforth, et al. (1977) Cuyahoga County (Cleveland) 1958–1974	Lundsgaarde (1977) Houston 1969	Dietz (1983) Detroit 1980	Wilbanks (1984) Dade County (Miami) 1980
Other civilian legal defensive homicides	(10)	0	n.a.	?	at least 1	57[c]	0
Total civilian legal defensive homicides (CLDH)[b]	(11)	122	8	c. 329	at least 20	73	72
Ratio, (11)/(7)	(12)	.195	.016	.101	at least .069	.130	.131
Ratio, (11)/(1)	(13)	.184	.013	.098	at least .064	.125	.127
Ratio, (11)/(3)	(14)	.242	.024	?	at least .071	.150	.151

Notes: [a] 14.7% of criminal homicide offenders prosecuted were charged with involuntary manslaughter. 147 × 588 = 86. 588 - 86 = 502. [b] (7)=(1)-(4)-(5)-(6) and (11) = (8) + (10). Homicides were classified according to their final legal classifications as reported in the study, whether police, coroner, or court-determined. See Kleck (1991, Appendix 5) for explanation of different types of noncriminal homicides. [c] Dietz reported 61 excusable homicides in 1980 (p. 203), but four of these were probably fatal gun accidents (analysis of U.S. NCHS 1983), leaving 57 other excusable homicides.

Sources: Bensing and Schroeder (1960, pp. 5, 59, 80); Wolfgang, (1958, pp.24, 228, 301, 303); Rushforth et al. (1977, pp. 531–533); Lundsgaarde (1977, pp. 68–69, 162, 219, 236, 237); Dietz (1983, p. 203); Wilbanks (1984, pp. 29-30,57,70-72,154).

nonnegligent manslaughters reported to the FBI, and that the ratio of the former to the latter will be roughly the same for the United States as a whole as it is for Detroit and Dade County. The combined totals for these two local areas were 1,062 killings counted by the FBI as murders and nonnegligent manslaughters (U.S. FBI 1981, pp. 74, 107) and 145 killings known to be CLDHs (Table 7.1), giving a ratio of the latter to the former of 0.1365. Multiplying this number times the 1994 national total of 23,310 murders and nonnegligent manslaughters (which includes some misclassified CLDHs) (U.S. FBI 1995, p. 58) yields an estimate of 3,183 CLDHs for the United States in 1994.

Alternatively, the national counts of civilian justifiable homicide reported to the FBI (1995, p. 22) could be used as a starting point, with an adjustment for its incomplete coverage of CLDHs (Estimation Method II). In 1980 there were 145 CLDHs in the two local jurisdictions, of which only 36 were reported to the FBI as CJHs (tabulations from 1980 SHR dataset, ICPSR 1984), yielding a ratio of 4.167 CLDHs to every CJH counted in the SHR program. Multiplying this times the 1994 national SHR total of 353 CJHs yields an estimate of 1,422 CLDHs. Of the 353 CJHs reported to the SHR program, 316, or 89.5 percent involved guns, so it is estimated that about 1,273 (.895 x 1,422) CLDHs involved guns, based on the lower estimate, or 2,849 (.895 x 3,183) based on the higher estimate. In sum, Method II implies about 1,300 to 2,800 felons killed by gun-wielding civilians in self-defense or some other legally justified or excusable cause in 1994.

The degree to which these estimates are meaningful for the nation as a whole is heavily dependent on the representativeness of the two local jurisdictions chosen as regards the critical ratios used in the estimates. However, the evidence indicates that the relative prevalence of CLDHs among homicides is not unusually high in these two areas. Row 14 of Table 7.1 indicates that the ratio of CLDHs to murders and nonnegligent manslaughters was 0.242 in the Bensing and Schroeder study of the Cleveland area, much higher than in Detroit and Dade County. As the ratio was lower in the Wolfgang and Rushforth, et al. studies and somewhat indeterminate in the Lundsgaarde study, it seems justifiable to tentatively regard the ratio based on Detroit and Dade County as a middle-range value. In any case, it is not claimed that the resulting numbers are anything more than rough estimates in-

TABLE 7.2 Estimated U.S. Totals, Police and Civilian Legal Defensive Homicides (LDHs), 1994[a]

Homicide Type	Justifiable Homicides Reported to FBI/SHR	Estimated Total LDHs Estimation Method I	Estimated Total LDHs Estimation Method II
Police, gun	461	289	578
Police, nongun	2	29	58
Police, total	463	318	636
Civilian, gun	316	2849	1273
Civilian, nongun	37	334	149
Civilian, total	353	3183	1422

Notes: SHR = Supplementary Homicide Reports. Estimation Methods — see text. [a] Method I police counts were taken from 1990 vital statistics system counts of deaths due to legal intervention.

Sources: U.S. Federal Bureau of Investigation (1995, p. 22); U.S. NCHS (1994, p. 222).

tended to support the very general claim that civilians use guns to legally kill a large number of felons each year.

The various estimates are summarized in Table 7.2. The police homicide estimates are simple totals for deaths by legal intervention as compiled by the vital statistics system (Estimation Method I) (U.S. NCHS 1994, p. 222), which were then doubled (Estimation Method II) to adjust for the fact that only about half of police killings get reported as such to the national vital statistics system (Sherman and Langworthy 1979, p. 552). FBI/SHR counts of police justifiable homicides are also reported here. Regardless of which counts of homicides by police are used, the results indicate that civilians legally kill far more felons than police officers do. The figures imply that, of 25,165 civilian (not by police) intentional homicide deaths in the United States in 1980 (U.S. NCHS 1985), about 1400 to 3200, or 5.7 to 12.6 percent were legal civilian defensive homicides.

This estimate was independently confirmed by the only study to ever examine a national sample of homicide dispositions. Analysis of all 231 gun homicides committed in the United States during May 1–7, 1989 indicated that 28 (12.1 percent) were ruled justifiable (*Time* 5-14-90, p. 30). The report was unclear whether 13 killings by police (*Time* 7-17-89, p. 31) had been excluded from the total of 28, so the number of civilian justifiable homicides with guns could have been as low as 15 (6.5 percent). Thus, the resulting range of nationally based estimates is 5.7 to 12.6 percent, almost identical to the 7.1 to 12.9 percent estimate based on extrapolation from local data.

Even if one had complete national counts of all homicides eventually declared lawful by the legal system, they would very likely understate certain categories of defensive homicide. Gillespie (1989, pp. xii–xiii) reviewed five local studies of homicides where women killed their husbands or men with whom they lived intimately and concluded that the majority were self-defense killings. She estimated that there were as many as 500 such defensive killings in the United States each year, but then she described case after case where women killed (usually with a gun) abusive husbands or boyfriends but were then convicted for criminal homicide, even in incidents where the circumstances seemed to clearly justify a legitimate claim of self-defense.

The following examples, adapted from brief case narratives in Wilbanks (1984, pp. 193–374), help give the flavor of typical defensive gun killings (V=victim, that is, the initial aggressor who was killed, O="offender" who used gun defensively).

> ◆ *Case 566.* V (Latin male) and O were both roomers in a "fleabag" hotel. O was a black male and did not speak or understand Spanish. V provoked O, pulled a knife on him and backed him into a corner (other Latins present tried to calm the V to no avail). O (a soft-spoken and quiet man) pulled out a gun and fired a warning shot. When the V kept coming the O fired again and killed the V (p. 373).

> ◆ *Case 228.* Black male V entered black female O's bedroom and told O not to be afraid as he just wanted to have sex. O got out her shotgun (by her bed) and advised V to leave. When V put his right leg on the bed, he was shot by the O. O keeps a loaded shotgun by her bed as she has been burglarized several times. V had a knife in his possession when he advanced on the O. O stated that she had never seen the V before (p. 270).

> ◆ *Case 288.* Two victims entered a pawn shop and attempted to pawn a bad stereo, which a store em-

ployee refused to accept. One V then jumped over the counter, armed with a revolver, and both victims were shot by the co-owner of the store (p. 278).

Case 566 is a clear case of excusable homicide, involving simple self-defense against an attacker, whereas cases 228 and 288 would probably be classified under FBI guidelines as justifiable homicides, involving defense against rape and robbery, respectively. A few homicides, although treated by authorities as noncriminal, are of a more dubious moral and legal character than these examples. The following incident is illustrative.

> ◆ *Case 159.* V and another person were burglarizing a residence when they were surprised by the owner of the house. Both V and accomplice ran from the house as owner fired shots and struck the V (p. 159). Although the victim was clearly committing a felony against the shooter, the latter was apparently no longer in danger when he fired his gun at the fleeing burglars.

Only four or five of the 72 civilian justifiable homicides in the Wilbanks dataset were similarly questionable, but Case 159 does illustrate that homicides can be legally classified as noncriminal even though they might be criminal under some legal doctrines. Likewise, cases that appear to be legitimate cases of self-defense can be wrongly classified as criminal homicides (Gillespie 1989). It is not known what the relative balance of these two types of errors are in general samples of homicides, so one cannot be sure whether they contribute to an overcount or an undercount of CLDHs, although Gillespie (1989) strongly suggests that there is a net undercount of lawful defensive killings among female-against-male homicides.

Defensive Woundings

Nonfatal gun woundings are far more frequent than fatal shootings. Cook (1985) reviewed data that indicate that only about 15 percent of gunshot wounds known to the police are fatal, implying a ratio of about 5.67 (85/15) nonfatal gun woundings to each fatal one. Assuming the same applies to legal civilian defensive shootings, there were between 8,700 and 16,600 nonfatal, legally permissible woundings of criminals by gun-armed civilians in 1980. Combining the defensive killings and nonfatal woundings, there are about 10,000 to 20,000 legal shootings of criminals a year, which would be less than 2 percent of all DGUs. The rest of DGUs, then, involve neither killings nor woundings but rather misses, warning shots fired, or guns pointed or referred to.

Keeping Loaded Guns

That DGUs, with or without a wounding, are so common is not surprising in light of how many Americans own guns for defensive reasons and keep them ready for defensive use. A 1989 national survey found that 27 percent of gun owners have a gun *mainly* for protection, and 62 percent said that protection from crime was at least *one* of the reasons they owned guns (Quinley 1990). The 1994 General Social Surveys indicated that 28 percent, or 53.9 million of the nation's adults personally own guns (Davis and Smith 1994), so these figures translate into about 15 million people who had guns mainly for protection, and about 33 million who had them at least partly for protection (using data on number of individual gun owners from Kleck 1991, p. 55).

Further, many gun owners, and almost certainly a majority of those who own guns primarily for protection, keep a household gun loaded. The 1989 Time/CNN survey found that 24 percent of gun owners always kept a gun loaded, and another 7 percent had a gun loaded at the time of the interview although they did not do so all the time, for a total of 31 percent. Guns were most commonly kept in the bedroom, where they would be ready for night-time use (Quinley 1990, pp. 4–6, 9). A 1994 national survey likewise found that 29 percent of gun owners reported that at least one of their guns was loaded at the time of the interview (Hemenway et al. 1995, p. 49).

Apparently nearly all of the guns kept loaded are handguns. Figures from the 1994 survey implied that 186 of the 206 loaded guns, or 90 percent, were handguns. A 1977 telephone survey of Illinois adults found that 35.4 percent of households that owned only handguns, and 31.9 percent of households that owned both handguns and long guns, kept a gun loaded, compared to only 1.6 percent of households that owned only long guns. Black gun owners were four times as likely as white owners to keep a gun loaded, Chicago residents were twice as likely to do so as other Illinois residents, and households with no adult male were twice as likely as other households to have a loaded gun (Bordua 1982). In short, keeping a gun loaded was most common in households where vulnerability to victimization was highest.

Carrying Guns for Protection

Carrying firearms for protection is one of the most active forms of gun use for both defensive and criminal purposes. Persons who wish to have guns available for defensive purposes in public spaces must carry guns, legally or illegally, to do so. Unlawful carrying of guns probably accounts for the majority of arrests for weapons violations (Bordua et al. 1985), and virtually all gun crime committed in public places necessarily involves carrying of firearms. Millions of Americans carry guns every year. A December 1993 Gallup poll indicated that 17 percent of adults who personally own a gun, or 5 percent of the entire adult population, carry a gun on their person for protection, whereas 25 percent of gun owners, and 8 percent of all adults, carry one in their vehicle (DIALOG 1995). These figures imply about 9 million people who carry a gun on their person and 13.5 million who carry in their vehicles. At most, 1.5 million gun carriers could be police, security guards, and the like (U.S. Bureau of the Census 1988, p. 389), leaving at least 7.5 million civilians who carry on their person and 12 million who do so in their vehicles. Given that handguns are involved in about 700,000 criminal incidents each year (U.S. Bureau of Justice Statistics 1994, pp. 82–83), with only some of these involving carrying, one implication of these numbers is that over 90 percent of gun carriers carry without any intention of committing a crime. Note that some of the guns may be carried in rural areas for protection against animals rather than criminals.

Carrying guns implies carrying deadly weapons in public spaces. What makes spaces public is that almost anyone may freely move through them without invitation. Therefore, unlike home spaces, they are places where unplanned encounters between strangers routinely occur. Such encounters are inherently more dangerous than encounters between family members, friends, and others who interact in private spaces, because the actors share no previously established understandings, commitments, emotional bonds, or obligations to restrain the open expression of hostility. Most people recognize this special character of public contacts with strangers and exercise caution accordingly. Gun carrying could have a number of effects in this setting. Carrying a gun might make people foolhardy, encouraging them to take unnecessary risks, and perhaps even to seek out risks. Or, by giving its possessor the quiet confidence of knowing he has a power advantage, a gun might prevent a potentially conflictual situation from progressing to the point where hostility was openly expressed, thereby making the resort to weapons unnecessary. Alternatively, display of the weapon could deter the unarmed party from further escalation of hostilities. However, once the situation did escalate to open hostilities, use of the gun might make it more likely that conflict could lead to a death.

Although gun laws regulating the carrying of firearms have been studied, especially the Massachusetts Bartley-Fox law (Pierce and Bowers 1981), and carrying by felons has recently been examined (Wright and Rossi 1986), research on carrying by the adult general public is rare (Kleck and Gertz 1998). A major review of research on guns and violence did not review a single study on the subject (Wright, Rossi and Daly 1983), and the handful of relevant studies are flawed and of limited generalizability. A 1962 study was descriptive in nature and limited to urban black arrestees, finding that 70 percent of 50 St. Louis blacks convicted of carrying concealed weapons did so because they anticipated attack (Schultz 1962).

Hassinger (1985) conducted a mail survey of Jefferson County (Birmingham) Alabama residents who had a legal permit to carry firearms. In this county, 10 percent of the adult population was licensed to carry a handgun. The most frequently endorsed reason for carrying a pistol was the belief that "the police cannot be everywhere; the pistol is a prudent precaution," and the second most common reason was worry about being a victim of crime (p. 115). The main sources of information that led to these concerns about crime were "actual prior incidents," "news reports about crime," and "common knowledge (word of mouth) about crime" (p. 117). Unfortunately, this survey had a return rate of only 21 percent, raising questions about generalizability.

Bankston et al. (1986) conducted a mail survey of Louisiana driver's license holders, which included an item that read: "Please indicate how often you do the following to protect yourself and your property. . . . Carry a firearm when you leave home." The possible responses were never, occasionally, frequently, and always (p. 7). The authors' regression analysis indicated that gun carrying was more likely, other things being equal, among persons with a crime victimization experience, people fearful of crime, younger people, males, and residents of Northern Louisiana, the area with the more traditionally Southern, non-Cajun, culture.

Unfortunately, there is strong indication that the sample surveyed was seriously biased. This survey indicated that 56.5 percent of white Louisiana households owned handguns, although only 37 percent of white households in the West South Central region (Louisiana, Texas, Oklahoma, and Arkansas) in the 1984 General Social Surveys reported a handgun (analysis of Davis and Smith 1984). Handgun owners appear to have been substantially more likely to return questionnaires. A return rate of less than 50 percent and the lack of follow-up mailings presumably contributed to this problem.

Psychological Effects of Keeping Guns for Protection

Before addressing the objective outcomes of actual defensive uses of guns, a more subjective issue should be addressed. If some people get guns in response to crime or the prospect of being victimized in the future (Kleck 1991, Ch. 2), does gun ownership have any reassuring effects? Once a gun is acquired, does it make its owner feel safer? Reducing fear would be an intangible benefit distinct from any objective utility a gun might have when it is actually used for defensive purposes.

A December 1989 CNN/Time national survey of 605 U.S. gun owners asked the following question: "Does having a gun in your house make you feel more safe from crime, less safe, or doesn't it make any difference?" Although 42 percent of the gun owners felt more safe, only 2 percent felt less safe, and the rest said it made no difference (Quinley 1990). Because only 27 percent of the owners had a gun mainly for protection from crime, and only 62 percent had a gun even partially for protection from crime, it is not surprising that some owners felt having a gun made no difference in their feelings of safety—it presumably was not supposed to make any difference, as their guns were owned for recreational reasons. Assuming that those who felt safer fell largely among those 62 percent (or 27 percent) of owners who had guns for protection, one can infer that a majority of defensive gun owners do feel safer from crime, or at least claim to feel that way. When asked, "Overall, do you feel comfortable with a gun in your house or are you sometimes afraid of it?," 92 percent of gun owners said they were comfortable, 6 percent were sometimes afraid, and 2 percent were not sure (p. 10).

A 1990 national survey indicated that nearly all defensive gun owners feel safer because they have a gun. Among persons whose primary reason for owning a gun was self-defense, 89 percent replied "yes" to the question: "Do you feel safer because you have a gun at home?" Among gun owners who did not feel safer, 96 percent were persons whose primary reason for owning was something other than defense (Mauser 1990).

These surveys confirmed what previous surveys had indicated. For example, in a national survey conducted in January 1981, Rs were asked: "How do you feel about having a gun in your house? Do you think it makes things safer, or do you think it makes things more dangerous?" This question wording differed from that of the CNN/Time and Mauser polls in that it focused on perception of actual dangers, a matter that is partly objective and partly subjective rather than on the purely subjective matter of how the gun made Rs feel. Among Rs in gun owning households giving nonmissing responses, 58 percent felt having a gun in their house "makes things safer," 30 percent felt things were about the same, and 11 percent felt it made things more dangerous (tabulation of data in the *Los Angeles Times* 1981). In sum, most gun owners, including many who do not even have a gun for defensive reasons, feel comfortable with guns, feel safer from crime because of them, and believe their guns actually do make them safer from crime.

Effectiveness and Risks
of Armed Resistance to Criminals

Of course, gun owners may be deceiving themselves. Their feelings of greater security, however real in emotional terms, may lack a factual foundation. Regardless, the belief that guns provide effective self-protection for at least some people some of the time is nearly universal. Even proponents of stringent gun control who assert that guns are not effective defensive devices for civilians nearly always make exceptions for police officers and the like. The rationale for police having guns is based at least partly on the idea that police need and can effectively use guns for defending themselves and others. Doubts about the defensive utility of guns, then, appear to rest on any of three beliefs: (1) civilians do not need any self-protective devices because they will never confront criminals, or at least will never do so while they have access to a gun; or (2) they can rely on the police for protection; or (3) they are not able to use guns effectively, regardless of need.

There is certainly some merit to the first belief. Most Americans rarely face a threat of serious physical assault, and some will never do so. Nevertheless, NCVS estimates indicate that 83 percent of Americans will, at some time over the span of their lives, be a victim of a violent crime, all of which by definition involve direct confrontation with a criminal (U.S. Bureau of Justice Statistics 1987a, p. 3). Further, the most common location for such a confrontation is in or near the victim's home, that is, the place where victims would be most likely to have access to a gun if they owned one (Curtis 1974, p. 176). Although it cannot be stated what share of these incidents will transpire in a way that would allow the victim to actually use a gun, it is clear that a large share of the population will experience such an incident.

The second idea, that citizens can depend on police for effective protection, is simply untrue. It implies that police can serve the same function as a gun in disrupting a crime in progress, before the victim is hurt or loses property. Police cannot do this, and indeed do not themselves even claim to be able to do so. Instead, police primarily respond reactively to crimes *after* they have occurred, questioning the victim and other witnesses in the hope that they can apprehend the criminals, make them available for prosecution and punishment, and thereby deter other criminals from attempting crimes.

Police officers rarely disrupt violent crimes or burglaries in progress; even the most professional and efficient urban police forces rarely can reach the scene of a crime soon enough to catch the criminal "in the act" (Walker 1989, pp. 134–135). More generally, the idea that modern police are so effective in controlling crime that they have rendered citizen self-protection obsolete is wildly at variance with a large body of evidence that police activities have, at best, only very modest effects on crime (Walker 1989, Chapter 7).

The third idea, that civilians are not generally able to use guns effectively, requires more extended consideration. Gun control proponents sometimes argue that only police have the special training, skills, and emotional control needed to wield guns effectively in self-defense. They hint that would-be gun users are ineffectual, panic-prone hysterics, as likely to accidentally shoot a family member as a burglar (for example, Alviani and Drake 1975, pp. 6–8; Yeager et al. 1976, pp. 3–7). Incidents in which householders shoot family members mistaken for burglars and other criminals do indeed occur, but they are extremely rare. Studies reviewed elsewhere (Kleck 1991, Chapter 7) indicate that fewer than 2 percent of fatal gun accidents (FGAs) involve a person accidentally shooting someone mistaken for an intruder. With 1,409 FGAs in 1992, this implies that there are fewer than 28 incidents of this sort annually. Compared with 2.5 million annual defensive uses of guns, this translates into about a 1-in-90,000 or less chance of a DGU resulting in this kind of accident.

It has been claimed that many people who attempt to use guns for self-protection have the gun taken from them by the criminal and used against them (for example, Shields 1981, pp. 49, 53; McNamara 1986, p. 989). This type of incident is not totally unknown, but it is extremely rare. In the 1979 to 1985 NCVS sample, it was possible to identify crime incidents in which the victim used a gun for self-protection and lost a gun to the offender(s). At most, 1 percent of DGUs resulted in the offender taking a gun away from the victim (author's analysis of NCVS data). Even these few cases did not necessarily involve the offender snatching a gun out of the victim's hands. Instead, a burglar might, for example, have been leaving a home with one of the household's guns when a resident attempted to stop him, using a different household gun. Thus, the 1 percent figure represents an upper limit estimate of the relative frequency of these events.

Reiss and Roth (1993, p. 266) presented a curious variation of this argument. They asserted that "firearm ownership can carry substantial risks," supporting this claim by citing misleading data on the frequency with which police officers are killed with their own guns. They report that 64 police officers, 19 percent of those killed with guns in 1984 to 1988, were killed "when their service weapons were turned against them." The purpose of citing the 19 percent figure was not made explicit, but in context the discussion clearly hinted that defensive gun use, even by experienced gun users like police, frequently leads to tragedy. This hinted inference is illogical, and the data do not in any way support the idea that defensive gun use frequently leads to a gun being taken away from the user by the criminal. A meaningful rate would have compared the number of police officers killed by their own gun with a measure of the frequency of exposure to this risk, such as the number of times they carried or used their guns defensively. There are about 600,000 police officers in the United States (U.S. FBI 1994, p. 288). Virtually all of them carry guns for defensive purposes, essentially every working day, 250 or more days per year. If each averaged just one actual defensive use of a gun (for example, it was drawn and at least pointed at someone) per year, this would imply a minimum of 600,000 annual DGUs by police, with 13 or fewer per year resulting in an officer losing his gun and being killed with it, a rate of 0.002 percent.

The Reiss-Roth figure was misleading in other ways as well. The authors misadded killings (there were 63 of this type, not 64) and managed to obtain a figure as high as 19 percent (actually 18 percent) only by using an unrepresentative time period. For the entire 1974 to 1990 period, only 13.5 percent of officers were killed with their own guns, a third less than 19 percent. Further, for the most recent year available to Reiss and Roth, 1990, there were only *three* officers killed with their own guns in the entire United States, or 5.4 percent of the total killed (U.S. FBI, *Law Enforcement Officers Killed and Assaulted,* annual issues covering 1974–1990). Even on those rare occasions when police officers are killed with their own guns, it does not involve guns being taken from the officers while they tried to use them defensively. A study of 11 such cases indicated that only one involved the gun being taken from the officer's hand (U.S. FBI 1992, p. 40), indicating that in a typical year there is probably only a single such case in the entire nation. Contrary to Reiss and Roth, gun owners of any kind, police or civilian, almost never have their weapons taken from them and used against them when using them for self-defense.

It is important to distinguish at this point two discrete issues: (1) the effectiveness of individual instances of civilian gun use against criminals in preventing injury and the completion of the crimes involved, and (2) whether such actions, and gun ownership in general, can deter criminal attempts from being made in the first place. Actual defensive use of guns by victims in specific criminal attempts could *disrupt* the attempt, preventing the criminal from injuring the victim or obtaining property. Also, the general fact of widespread civilian gun ownership, or ownership by specific individuals or identifiable groups, could *deter* some criminals from making the criminal attempts in the first place. It is even hypothetically possible that defensive actions could often be effective in preventing completion of crimes, yet fail to exert any general deterrent effect on the criminal population; the opposite could also be true. Nevertheless, one would expect, a priori, that gun ownership would be more likely to deter if DGUs were effective in disrupting those individual crimes in which victims used guns.

Disrupting (Preventing Completion of) the Crime.   It has been argued that resistance by crime victims, especially forceful resistance, is generally useless and even dangerous to the victim (Block 1977; Yeager et al. 1976). Although evidence supports this position as it applies to some forms of resistance, it does not support the claim as it applies to resistance with a gun. Yeager and his colleagues (1976) examined data from victim surveys in eight large U.S. cities that included information on the fraction of robberies and assaults that were completed against the victim and on victim use of self-protection measures. They did not report results separately for victims resisting with a gun but analyzed a category including victims using any weapon to resist. For robbery, the completion rate was 37 percent in crimes where the victim resisted with a weapon, a rate lower than that of any other form of self-protection and far lower than among those who did not resist in any way (p. 13). Because guns are regarded as more intimidating and deadly weapons than knives and other lesser weapons, one would expect gun-armed resisters to experience lower completion rates than victims resisting with other weapons. Therefore, had gun resisters been separately analyzed by Yeager et al., the results should have indicated even greater effectiveness of gun resistance relative to other forms of self-protection.

This is confirmed by the national data reported in Table 7.3, which break out gun-armed resistance from other armed resistance. In 1979, NCVS interviewers began to separately code self-protection with a gun. These figures are derived from analysis of the 1979 to 1985 incident-level files of the NCVS public use computer tapes (ICPSR 1987b). This dataset contains information on over 180,000 sample crime incidents reported by nationally representative samples of noninstitutionalized persons aged 12 and over. Respondents were asked if they had been a victim of crime in the previous six months, if they used any form of self-protection, if they were attacked, if they suffered injury, and if the crimes were completed. For assaults, "completion" means injury was inflicted; thus, completion and injury rates are the same for assaults. For robbery, "completion" means the robber took property from the victim.

The figures in Table 7.3 indicate that robbery victims who resisted with a gun or with a weapon other than a gun or knife were less likely to lose their property than victims using any other form of self-protection or who did not resist at all.

The remarkably successful outcomes of DGUs might seem surprising if one imagines the incidents to usually involve gun-armed offenders and shoot-outs between criminal and victim. This, however, does not describe most gun uses. Among the 1979 to 1985 violent incidents reported in the NCVS, 70.4 percent of DGUs were against offenders who did not even have a gun (or at least none visible to the victim). Even in the remaining cases it is unlikely that many involved the victim and offender shooting at one another, as less than 13 percent of handgun assaults involve a gun actually being fired (U.S. Bureau of Justice Statistics 1990) and only about one fourth of DGUs involve the defender shooting. This was confirmed in a later analysis of NCVS-reported robberies — less than 2 percent of robberies where a victim used a gun for protection involved both parties shooting (Kleck and DeLone

TABLE 7.3 Attack, Injury and Crime Completion Rates in Robbery and Assault Incidents, by Self-Protection Method, U.S., 1979–1985[a]

| Method of Self-Protection | (1) Percent Completed | Robbery | | | (5) Percent Attacked | Assault | |
		(2) Percent Attacked	(3) Percent Injured	(4)[b] Estimated Number Times Used		(6) Percent Injured	(7)[b] Estimated Number Times Used
Used gun	30.9	25.2	17.4	89,009	23.2	12.1	386,083
Used knife	35.2	55.6	40.3	59,813	46.4	29.5	123,062
Used other weapon	28.9	41.5	22.0	104,700	41.4	25.1	454,570
Used physical force	50.1	75.6	50.8	1,653,880	82.8	52.1	6,638,823
Tried to get help or frighten offender	63.9	73.5	48.9	1,516,141	55.2	40.1	4,383,117
Threatened or reasoned with offender	53.7	48.1	30.7	955,398	40.0	24.7	5,743,008
Nonviolent resistance, including evasion	50.8	54.7	34.9	1,539,895	40.0	25.5	8,935,738
Other measures	48.5	47.3	26.5	284,423	36.1	20.7	1,451,103
Any self-protection	52.1	60.8	38.2	4,603,671	49.5	30.7	21,801,957
No self-protection	88.5	41.5	24.7	2,686,960	39.9	27.3	6,154,763
Total	65.4	53.7	33.2	7,290,631	47.3	29.9	27,956,719

Notes: [a] See U.S. Bureau of Justice Statistics (1982) for exact question wordings, definitions, and other details of the surveys. [b] Separate frequencies in columns (4) and (7) do not add to totals in "Any self-protection" row since a single crime incident can involve more than one self-protection method.

Source: Incident files of 1979–1985 National Crime Survey public use computer tapes (ICPSR 1987b).

1993, p. 74). Likewise, in a general sample of DGU incidents of all kinds, only 3 percent involved both parties shooting at each other (Kleck and Gertz 1995, p. 175). More commonly, gun-armed defenders face a criminal without a gun, therefore have a strong power advantage, and successfully prevent the completion of the crime without shooting.

Avoiding Injury. Some might concede that DGU can be effective, yet also argue that it is dangerous, that defensive gun users raise their risks of injury even if they do successfully retain their property. The best available evidence contradicts this. National data on attack and injury rates in robberies and assaults, by victim protection method, for the entire nation are also shown in Table 7.3. Robbery and assault victims who used a gun to resist were less likely to be attacked or to suffer an injury than those who used any other methods of self-protection or those who did not resist at all. Only 17.4 percent of gun resisters in robberies, and 12.1 percent in assaults, were injured.

The other course of action least likely to involve victim injury is nonresistance. However, this strategy is also the worst at preventing completion of the crime. Further, passivity is not a completely safe course either, as a quarter of victims who did not resist were injured anyway. This may be because some robbers use violence preemptively, as a way of deterring or heading off victim resistance before it occurs. Thus, they may use violence instrumentally to assure victim compliance against those victims for whom this seems to be a safe course of action (Conklin 1972, Chapter 6). Other robbers may simply enjoy assaulting victims for its own sake, using violence expressively (Cook and Nagin 1979, pp. 36–37). Note also that the misleading consequences of lumping gun resistance in with other forms of forceful resistance (ala Yeager et al. 1976; Cook 1986) are made clear by these data, as other forms of forceful self-protection are far more risky than resisting with a gun.

Some analysts of robbery data have uncritically assumed that where crimes involve victims who resisted and were also injured resistance must somehow have lead to the injury (for example, Yeager et al. 1976). It is tempting to assume that resistance to a robber provokes attack, but the reverse may also be true. That is, victims otherwise reluctant to resist may do so out of desperation or anger after being attacked by the robber — injury may provoke victim resistance. (NCVS surveys have only recently begun to establish the sequence of offender attack and victim self-protection actions, and they still provide too few sample DGU cases for meaningful analysis.) Consequently it is not certain if any of the 17.4 percent of robberies with an injured, gun resisting victim involved an attack provoked by the victim's resistance. Nevertheless, even after acknowledging that their police record data do not allow them to confidently establish the sequence of events, Zimring and Zuehl (1986, p. 19) claimed that active victim resistance escalates victim risk of death and recommended that victims refrain from resisting.

Based on work of a former Zimring collaborator, it is evident that such a conclusion is questionable. In a study of robberies reported to the Chicago police in 1975, Block (1977) examined offense reports to determine which came first, victim resistance or robber use of force. In robberies where the victim resisted with force (including the use of weapons), victim resistance came *after* the offender's initial use of force in 68 percent of the cases (1977, pp. 81–82). Presumably the remaining 32 percent involved resistance first, followed by offender use of force. If this applied nationally to the 17.4 percent of robbery gun resisters who were injured, it would mean that only about 6 percent (.32 x .174 = .058) were injured after they used their guns to resist. And because some of these injuries surely would have occurred even without resistance, it means that fewer than 6 percent of these victims provoked the injury by their use of a gun. In any case, even if all gun resister injuries had been directly caused by the resistance, a dubious assumption, it is still clear that a robbery victim's resistance with a gun rarely provokes a robber into injuring him. Based on the present findings and those of Block, the chances of this happening are probably less than 1 in 20.

In contrast, Block noted that among victims who resisted nonforcefully, by fleeing or yelling for help, it was resistance that came first in 70 percent of the cases. The evidence is thus compatible with the hypothesis that active physical resistance without a gun often provokes offender attack, whereas resistance with a gun deters attack.

These conclusions are supported by special NCVS data. Although the regular NCVS did not, until recently, routinely ask questions about the sequence of resistance and injury, sequence questions were asked in a limited one-month-only Victim Risk Supplement (VRS) administered to 14,258 households as part of the NCVS in February of 1984. In assaults that involved both *forceful* self-protection actions and an attack on the victim, the victim actions preceded attack in only 9.8 percent of the incidents. For assaults involving *nonforceful* resistance, only 5.7 percent of victim actions preceded attack. For robbery incidents with both attack on the victim and self-protection actions, *forceful* self-protective actions *never* preceded attack. Even among incidents involving *nonforceful* victim actions, victim defensive actions preceded the attack in only 22 percent of the cases (author's analysis of ICPSR 1987a). Thus, even in those few incidents in which forceful resistance was accompanied by attacks on the victim, the sequencing was incompatible with the contention that the victim's resistance provoked the attack. The national victim survey data, then, even more strongly indicate that gun-armed victim resistance to robbery or assault almost never provokes the offender to injure the victim.

It has been conjectured that these low rates of injury and property loss are not really due to victim DGU but rather that the association is a spurious one attributable to unusual scenarios where, for example, the criminal failed to surprise the victim. The lack of surprise can both make the criminal more vulnerable to any form of self-defense and allow the victim to get a gun (Reiss and Roth 1993, p. 266). This is a clever speculation whose chief advantage for its authors is that it cannot be tested with the NCVS or any other existing body of evidence.

The NCVS does, however, provide data relevant to the general underlying idea that defensive gun users faced "easier" crime circumstances. These data indicate that victims who use guns for self-protection are more likely to face armed criminals (Kleck and DeLone 1993). Likewise, Kleck and Gertz (1995, pp. 175–176) found that victims who used guns to defend themselves were both more likely to face armed adversaries and more likely to face multiple offenders than were other victims. These findings support the idea that such gun-wielding victims actually face *tougher* circumstances than other victims, and that many victims may resort to more extreme defensive measures only when forced to do so by more threatening actions by the criminals they face.

Robbery and Resistance

The simple percentage table results concerning robbery completion and injury rates were confirmed by more sophisticated multivariate analysis of NCVS robbery incidents. In a logistic
regression analysis, Kleck and DeLone (1993) found that robbery
victims who used guns in self-protection were significantly less
likely to either be injured or lose their property than victims who
used any other form of self-protection or who did nothing to resist.
This was true even controlling for other characteristics of the
robbery situation that could influence the effectiveness of defensive actions, such as the number of robbers, the number of victims,
whether the robbery occurred in a private place, whether it occurred when it was dark, whether the robbers were armed, the age
and gender of victims, and so on.

Rape and Resistance

Previous discussion addressed gun resistance only in robberies
and assaults. Rape, the third major violent crime covered in NCVS
data, had to be excluded because there are so few relevant sample
cases to analyze. Less than 1 percent of NCVS rape victims report
resistance with a gun (for example, U.S. Bureau of Justice Statistics
1985c). However, one may gain some strong hints about the results
of gun resistance by examining all instances of armed resistance
by rape victims. Grouping together instances of resistance with
guns, knives, or other weapons, Kleck and Sayles (1990) found, in
a multivariate probit analysis of national victim survey data, that
rape victims using armed resistance were less likely to have the
rape attempt completed against them than victims using any other
mode of resistance. These results confirmed those of Lizotte (1986)
using city victim surveys. Further, there was no significant effect
of armed resistance on the rapist inflicting additional injury beyond the rape itself. In light of the robbery and assault findings
indicating that gun resistance is generally more effective than
armed resistance using other weapons, it would seem to be a
reasonable inference that the same is true for rape. Indeed, this
would seem especially likely with rapes, given that rape victims

are nearly all women, and guns are the weapon type whose effectiveness is least dependent on the physical strength of its user.

The Police Chief's Fallacy

Joseph McNamara, former Chief of the San Jose, California, Police Department, testified before a Congressional committee considering gun legislation: "We urge citizens not to resist armed robbery, but in these sad cases I described, the victims ended up dead because they produced their own handguns and escalated the violence. Very rarely have I seen cases where the handgun was used to ward off a criminal" (McNamara 1986, p. 989). Why do some police give such advice? Although some, like Chief McNamara, a strong gun control advocate, may be motivated by political considerations, it is doubtful if this is true for most officers. Instead, police advice may well logically follow from the resistance experiences of victims with whom officers have had contact. The problem with relying on this sample of resistance cases is that it is substantially unrepresentative of the experiences of crime victims in general — the cases McNamara and other police officers have seen are not like those they have not seen, and the latter outnumber the former by a wide margin.

Most crimes are not reported to the police, and the crimes most likely to go unreported are the ones that involve neither injury nor property loss, that is, those that had successful outcomes from the victim's viewpoint. For example, among robberies reported to the NCVS, only 24 percent of those with no injury or property loss were reported to police, whereas 72 percent of those with both were reported. Likewise, assaults without injury are less likely to be reported than those with injury (U.S. Bureau of Justice Statistics 1985c, p. 3). By definition, all successful DGUs fall within the no-injury, no-property-loss category and thus are largely invisible to the police. Consequently, police never hear about the bulk of successful DGUs, instead hearing mostly about an unrepresentative minority of them that include a disproportionately large number of failures. To conclude that armed resistance is ineffective or dangerous, based on the experiences of this sort of unrepresentative sample of victims, can be called, in honor of former Chief McNamara, "the police chief's fallacy." At present, advising victims not to use guns to resist criminal attempts seems imprudent at best, reckless at worst. As Ziegenhagen and Brosnan (1985, p. 693) have commented: "Victims can and do play an active part in the control of crime outcomes regardless of well-intentioned but ill-conceived efforts to encourage victims to limit the range of responses open to them. Victims can, and do, exercise a range of optional responses to robbery far beyond those conceived of by criminal justice professionals."

An Exercise in Ingenious Speciousness

When gun control advocates and public health scholars consider whether keeping a gun for defensive purposes is sensible, they frequently bring up one of the oddest statistics in the gun control debate. In 1975 four physicians published an article based on data derived from medical examiner files in Cuyahoga (Cleveland) County. They noted that during the period 1958 to 1973, there were 148 fatal gun accidents (78 percent of them in the home) and 23 "burglars, robbers or intruders who were not relatives or acquaintances" killed by people using guns to defend their homes. They stated that there were six times as many home fatal gun accidents as burglars killed. (This appears to have been a miscomputation — the authors counted all 148 accidental deaths in the numerator instead of just the 115 occurring in the home. Although the value of the number does not matter much, the correct ratio was five rather than six.) On the basis of these facts, the authors concluded that "guns in the home are more dangerous than useful to the homeowner and his family who keep them to protect their persons and property" and that "the possession of firearms by civilians appears to be a dangerous and ineffective means of self-protection" (Rushforth et al. 1975, pp. 504–505; see also Newton and Zimring 1969, p. 64, for an earlier version of this argument).

These conclusions were a breath-taking non sequitur. The authors presented no evidence of any kind having any bearing on the issue of whether guns are "ineffective" means of self-protection — no counts of defensive uses, no estimates of the fraction of defensive uses that prevented completion of crimes or resulted in injury — nothing. As to how dangerous keeping a gun for protection is, the authors cited only accidental gun deaths. Yet they did not establish that any of the accidents occurred in connection with defensive uses or even that the guns involved were owned for defensive reasons. The connection between the accidents and defensive gun ownership was simply assumed, rather than demonstrated.

The authors treated the 6:1 ratio as if it were somehow a cost-benefit ratio, a comparison that could say something about the relative benefits and risks of defensive gun ownership. The ratio cannot serve such a purpose. The numerator is not a meaningful measure of risk for the average gun-owning household, and the denominator has no bearing at all on the defensive benefits of keeping a gun. Gun accidents are largely concentrated in a very small, high-risk subset of the population (Kleck 1991, Chapter 7). For everyone else, the risks of a fatal gun accident are negligible. Therefore, the population-wide accident rate is an exaggeration of the risk born by the typical defensive gun-owning household.

More important, the number of burglars killed does not in any way serve as a measure of the defensive benefit of keeping a gun. As Barry Bruce-Briggs wryly noted, "The measure of the effectiveness of self-defense is not in the number of bodies piled up on doorsteps" (1976, p. 39). Thus, the one protection-related event the authors did count is not even itself a benefit. Defensive gun owners do not have guns for the purpose of getting a chance to "bag a burglar." Being forced to kill another human being, burglar or not, is a nightmare to be suffered through for years. To assess defensive benefits might entail estimating the number of burglars captured, frightened off, deterred from attempting burglaries, or displaced to unoccupied premises where they could not injure any victims. The authors measured none of these things. As previously noted, well under 1 percent of DGUs involve a criminal being killed, so a count of justifiable homicides covers a minuscule share of DGUs beneficial to crime victims. Thus, the authors counted one of the most serious costs possibly associated with defensive guns in the home (that is, accidental gun deaths), yet counted *none* of the possible benefits. The value of computing a cost-benefit ratio from such numbers is difficult to discern.

Even the number of home defensive gun homicides was artificially reduced in this study by excluding killings of aggressors who were relatives or acquaintances; the authors apparently felt that killings by, for example, a wife defending herself against a homicidally abusive husband, or a woman defending herself against an estranged husband or ex-boyfriend trying kill or rape her, were not legitimate defensive homicides suitable to be counted along with shootings of burglars (see Kates 1990, pp. 24-32 for an extended discussion of this exclusion).

Bruce-Briggs described this sort of study as "ingeniously specious" (1976, p. 39) and briefly dismissed it. Most serious gun scholars ignore this particular study (for example, the massive review by Wright et al. does not mention it at all), but it is a favorite of pro-control propagandists (for example, Yeager et al. 1976, p. 4; Alviani and Drake 1975, p. 8). It was even unwittingly replicated 11 years later by two other physicians (Kellermann and Reay 1986) who apparently were unaware of the Rushforth et al. study (or at least did not cite it) or of the harsh criticism to which it had been subjected. This later analysis had all the same problems as its predecessor, used the same specious reasoning and, inevitably, arrived at essentially the same non sequitur conclusion: "The advisability of keeping firearms in the home for protection must be questioned." Those who have uncritically cited the Kellermann and Reay evidence as relevant to an assessment of the relative risks and benefits of keeping guns for self-defense include McDowall and Wiersema (1994) and Reiss and Roth (1993, p. 267).

The benefit of defensive gun ownership that would be parallel to innocent lives *lost* to guns would be innocent lives *saved* by guns. However, it is probably impossible to count the latter, so it may never be possible to form a meaningful ratio of genuinely comparable quantities. Nevertheless, it is worth considering what a more meaningful comparison of lives lost and saved due to guns might look like. In 1992, there were about 38,000 deaths involving guns, including homicides, suicides, fatal gun accidents, deaths by legal intervention, and deaths where it was undetermined whether the injury was accidentally or purposely inflicted (Kochanek and Hudson 1994). Results to be discussed in Chapter 8 indicate that each year there are 340,000 to 400,000 defensive uses of guns where the user would claim that the use saved a life. Even if as little as a tenth of these users were correct in their assessments, the number of life-saving defensive uses of guns would equal or exceed the number of gun-related deaths.

Of course, many deaths involving guns would have occurred even in the absence of the guns, so the gun death count is not a count of deaths that are uniquely attributable to guns, that is, that would have been avoided had guns not been available. That number would necessarily be smaller than the number of deaths in which a gun was used. Conversely, no one can be sure a death would have occurred had a victim not used a gun defensively, so we cannot obtain a conclusive count of lives saved by defensive uses of guns either. This exercise serves only to indicate what a more meaningful comparison of comparable quantities would look like and to show that one cannot dismiss out of hand the possibility that guns save as many lives as they take. In contrast, the ratios computed by Kellermann and Reay and their predecessors have literally no bearing whatsoever on the relative merits of keeping a gun in the home for self-defense.

Note

1. The gun accident death figure was obtained from secondary analysis of the 1969 to 1978 Mortality Detail File (ICPSR 1985) and the 1979 and 1980 Mortality Detail Files (U.S. NCHS 1982; 1983).

Chapter 8

The Nature of Defensive Gun Use and the Deterrence and Displacement of Crime*

Gary Kleck

The Nature of Defensive Gun Use

The National Self-Defense Survey (Kleck and Gertz 1995) provides some details on exactly who is involved in defensive gun use (DGUs), and what they do in those incidents. A total of 222 sample cases of defensive gun use against humans were obtained. For nine of these, the R broke off discussion of the incident before any significant amount of detail could be obtained beyond the fact that the use was against a human. This left 213 cases with fairly complete information. Although this dataset constitutes the most detailed body of information available on defensive gun use, the sample size is nevertheless fairly modest. Estimates of DGU frequency are reliable because they were based on a very large sample of 4,977 cases, but results pertaining to the details of DGU incidents are based on 213 or fewer sample cases, and readers should treat these results with appropriate caution.

Quite apart from the sample size, we believe that the results

*References for this chapter appear on pages 258–268.

from this survey are also affected by sample censoring. Beyond the incidents our interviewers were told about, almost certainly other DGUs did occur in the recall period that Rs did not mention to interviewers. In debriefings by the authors, almost all of our interviewers reported that they had experienced something like the following: they asked the key DGU question, which was followed by a long silence on the other end of the line or the R asking something like "Who wants to know?" or "Why do you want to know?" or some similarly suspicious remark, followed by a "no" answer. In contrast, only one interviewer, in a single interview, spoke with a person they thought was inventing a nonexistent incident. One obvious implication is that the true frequency of DGU is probably even higher than our estimates indicate, and another implication is that the incidents that were reported might differ from those that were not.

We believe that two rather different kinds of incidents are especially likely to go unreported: (1) cases that Rs do not want to tell strangers on the phone about, because the Rs deem them legally or morally dubious (or think the interviewer will regard them that way), and (2) relatively minor cases that Rs honestly forget about or did not think were serious enough to qualify as relevant to our inquiries. Thus, in addition to the mostly legitimate and serious cases covered in our sample, there are still other, less legitimate or less serious, DGU incidents that this or any other survey is likely to miss. This supposition would imply two kinds of bias in our descriptive results: (1) our DGUs would look more consistently "legitimate" than the entire set of all DGUs actually are, and (2) the DGUs would look more serious, on average, than the entire set of DGUs really are. These possibilities should be kept in mind when considering the following descriptive information.

Table 8.1 summarizes what our sample DGU incidents were like. The data support a number of broad generalizations. First, much like the typical gun crime, many of these cases were relatively undramatic and minor compared to fictional portrayals of gun use. Only 24 percent of the gun defenders in the present study reported firing the gun, reporting wounding an adversary in just 8 percent of the incidents (Panel A). This parallels the fact that only 17 percent of the gun crimes reported in the NCVS involve the offender shooting at the victim, and only 3 percent involve the victim suffering a gunshot wound (Rand 1994).

TABLE 8.1 The Nature of Defensive Gun Use Incidents[a]

	%
A. What the Defender Did with the Gun[b]	
Brandished or showed gun	75.7
Verbally referred to gun	57.6
Pointed gun at offender	49.8
Fired gun (including warning shots)	23.9
Fired gun at offender, trying to shoot him/her	15.6
Wounded or killed offender	8.3
B. Location of Incident	
In defender's home	37.3
Near defender's home	35.9
At, in, near home of friend, relative, neighbor	4.2
Commercial place (bar, gas station, office, factory)	7.5
Parking lot, commercial garage	4.5
School (in building, on school property, playground)	0.3
Open area, on street or public transportation	7.4
Other locations	2.3
C. Type of Crime Defender Thought Was Being Committed[b]	
Burglary	33.8
Robbery	20.5
Other theft	6.2
Trespassing	14.8[c]
Rape, sexual assault	8.2
Other assault	30.4
Other crime	9.5
D. Did Offender Get Away with Money or Property?	
% of property crimes with property loss	11.0
E. Violence Directed at Defender	
No threat or attack	46.8
Threatened only	32.3
Attacked but not injured	15.3
Attacked and injured	5.5
(In incidents where defender was threatened or attacked): Who was first to threaten or use force?	
Defender	15.3
Offender	83.5
Someone else	1.3
F. Offender's Weapons[b]	
None (unarmed)	51.9
Weapon	48.1
Handgun	13.4
Other gun	4.5
Knife	17.8
Other sharp object	2.0
Blunt object	9.9
Other weapon	5.9

TABLE 8.1 The Nature of Defensive Gun Use Incidents[a] *(continued)*

	%
G. Shooting	
Did offender shoot at defender?	
% of all incidents	4.5
% of incidents with offender armed with gun	26.2
Did both parties shoot?	
% of all incidents	3.1
H. Type of Gun Used by Defender	
Revolver	38.5
Semi-automatic pistol	40.1
Other, unspecified handgun	1.1
Rifle	6.4
Shotgun	13.9
I. Relationship of Offender to Defender	
Stranger	73.4
Casual acquaintance	8.3
Neighbor	1.3
Boyfriend, girlfriend	1.0
Other friend, co-worker	1.0
Brother, sister	0.0
Son, daughter	0.5
Husband, wife	3.1
Other relationship	4.2
Unknown	7.3
J. Number of Offenders	
1	47.2
2	26.1
3-4	17.6
5-6	4.0
7 or more (includes 3 cases where defender could only say there was a very large number)	5.0
K. Defender's Perceived Likelihood that Someone Would Have Died Had Gun Not Been Used for Protection	
Almost certainly not	20.8
Probably not	19.3
Might have	16.2
Probably would have	14.2
Almost certainly would have	15.7
Could not say	13.7
L. Were Police Informed of Incident or Otherwise Find Out?	64.2

Notes: [a] Table covers only defensive uses against persons, and excludes 9 cases where respondents refused to provide enough detail to confirm incidents as genuine defensive uses. [b] Percentages will sum to more than 100 percent because respondents could legitimately select or report more than one category. [c] Only 3.7 percent of incidents involved trespassing as *only* crime.

Low as it is, even an 8 percent wounding rate is probably too high, both because of censoring less serious cases (which in this context would be cases without a wounding) and because we did not establish how Rs knew they had wounded someone. We suspect that in incidents where the offender left without being captured, some Rs "remembered with favor" their marksmanship and assumed they had hit their adversaries. If 8.3 percent really had hit their adversaries, and a total of 15.6 percent had fired at their adversaries, this would imply a 53 percent (8.3/15.6) "incident hit rate," a level of combat marksmanship far exceeding that typically observed even among police officers. In a review of 15 reports, police officers inflicted at least one gunshot wound on at least one adversary in 37 percent of the incidents in which they intentionally fired at someone (Geller and Scott 1993, pp. 100–106). A 53 percent hit rate would also be triple the 18 percent hit rate of criminals shooting at crime victims (Rand 1994). Therefore, we believe that even the rather modest 8.3 percent wounding rate we found is probably too high, and that typical DGUs are less serious or dramatic in their consequences than our data suggest. In any case, the 8.3 percent figure was produced by just 17 sample cases in which Rs reported that they wounded an offender.

About 37 percent of these incidents occurred in the defender's home, with another 36 percent near the defender's home (Panel B). This implies that the remaining 27 percent occurred in locations where the defender must have carried a gun through public spaces. Adding in the 36 percent that occurred *near* the defender's home and that may or may not have entailed public carrying, 36 to 63 percent of the DGUs entailed gun carrying.

Guns were most commonly used for defense against burglary, assault, and robbery (Panel C). Cases of "mutual combat," where it would be hard to tell who is the aggressor, or where both parties are aggressors, would be some subset of the 30 percent of cases where assault was the crime involved. However, only 19 percent of all DGU cases involved *only* assault and no other crime where victim and offender are more easily distinguished. Further, only 11 percent of all DGU cases involved only assault and a male defender (we had no information on gender of offenders); some subset of these could have been male-on-male fights. Thus, very few of these cases fit the classic mutual combat model of a fight between two males. This is not to say that such crimes where a gun-using combatant might claim that his use was defensive are rare but rather that few of them are in this sample. Instead, cases where it is hard to say who is victim and who is aggressor apparently constitute an additional set of questionable DGUs lying largely outside the universe of more one-sided events that our survey methods could effectively reach.

It was not our intention to compare the effectiveness of armed resistance with other forms of victim self-protection as this sort of work has already been done (and was reviewed in Chapter 7). Panels D and E nevertheless confirm previous research on the effectiveness of self-defense with a gun—crime victims who use this form of self-protection rarely lose property and rarely provoke the offender into hurting them. In incidents where a property crime (burglary, robbery or other theft) was attempted, victims lost property in just 11 percent of the cases. Gun defenders were injured in just 5.5 percent of all DGU incidents. Further, in 84 percent of the incidents where the defender was threatened or attacked, it was the offender who was the first to threaten or use force. In *none* of the 11 sample cases where gun defenders were injured was the defender the first to use or threaten force. Instead, the victim used a gun to threaten or attack the offender only *after* the offender had already attacked or threatened them, and thus usually after the offender had inflicted the injury. There is no support in this sample for the hypothesis that armed resistance provokes criminals into attacking victims, confirming the findings of prior research (Kleck 1988, pp. 7–9; Kleck and DeLone 1993, pp. 75–77).

Although only 14 percent of *all* violent crime victims face offenders armed with guns (U.S. Bureau of Justice Statistics 1994, p. 83), 18 percent of the gun-using victims in our sample faced adversaries with guns (Panel F). Thus, although the gun defenders usually faced unarmed offenders or offenders with lesser weapons, they were more likely than other victims to face gun-armed criminals. This is consistent with a view that more desperate circumstances call forth more desperate defensive measures. The findings undercut the view that victims are prone to use guns in "easy" circumstances that were likely to produce favorable outcomes for the victim regardless of their gun use (for a related speculation, see Reiss and Roth 1993, p. 266). Instead, gun defenders appear to face more difficult circumstances than other crime victims, not easier ones.

Nevertheless, one reason crime victims are willing to take the risks of forcefully resisting the offender is that most offenders faced by victims choosing such an action are unarmed, or armed only with less lethal weapons. Relatively few victims try to use a gun against adversaries who are themselves armed with guns — offenders were armed with some kind of weapon in 48 percent of DGU incidents, but had guns in only 18 percent of them (Panel F).

The distribution of guns by type in DGUs is similar to that of guns used by criminals. NCVS and police-based data indicate that about 80 percent of guns used in crime are handguns (U.S. Bureau of Justice Statistics 1994, p. 83; U.S. Federal Bureau of Investigation 1993, p. 18), and the present study indicates that 80 percent of the guns used by victims are handguns (Panel H).

Incidents where victims use a gun defensively are almost never gunfights where both parties shoot at one another. Only 24 percent of the incidents involved the defender firing their gun, and only 16 percent involved the defender shooting *at* their adversary (Panel A). Likewise, the offender shot at the defender in only 4.5 percent of the cases (Panel G). Consequently, it is not surprising that only 3 percent of all the incidents involved both parties shooting at each other.

Among our sample cases, the offenders were strangers to the defender in nearly three quarters of the incidents (Panel I). We suspect that this again reflects the effects of sample censoring. Just as the NCVS appears to detect less than a tenth of domestic violence incidents (Loftin and MacKenzie 1990, pp. 22–23), our survey is probably missing many cases of DGU against family members and other intimates.

Although victims face multiple offenders in only about 24 percent of *all* violent crimes (U.S. Bureau of Justice Statistics 1994, p. 82), the victims in our sample who used guns faced multiple offenders in 53 percent of the incidents (Panel J). This mirrors the observation that criminals who use guns are also more likely than unarmed criminals to face multiple victims (Cook 1991). Having a gun allows either criminals or victims to handle a larger number of adversaries. Many victims facing multiple offenders probably would not resist at all if they were without a gun or some other weapon. Another possible interpretation is that some victims will resort to a defensive measure as serious as wielding a gun only if they face the most desperate circumstances. Again, this finding contradicts a view that gun defenders face easier circumstances than other crime victims.

Another way of assessing how serious these incidents appeared to the victims is to ask them how potentially fatal the encounter was. We asked Rs: "If you had *not* used a gun for protection in this incident, how likely do you think it is that you or someone else would have been *killed?* Would you say almost certainly *not*, probably not, might have, probably would have, or almost certainly would have been killed?" Panel K indicates that 15.7 percent of the Rs stated that they or someone else "almost certainly would have" been killed, with another 14.2 percent responding "probably would have" and 16.2 percent responding "might have." Thus, nearly half claimed that they perceived some significant chance of someone being killed in the incident had they not used a gun defensively.

It should be emphasized that these are just stated perceptions of participants, not objective assessments of actual probabilities. Some defenders might have been bolstering the justification for their actions by exaggerating the seriousness of the threat they faced. Our cautions about sample censoring should also be kept in mind—more minor, less life-threatening events are likely to have been left out of this sample, either because Rs forgot them or because they did not think them important enough to qualify as relevant to our inquiries.

If we consider only the 15.7 percent who believed someone almost certainly would have been killed had they not used a gun, applying this figure to estimates in the first two columns of Table 6.2 yields national annual estimates of 340,000 to 400,000 defensive uses of guns of any kind, and 240,000 to 300,000 uses of handguns, where defenders would state, if asked, that they believed they almost certainly had saved a life by using the gun. How many of these truly were life-saving gun uses is impossible to know. As a point of comparison, the largest number of deaths involving guns, including homicides, suicides and accidental deaths, in any one year in U.S. history was 39,595 in 1993 (U.S. National Center for Health Statistics 1996, p. 32).

Finally, we asked if Rs had reported these incidents to the police, or if the police otherwise found out about them; 64 percent of the gun-using victims claimed that the incidents had become known to the police. This figure should be interpreted with caution because victims presumably want to present their use of guns as legitimate, and being willing to report the incident to the police would help support an impression of legitimacy. Rs who had in fact not reported the incident to the police might have wondered whether a "no" reply might not lead to discomfiting follow-up questions like "why not?" (as indeed it does in the NCVS). Further, it is likely that some Rs reported these incidents but did not mention their use of a gun.

Who Is Involved in Defensive Gun Use?

Finally, we consider what sorts of people use guns defensively, and how they might differ from other people. Table 8.2 presents comparisons of five groups: (1) "defenders," that is, persons who reported using a gun for defense; (2) those who personally own guns but did not report a DGU; (3) those who do not personally own a gun; (4) all those who did not report a DGU, regardless of whether they own guns; and (5) all persons who completed the full interview.

Some of the earlier gun surveys asked the DGU question only of Rs who reported owning a gun. The cost of this limitation is evident from the first two rows of Table 8.2. Nearly 40 percent of the people reporting a DGU did not personally own a gun at the time of the interview. They either used someone else's gun or had gotten rid of a gun since the DGU incident. About a quarter of the defenders reported that they did not even have a gun in their household at the time of the interview, irrespective of who it belonged to. Another possibility is that many gun owners were falsely denying their ownership of the "incriminating evidence" of their defensive gun use.

Many of the findings in Table 8.2 are unsurprising. Gun defenders are more likely to carry a gun for self-protection, consistent with the large share of DGUs that occurred away from the defender's home. They were also obviously more likely to have been a victim of a burglary or robbery in the past year, a finding that is a tautology for those Rs whose DGU was in connection with a robbery or burglary committed against them in the preceding year. They were also more likely to have been a victim of an assault since becoming an adult.

TABLE 8.2 Comparison of Defenders with Other People (weighted percentages)

	Defenders	No-DGU Gun owners	Sample[a] Non- owners	No DGU	All Persons
Personally owns gun	59.5	100.0	0.0	23.9	25.5
Gun in household	79.0	100.0	16.3	36.3	37.9
Carries gun for protection	47.3	23.3	2.1	7.3	8.8
Burglary victim, past year	19.3	4.5	4.9	4.9	5.5
Robbery victim, past year	12.9	1.9	2.0	2.1	2.5
Assault victim as adult	46.8	29.3	18.3	21.5	22.5
Nights away from home, monthly average					
0	8.2	5.2	8.9	8.2	8.2
1–6	27.5	24.1	33.4	31.5	31.2
7–13	23.2	28.2	22.7	23.8	23.9
14+	42.0	42.5	35.0	36.8	36.6
Must depend on self rather than cops	80.4	69.7	50.0	55.0	55.8
Supports death penalty	72.4	85.2	65.8	70.5	70.6
Courts not harsh enough	75.2	78.9	71.5	74.0	74.0
Gender (% male)	53.7	75.4	37.1	46.4	46.7
Age					
18–24	25.7	10.2	14.3	13.1	13.5
25–34	36.9	21.6	22.6	22.1	22.6
35–44	20.6	26.8	25.2	25.5	25.4
45–64	14.2	30.6	25.9	27.3	26.8
65+	2.6	10.9	12.1	12.0	11.7
Race					
White	72.4	90.3	83.0	84.6	84.1
Black	16.8	5.1	9.7	8.6	8.9
Hispanic	8.0	3.2	4.9	4.6	4.8
Other	2.8	1.3	2.4	2.2	2.1

Spending time away from home at night places people at greater risk of victimization, but defenders spend no more of their time like this than other gun owners, and these two groups spend only slightly more time like this than those who do not own guns.

Defenders are more likely to believe that a person must "be prepared to defend their homes against crime and violence" rather than letting "the police take care of that," compared to either gun owners without a DGU or nonowners. Whether this is cause or consequence of defenders' defensive actions is impossible to say with these data.

TABLE 8.2 *(continued)*

	Defenders	No-DGU Gun owners	Sample[a] Non-owners	No DGU	All Persons
Place of Residence					
Large city (over 500,000)	32.5	14.7	24.7	22.2	22.6
Small city	29.8	32.2	27.7	29.4	29.3
Suburb of large city	25.5	28.1	32.6	31.3	31.1
Rural area	12.2	24.9	15.1	17.2	17.0
Marital Status					
Married	50.8	69.1	57.5	60.5	60.1
Widowed	0.6	2.2	6.5	6.2	6.0
Divorced/Separated	15.3	10.9	11.2	11.8	12.0
Never married	33.3	17.8	24.8	21.4	21.9
Annual Household Income					
Under $15,000	12.3	7.4	15.3	13.6	13.5
$15,000–29,999	30.1	23.2	27.9	26.9	27.2
$30,000–44,999	22.2	30.3	23.0	24.5	24.4
$45,000–59,999	18.6	17.8	20.0	19.2	19.2
$60,000–79,999	7.9	12.1	8.0	8.9	8.9
$80,000 or more	8.8	9.2	5.8	6.8	6.9
Gun-related occupation	2.4	4.9	2.0	3.2	3.1

Notes: [a] "Defenders" are persons who reported a defensive gun use against another person in the preceding five years, excluding uses in connection with military, police, or security guard duties. This sample includes nine cases where such a use was reported but the respondent did not provide further details. "No-DGU gun owners" are persons who report personally owning a gun but did not report a defensive gun use. "Nonowners" are persons who did not report personally owning a gun and who did not report a defensive gun use. These persons may, however, live in a household where others own a gun. "No DGU" are persons who did not report a defensive gun use, regardless of whether they reported owning a gun.

It might be suspected that supposedly defensive uses of guns were actually the aggressive acts of vengeful vigilantes intent on punishing criminals. If this were true of gun defenders as a group, one might expect them to be more supportive of punitive measures like the death penalty. In fact, those who reported a DGU were no more likely to support the death penalty than those without such an experience, and were somewhat *less* likely to do so compared with gun owners as a group. Similarly, gun defenders were no more likely than other people to endorse the view that the courts in their area do not deal harshly enough with criminals.

Perhaps the most surprising finding of the survey was the large share of reported DGUs that involved women. Both because of their lower victimization rates and lower gun ownership rates, one would expect women to account for far less than half of DGUs. Nevertheless, 46 percent of our sample DGUs involved women. We are skeptical about this finding and suspect that it could be due to males reporting a lower fraction of their DGUs than women. If a larger share of men's allegedly defensive uses of guns were actual partly aggressive actions, this would imply that a larger share would be at the "illegitimate" end of the scale and thus less likely to be reported to interviewers. Further, women may be more likely than men to report their DGUs because they are less afraid of prosecution. Consequently, although we have no reason to doubt that women use guns defensively as often as this survey indicates, we strongly suspect that males account for a larger number, and larger share, of DGUs than these data indicate.

A disproportionately large share of defenders are black or Hispanic compared to the general population, and especially in comparison to gun owners. Likewise, defenders are disproportionately likely to reside in big cities compared to other people, and especially so when compared to gun owners, who are disproportionately from rural areas and small towns. Finally, defenders are disproportionately likely to be single. These patterns are all presumably due to the higher rates of crime victimization among minorities, big city dwellers, and single persons (U.S. Bureau of Justice Statistics 1994, pp. 25–26, 31, 38–39). However, defenders are not especially likely to be poor. The effect of higher victimization among poor people may be canceled out by the lower gun ownership levels among the poor (Kleck 1991, p. 56).

It might be suspected that, despite instructions to not report such events, some of the Rs reporting a DGU might have been describing an event that occurred as part of their occupational activities as a police officer, member of the military, or security guard. This could not have been true for more than a handful of our DGU cases, as only 2.4 percent of them (5 sample cases) involved a person who had this type of occupation. Even these few cases may have occurred off-duty and thus would not necessarily be occupational DGUs. Gun defenders were in fact somewhat*less* likely to have a gun-related occupation than other gun owners.

Deterrence

Gun Deterrable Crimes

To deter a crime means to cause a criminal to refrain from even attempting the crime, due to fear of some negative consequence. If there is a deterrent effect of defensive gun ownership and use, it should be facilitated by a criminal being able to realistically anticipate a potential victim using a gun to disrupt the crime. The types of crimes most likely to be influenced by this possibility are crimes occurring in homes — where victims are most likely to have access to a gun — and in the kinds of business establishments where proprietors keep guns. In line with the preceding information about where defensive uses commonly occur, crimes such as assault in the home, residential burglary, and retail store robbery would seem to be the most likely candidates to be deterred. About one in eight residential burglaries occurs while a household member is present (U.S. Bureau of Justice Statistics 1985a, p. 4), and, by definition, all robberies, rapes, assaults, and homicides involve direct contact between a victim and an offender. To be sure, in many of these incidents the offender has the initiative, often taking the victim by surprise, and the situations often develop too quickly for victims to get to their guns. However, the most common single location for violent crimes, especially homicides and assaults between intimates, is in or near the home of the victim or the home of both victim and offender, where access to a gun would be easier (U.S. Bureau of Justice Statistics 1980, p. 22; Curtis 1974, p. 176).

Strategic attributes of some crime types make them better-than-average candidates for disruption by armed victims. For example, violent acts between intimates are typically part of a persistent, ongoing pattern of violence (Wilt et al. 1977). Prospective victims of such violence may not ordinarily be able to predict the exact time of the next violent episode, but they often are able to recognize common precursors of repetitive violence. Wives and girlfriends of violent men, for example, may understand well the significance of their husband or boyfriend getting drunk and verbally abusive (Gillespie 1989; Kates 1990). This implies a distinct tactical difference between violence among intimates and other crimes. Victims of intimate violence can take advantage of behavioral cues that serve as advance warning signs and can ready themselves accordingly. In the most threatening situations, advance preparations could include securing a weapon.

Plausibility of Deterrent Effects

Demonstrating deterrent effects of criminal justice system punishment has proven difficult (for example, Blumstein et al. 1978) and the same must certainly be true for the private use of force, which is even less well measured than the risk-generating activities of the criminal justice system. Therefore, the following evidence should be regarded only as suggestive.

Results from deterrence research have been highly mixed and often negative. Why then should one expect deterrence from the armed citizenry when the legal system appears to have so little impact? The deterrence doctrine states that punishment deters more as its certainty, severity, and celerity (promptness) increase (Gibbs 1975). One obvious difference between the risk for the criminal from criminal justice activity and that from civilian gun use is that the maximum potential severity of citizen self-help is far greater than legal system responses to crime. The maximum legal penalty a burglar, robber, or even a murderer is likely to face is a few years in prison: only 143 persons were legally executed, all for murders, between mid-1967 and the end of 1990 (U.S. Bureau of Justice Statistics 1991). In contrast, 1,300 to 2,800 criminals are killed by gun-wielding private citizens each year.

The frequency of DGUs exceeds the total number of U.S. arrests for violent crime and burglary, which numbered about 1,160,000 in 1993 (U.S. FBI 1994, p. 217). Being threatened or shot at by a gun-wielding victim is more likely than arrest and far more likely than conviction or incarceration. This is not surprising as there are only about 600,000 police officers in the United States, fewer than a quarter of whom are on duty at any one time (U.S. FBI 1994, p. 288). There are, however, tens of millions of civilians who have immediate access to firearms and are well motivated to disrupt crimes directed at themselves, their families, or their property.

Finally, victims who use guns defensively almost always do so within minutes of the attempted crime. In contrast, when an arrest occurs, it can follow the crime by days or even weeks. At the very soonest, it comes after the several minutes it takes a patrol car to respond to a citizen's call. In any case, the average swiftness of even arrest is much lower than for victim gun use, and the celerity of conviction and punishment is lower still. Thus, the certainty, severity, and swiftness of DGU would seem at least as great as that of criminal justice system punishment activities. If the possibility of deterrence due to CJS activities is taken seriously, then so should the possibility of deterrence due to private gun ownership and defensive use.

Evidence from Surveys of Criminals

There is direct, albeit not conclusive, evidence on the deterrent effects of victim gun use from surveys of imprisoned criminals. Wright and Rossi (1986) interviewed 1,874 felons in prisons in ten states and asked about their encounters with armed victims and their attitudes toward the risks of such encounters. Among felons who reported ever committing a violent crime or a burglary, 42 percent said they had run into a victim who was armed with a gun, 38 percent reported they had been scared off, shot at, wounded, or captured by an armed victim (these were combined in the original survey question), and 43 percent said they had at some time in their lives decided not to commit a crime because they knew or believed the victim was carrying a gun (author's tabulations from ICPSR 1986). Note that the 38 percent of felons who were scared off or shot at by an armed victim are necessarily a subset of those 42 percent who encountered an armed victim. This implies that 90 percent (38/42=.90) of the prisoners who had encountered an armed victim had been scared off, shot, wounded, or captured at least once by such a victim.

Concerning the felons' attitudes toward armed victims, 56 percent agreed with the statement that "most criminals are more worried about meeting an armed victim than they are about running into the police," 58 percent agreed that "a store owner who is known to keep a gun on the premises is not going to get robbed very often," and 52 percent agreed that "a criminal is not going to mess around with a victim he knows is armed with a gun." Only 27 percent agreed that committing a crime against an armed victim is an exciting challenge" (author's tabulations from ICPSR 1986). Further, 45 percent of those who had encountered an armed victim reported that they thought regularly or often about the possibility of getting shot by their victims. Even among those without such an encounter, the figure was 28 percent (Wright and Rossi 1986, p. 149). These results agree with earlier findings from less sophisticated surveys of prisoners (Firman 1975; Link 1982).

Many objections to prison survey research on deterrence concern flaws whose correction would tend to strengthen conclusions that there are deterrent effects. For example, Zimring and Hawkins (1973, pp. 31–32) discussed the "warden's survey fallacy" whereby prison wardens concluded that the death penalty could not deter murder because all the killers on death row to whom they spoke said the penalty had not deterred them. Clearly, prisoners are biased samples of criminals and prospective criminals; their presence in prison itself indicates that deterrence was not completely effective with them. In light of this bias, prison survey results supporting a deterrence hypothesis are all the more impressive. Caveats about the validity of prisoners' responses to surveys are discussed throughout the Wright and Rossi book (1986, but especially pp. 32–38). Being "scared off by a victim" is not the sort of thing a violent criminal is likely to want to admit, especially in prison, where maintaining a fearless image can be critical to survival. Therefore, incidents of this nature may well have been underreported. Even more significantly, the most deterrable prospective criminals and those deterred from crime altogether will not be included in prison samples. These results, therefore, may reflect a minimal baseline picture of the deterrent potential of victim gun use.

Quasi-Experimental Evidence

There is no serious multivariate research on the deterrent effects of civilian gun ownership or defensive use. Instead, there is mostly anecdotal evidence concerning incidents in which civilian gun training programs were implemented or guns were used for self-defense, followed by substantial news media coverage. Highly publicized incidents of this sort are worth studying because they arguably can be expected to produce sharp changes among prospective criminals in awareness of the risks of encountering an armed victim. For example, highly publicized programs to train citizens in gun use amount to "gun awareness" programs that could conceivably produce sharp changes in prospective criminals' awareness of gun ownership among potential victims. If citizen gun ownership does exert any deterrent effect, then this effect should be intensified during these episodes of victim gun-related publicity. Thus, an ongoing, pervasive deterrent effect that would ordinarily be invisible becomes potentially detectable through examination of trends in deterrable crimes. Further, unlike gradual increases in mass gun ownership, the impact of these programs can be examined because they have specific times of onset and specific spans of operation that make it easier to say when they might be most likely to affect crime.

From October 1966 to March 1967 the Orlando Police Department trained more than 2,500 women to use guns (Krug 1968). Organized in response to demands from citizens worried about a sharp increase in rape, this was an unusually large and highly publicized program. It received several front-page stories in the local daily newspaper, the *Orlando Sentinel*, a co-sponsor of the program. An analysis of Orlando crime trends showed that the rape rate decreased by 88 percent in 1967, compared to 1966, a decrease far larger than in any previous one-year period. The rape rate remained constant in the rest of Florida and in the United States. Interestingly, the only other crime to show a substantial drop was burglary. Thus, the crime targeted decreased, and the offense most likely to occur where victims have access to guns, burglary, also decreased (Kleck and Bordua 1983, pp. 282–288).

Green (1987, p. 75) interpreted the results of the Orlando study as indicating a partial "spillover" or displacement of rape from the city to nearby areas, that is, a mixture of absolute deterrence of some rapes and a shift in location of others. Green also suggested that the apparent rape decrease might have been due to allegedly irregular crime recording practices of the Orlando city police department, without, however, presenting any evidence of police reporting changes over this period beyond the sharp changes in the rape rates themselves.

McDowall, Lizotte and Wiersema (1991) applied Box-Tiao ARIMA methods to the annual Orlando rape data. Despite their claims to the contrary (fn. 9), 14 time points are not sufficient for purposes of diagnosis and model identification, so it is generally considered inappropriate to apply ARIMA methods to such short series (for example, McCleary and Hay, with Meidinger and McDowall 1980, p. 20). Further, such a small sample makes it unlikely any but the most extreme causal effects can pass a significance test. As the authors blandly put it (fn. 9): "small numbers of observations imply. . . low power against a maintained hypothesis." In this case, a more informative observation would have been that even the largest possible causal effect, a 100 percent reduction in rape, would have been "insignificant" by the authors' standards. Because Orlando averaged 14 rapes per year before the training program, the authors' impact parameter of -11.3846 implied an 81 percent drop (-11.3846/14 = -0.81), virtually identical to the simple before-and-after 88 percent drop computed from the simpler analysis (Kleck 1988), yet this huge decrease was insignificant. Indeed, even a parameter of -14, implying a 100 percent drop, would have been insignificant.

Given this, the purpose of applying significance tests in this context is difficult to discern. The authors state that the observed crime changes "could easily be attributed to chance" (p. 504), by which they apparently meant that there was at least a 5 percent chance of this. Because the series was not selected by a random chance selection process, it is unclear exactly what chance process the authors thought produced the huge drops in rape. If the significance test was inappropriate or unimportant, then the main finding of McDowall et al. was that the Orlando program was indeed associated with a huge (81 percent) drop in rape, the ARIMA results confirming the conclusions of the earlier study. Interestingly, in a previous study, when a statistically insignificant finding supported a hypothesis they favored, McDowall and Loftin favorably cited and accepted the finding as relevant and supportive, with no stress on the significance test results (1983, p. 1150, citing Kleck 1979).

A much smaller training program was conducted with only 138 people from September through November 1967 by the Kansas City (Missouri) police in response to retail businessmen's concerns about store robberies (U.S. Small Business Administration 1969, pp. 253–256). The city had a population of 507,000 (U.S. Bureau of the Census 1982, p. 23), so the participation rate was less than 1/90 of that achieved in Orlando. Nevertheless, results from

TABLE 8.3 Crime Trends in Kansas City and Comparison Areas, 1961–1974

			Kansas City, Missouri			
Year	Robbery	MNNM	Aggravated Assault	Rape	Burglary	Auto Theft
1961	1,169	49	1,194	222	6,020	1,995
1962	1,069	49	946	147	5,337	2,336
1963	1,164	60	935	197	5,600	2,911
1964	1,180	48	1,126	205	6,484	2,701
1965	1,212	71	1,180	209	7,219	3,054
1966	1,574	59	1,315	205	7,495	3,689
1967	2,120	62	1,711	231	9,455	4,835
1968	2,171	92	1,995	307	10,020	4,929
1969	2,679	105	1,921	375	12,269	6,926
1970	2,982	120	1,805	401	11,265	5,570
1971	2,473	103	1,961	371	11,550	5,408
1972	2092	71	1,960	344	9,472	3,921
1973	2,333	81	2,433	302	10,394	3,884
1974	3,002	109	2,575	363	13,406	3,719
% Change, 1967–68	2	48	25	33	6	2

			Kansas City SMSA, Excluding Kansas City			
Year	Robbery	MNNM	Aggravated Assault	Rape	Burglary	Auto Theft
1961	202	14	135	42	2,430	622
1962	239	21	184	38	2,680	840
1963	347	20	234	47	2,937	958
1964	270	26	745	83	3,416	1,109
1965	261	25	770	100	4,234	1,148
1966	432	27	674	124	4,917	1,414
1967	644	41	760	93	6,612	1,925
1968	563	33	874	170	6,219	2,319
1969	559	33	879	174	6,733	2,810
1970	712	38	1,102	183	7,554	2,815
1971	641	48	1,389	173	8,104	2,666
1972	742	35	1,295	200	8,391	2,607

TABLE 8.3 Crime Trends in Kansas City and Comparison Areas, 1961–1974 *(continued)*

			Kansas City SMSA, Excluding Kansas City			
Year	Robbery	MNNM	Aggravated Assault	Rape	Burglary	Auto Theft
1973	715	64	1,288	185	10,073	2,554
1974	1,087	57	1,856	201	12,585	2,761
% change, 1967–68	-13	-20	15	83	-6	20

		Robbery	
	Missouri, excl.K.C. SMSA	West North Central	U.S.
1961	2,266	5,702	106,670
1962	2,166	5,597	110,860
1963	2,277	6,241	116,470
1964	2,505	6,594	130,390
1965	2,722	6,938	138,690
1966	2,763	8,022	157,990
1967	3,241	10,624	202,910
1968	4,374	12,724	262,840
1969	5,245	14,272	298,850
1970	5,699	16,279	349,860
1971	5,419	14,582	387,700
1972	5,513	14,928	376,290
1973	6,153	16,571	384,220
1974	6,364	19,894	442,400
% change, 1967–68	35	20	30

Notes: Figures before 1961 for Kansas City are not comparable with later years (U.S. FBI, 1962:131). The Kansas City Metropolitan Police Department firearms training program sessions were held in September through November 1967 (U.S. Small Business Administration 1968). MNNM = Murders and nonnegligent manslaughters. SMSA = Standard Metropolitan Statistical Area.

Sources: Annual issues, Uniform Crime Reports (U.S. FBI, 1962–1975).

the Kansas City program are consistent with the hypothesis that the program caused crime levels to be lower than they otherwise would have been. Table 8.3 displays crime trends in Kansas City and its metropolitan area, as well as robbery trends in the rest of Missouri, the region of which Kansas City is a part, and in the United States. The frequency of robbery increased sharply from 1967 to 1968, by 35 percent in the rest of Missouri, 20 percent in the region, and 30 percent in the United States, but it essentially leveled off in Kansas City and declined by 13 percent in surrounding areas, even though robberies had been increasing in the five years prior to the training program and continued to increase again in 1968. Thus, the upward trend showed a distinct interruption in the year immediately following the program. This cannot be attributed to some general improvement in conditions generating robbery rates elsewhere in the nation, because robbery rates were increasing elsewhere. Nor can it be attributed to improvements in conditions producing violent crime in general in Kansas City, because robbery was the only violent crime to level off—a pattern not generally evident elsewhere. Something occurred in the Kansas City area in the 1967 to 1968 period that caused an upward trend in robberies to level off, something that was not occurring in other places and that was specifically related to robbery. Interestingly, Kansas City also experienced a leveling off in its sharply upward trend in burglary, suggesting a possible "by-product" deterrent effect like that suggested by the Orlando data.

The finding of no change in robberies in Kansas City, even though robberies were increasing in control areas, suggests that the training program had a "dampening" effect, preventing the city from experiencing the increases occurring elsewhere. McDowall et al. (1991) confirmed these findings with ARIMA methods (pp. 548–549), yet paradoxically concluded that they indicated "no effect." Interestingly, two of the authors (McDowall and Wiersema), when faced with an essentially identical combination of findings in another study (no significant change in the target crime, combined with significant increases in control series), concluded that the intervention had a "dampening effect" (O'Carroll et al. 1991, p. 578). The most obvious difference is that the intervention they felt had a dampening effect was a gun control law. The authors neither mentioned nor accounted for this apparent inconsistency in interpretation of results. Applying a more consistent set of interpretive standards, the McDowall et al. Kansas City results confirmed those of the earlier study, supporting the deterrence hypothesis.

The two gun training episodes are not unique. They resemble instances of crime drops following gun training programs elsewhere, including decreases in grocery store robberies in Detroit after a grocer's organization began gun clinics, and decreases in retail store robberies in Highland Park, Michigan, attributed to "gun-toting merchants" (Krug 1968, p. H571).

Awareness of the risks of confronting an armed victim may also be increased by highly publicized instances of defensive gun use. After Bernhard Goetz used a handgun to wound four robbers on a New York City subway train on December 22, 1984, subway robberies decreased by 43 percent in the next week compared to the two weeks prior to the incident, and decreased in the following two months by 19 percent compared to the same period in the previous year, even though nonrobbery subway crime increased and subway robberies had been increasing prior to the shootings (*Tallahassee Democrat* 1-25-85, p. 1A; *New York Times* 3-22-85, p. B4; 4-18-85, p. 87). However, because New York City transit police also increased manpower on the subway trains immediately after the shootings, any impact uniquely attributable to the Goetz gun use was confounded with potential effects of the manpower increase.

The hypothesis of deterrent effects of civilian gun ownership is also supported by the experience of Kennesaw, Georgia, a suburb of Atlanta with a 1980 population of 5,095 (U.S. Bureau of the Census 1983, p. 832). To demonstrate their disapproval of a ban on handgun ownership passed in Morton Grove, Illinois, the Kennesaw city council passed a city ordinance requiring heads of households to keep at least one firearm in their homes. Only a token fine of $50 was provided as a penalty. Citizens could exempt themselves simply by stating that they conscientiously objected to gun possession, and there was no active attempt to enforce the law by inspecting homes. It is doubtful that the law substantially increased household gun ownership; the mayor of Kennesaw guessed that "about 85% of Kennesaw households already possessed firearms before the ordinance was passed" (Schneidman 1982). Instead, the significance of the ordinance and the associated publicity is that they presumably increased the awareness among criminals of the prevalence of guns in Kennesaw homes.

In the seven months immediately following passage of the ordinance (March 15, 1982 to October 31, 1982), there were only five residential burglaries reported to police, compared to 45 in the same period in the previous year, an 89 percent decrease (Benenson 1982). This drop was far in excess of the modest 10.4 percent decrease in the burglary rate experienced by Georgia as a whole from 1981 to 1982, the 6.8 percent decrease for South Atlantic states, the 9.6 percent decrease for the nation, and the 7.1 percent decrease for cities under 10,000 population (U.S. FBI 1983, pp. 45-7, 143).

This decrease, however, is not conclusive evidence of a deterrent effect because small towns have small numbers of crimes and monthly trends can be very erratic. It is not clear that any deterrent effect, no matter how large, would be detectable in an area with monthly crime trends as erratic as those found in small towns. For example, an ARIMA analysis of monthly burglary data found no evidence of a statistically significant drop in burglary in Kennesaw (McDowall, Wiersema and Loftin 1989; see also McDowall et al. 1991). This study, however, was both flawed and largely irrelevant to the deterrence hypothesis. The Kennesaw ordinance pertained solely to home gun ownership, and thus its deterrent effects, if any, would be evident with *residential* burglaries. This study blurred any such effects by using a data source that lumped all burglaries together (see their footnote 1). The difference between the two numbers apparently can be very large — the authors report 32 total burglaries for 1985, whereas a *New York Times* article, which the authors cited, reported only 11 "house burglaries" for that year (Schmidt 1987). The authors also used raw numbers of burglaries rather than rates. Kennesaw experienced a 70 percent increase in population from 1980 to 1987. Burglary increases due to sheer city growth would obscure any crime-reducing effects of the ordinance. The effects of these two errors can be very large, as indicated in Table 8.4.

Thus the authors' methods apparently obscured much of the decrease in the residential burglary rate. Also, their use of total burglary data ignores the implications of an extended discussion in Kleck (1988, pp. 15-16, immediately following the Kennesaw discussion cited by the authors), in which it was argued that a

TABLE 8.4 Differences Due to Using Raw Data versus Rates

Raw Numbers or Rate?	Total Burglaries or Just Residential?	% Change	
		1981–82	1981–86
Raw	Total	-35	-41
Rate[a]	Total	-40	-56
Raw	Residential[b]	-53	-80
Rate[a]	Residential[b]	-57	-85

Notes: [a] Based on linear interpolation of 1980 and 1987 population figures reported in Schmidt (1987). [b] Based on counts of "house burglaries" reported in Schmidt (1987).

major effect of residential gun ownership may be to displace burglars from occupied homes to less dangerous targets (see also next section). Because nonresidential targets, especially stores and other businesses left unoccupied at night, would fit into the latter category, one would expect a displacement from residential burglaries to nonresidential burglaries, as well as a shift from occupied residences to unoccupied ones. Thus, the hypothesized deterrent effect on occupied residential burglary could occur with no impact at all on total burglaries. Consequently, the exercise by McDowall and his colleagues has no clear relevance to the gun deterrence hypothesis.

Even as a test of the impact on total burglary, this study was affected by two other related flaws. The authors specified an intervention model that assumed an abrupt and *permanent* change in crime. However, a deterrence model stresses the critical importance of increases in offenders' perceptions of risk. Any such subjective shift is almost certainly temporary, fading along with memories of the passage of the ordinance. A temporary-change model would be theoretically preferable, regardless of issues of fit to the data. (The authors reported that a model assuming a temporary effect did not fit the data as well as the one they preferred.)

Although the intervention occurred in March of 1982, the authors extended their time series all the way to the end of 1986. More time points are desirable from a narrow statistical viewpoint, but a longer post-intervention period will also tend to obscure any effects that were temporary and followed by rising crime rates. This suspicion is supported by the authors' footnote 3 and Figure 1, which indicate that, beginning about three years after the intervention, total burglaries increased substantially (probably at least partly due to the large population increases and related changes). When the authors excluded 1986 time points, the parameter measuring impact of the intervention reversed sign, going from small positive to small negative. This raises the possibility that if the time series had been further limited just to time points closer to the intervention (say, within three years), this alteration alone might have made the impact parameter negative and significant, supporting the deterrence thesis.[1] Some intriguing findings concerning the impact of handgun bans have been reported by McDowall et al. (1991). Evanston and Morton Grove, Illinois, passed local bans on handgun possession in the 1980s. Both ordinances applied only to handguns, allowing homeowners to remain armed with the more lethal shotguns and rifles. Therefore, the only households that even hypothetically could have become gunless as a result of the ordinances would have been those that (1) owned only handguns, (2) obeyed the law and got rid of handguns, and (3) did not replace the handguns by acquiring long guns. Although half of U.S. households own guns, only 7 percent own only handguns (Kleck 1991, p. 55). Thus, only some very law-abiding subset of this 7 percent could potentially be disarmed by handgun-only bans.

Citizens would have had to have been very law-abiding indeed to be disarmed by these measures, as authorities depended almost entirely on purely voluntary compliance. The ordinances were not seriously enforced; the Evanston deputy police chief publicly announced that the police would not actively search out handguns. Only 74 charges were brought for violations over the first three years after the ordinance was passed, and only 116 handguns were handed in or confiscated, all this in a city with over 5,000 admitted handgun owners (Kleck 1991, pp. 408–411). Thus, there is no reason to believe that there was any actual reduction in gun-armed households in either city, nor any reason to believe that prospective burglars believed there was a reduction. Indeed, to the extent that burglars perceived any change at all, some might have reasonably supposed that at least a few gun owners upgraded their weapons by exchanging their less-lethal handguns for more lethal long guns.

Both of these measures, however, were preceded by extended and highly publicized debate, with advocates stressing the "handgun scourge" in their communities and emphasizing the need to reduce the excessive prevalence of handguns. Thus, in the absence of any significant amount of actual disarming, the dominant effect of these episodes should have been an increased awareness of victim gun possession among prospective criminals engendered by the public debate over the measures. This analysis would lead one to expect, if there were any crime changes at all, a reduction in burglary due to intensified deterrent effects of ongoing citizen gun ownership.

Applying ARIMA methods to substantial (132 time points) monthly burglary series, McDowall et al. detected burglary declines in both cities (significant in Morton Grove and not significant in Evanston). Thus, the results, at least in Morton Grove, supported the gun deterrence hypothesis. The authors, however, did not interpret the results this way. They asserted that passage of the ordinances should have led burglars to believe that fewer homes were armed with guns, leading to a *reduced* deterrent effect of guns and an increase in burglary, if a gun deterrence effect had previously been operating. The lack of significant increases in burglaries, they argued, was evidence that no such deterrent effect had been operating. The authors presented neither evidence nor theoretical rationale for the notion that burglars would somehow come to believe that fewer local homes were armed with guns after the passage of largely unenforced bans applying only to handguns; therefore their seemingly counter-intuitive interpretation must be tentatively rejected. One advantage of the present interpretation is that it can explain what McDowall et al. could not. They were puzzled by the burglary declines, insisting that "there is no convincing mechanism to explain how a handgun ban could generate such a reduction" (pp. 553–554). There is, of course, such a mechanism, although apparently not one that would be "convincing" to these authors. These handgun ban episodes were consistent with the gun deterrence hypothesis.

It needs to be stressed that the results of these natural "experiments" are not cited for the narrow purpose of demonstrating the short-term deterrent effects of gun training programs or victim gun use per se. There is no reason to believe that citizens used the gun training in any significant number of real-life defensive situations, nor any solid evidence that gun ownership or defensive uses increased in the affected areas. Rather, the results are cited as evidence on the question of whether routine gun ownership and defensive use by civilians have a pervasive, *ongoing* impact on crime, with or without such programs or incidents. This ongoing impact is merely intensified and made more salient at times when criminals' awareness of potential victims' gun possession is dramatically increased, thereby offering an opportunity to detect an effect that is ordinarily invisible. A few diverse examples of how this awareness might come to be increased have been described. Other examples would be general stories in the news media about gun ownership, increases in gun sales, and so on.

All of these cases, although very consistent with the gun deterrence hypothesis, can provide only weak anecdotal evidence. There is no technically sound nonexperimental methodology that allows researchers to separate the effects of an intervention, whether a gun training program or a new gun control law, from the effects of thousands of contemporaneous changes in variables that affect crime trends. Consequently, at present it seems unlikely we will ever have strong evidence bearing on the gun deterrence hypothesis, or at least none based on local case studies like those discussed here. In particular, the univariate interrupted time series design, with or without ARIMA analysis, cannot be considered adequate for this purpose (Kleck, Britt and Bordua 1993; Britt, Kleck and Bordua 1996).

Guns and the Displacement of Burglars from Occupied Homes

Residential burglars devote considerable thought, time, and effort to locating homes that are unoccupied. In interviews with burglars in a Pennsylvania prison, Rengert and Wasilchick (1985) found that nearly all of the two hours spent on the average suburban burglary was devoted to locating an appropriate target, casing the house, and making sure no one was home. There are at least two reasons why burglars make this considerable investment of time and effort: to avoid arrest and to avoid getting shot. Several burglars in this study reported that they avoided late night burglaries because it was too difficult to tell if anyone was home, explaining "That's the way to get shot" (Rengert and Wasilchick

1985, p. 30). Burglars also stated that they avoided neighborhoods occupied largely by persons of a different race because "You'll get shot if you're caught there" (p. 62). Giving weight to these opinions, one of the 31 burglars admitted to having been shot on the job (p. 98). In the Wright-Rossi survey, 73 percent of felons who had committed a burglary or violent crime agreed that "one reason burglars avoid houses when people are at home is that they fear being shot" (author's analysis of ICPSR 1986).

The nonconfrontational nature of most burglaries is a major reason why associated deaths and injuries are so rare—an absent victim cannot be injured. Don Kates (1983) has argued that victim gun ownership is a major reason for the nonconfrontational nature of burglary and is therefore to be credited with reducing deaths and injuries by its deterrent effects. This possible benefit would be enjoyed by all potential burglary victims, not just those who own guns, because burglars seeking to avoid confrontations usually cannot know exactly which homes have guns and therefore must attempt to avoid all occupied premises.

Under hypothetical no-guns circumstances, the worst a burglar would ordinarily have to fear would be breaking off a burglary attempt if faced with an occupant who called the police. A typical strong, young burglar might have little reason to fear attack or apprehension by unarmed victims, especially if the victim confronted was a woman or an older person. Further, there would be positive advantages to burglary of occupied premises as this would give the burglar a much better chance to get the cash in victims' purses or wallets, cash being the most attractive of all theft targets.

To be sure, even under no-guns conditions, many burglars would continue to avoid occupied residences simply because contact with a victim would increase their chances of apprehension by the police. Others may have chosen to do burglaries rather than robberies because they were emotionally unable or unwilling to confront their victims and thus would avoid occupied premises for this reason. However, this does not seem to be true of most incarcerated burglars. Prison surveys indicate that few criminals specialize in one crime type; most imprisoned burglars report having also committed robberies. In the Wright and Rossi survey, of those who reported ever committing a burglary, 62 percent also reported committing robberies (author's secondary analysis of

ICPSR 1986). Thus, most of these burglars were temperamentally capable of confronting victims, yet they presumably preferred to avoid them when committing a burglary.

Results from victim surveys in three foreign nations indicate that in countries with lower rates of gun ownership than the United States, residential burglars are much more likely to enter occupied homes. A 1977 survey in the Netherlands found an occupancy rate of 48 percent for all burglaries, compared to 9 percent in the United States the previous year (Block 1984, p. 26). In the British Crime Surveys of 1982, 1984, 1988 and 1992, 43 percent of burglaries were committed with someone at home (Mayhew et al. 1993, Table A4.6). And Waller and Okihiro (1978, p. 31) reported that 44 percent of burglarized Toronto residences were occupied during the burglaries, with 21 percent of the burglaries resulting in confrontations between victim and offender. The huge differences between the United States and Great Britain and Canada cannot be explained by more serious legal threats in this country, because the probability of arrest and imprisonment and the severity of sentences served for common crimes are no higher in the United States than in these other nations (Wilson 1976, pp. 18–19; U.S. Bureau of Justice Statistics 1987b).

If widespread civilian gun ownership helps deter burglars from entering occupied premises, what might this imply regarding the level of burglary-linked violence? NCVS data indicate that when a residential burglary is committed with a household member present, it results in a threat or attack on the victim 30.2 percent of the time (U.S. Bureau of Justice Statistics 1985a, p. 4). Although only 12.7 percent of U.S. residential burglaries are against occupied homes, the occupancy rate in three low gun-ownership nations averaged about 45 percent. What would happen if U.S. burglars were equally likely to enter occupied premises? In 1985 the NCVS counted 5,594,420 household burglaries, with about 214,568 resulting in assaults on a victim (5,594,420 x .127 x .302). Assume that 30.2 percent of the occupied premise burglaries resulted in assaults on a victim, the same as now, but also assume that the occupancy rate increased to 45 percent, as in low gun-ownership nations. This would imply about 760,282 assaults on burglary victims (5,594,420 x .45 x .302 = 760,282), 545,713 more than now. This change alone would have represented a 9.4 percent increase in all NCVS-counted violent crime in 1985. If high home gun ownership rates in the United States really do account for the difference in burglary occupancy rates between the United States and other nations, these figures indicate that burglary displacement effects of widespread gun ownership may have a significant downward impact on violence rates.

Conclusions

To briefly summarize, gun use by private citizens against violent criminals and burglars is common and about as frequent as legal actions like arrests, is a more prompt negative consequence of crime than legal punishment, and is more severe, at its most serious, than legal system punishments. However, only a minority of criminal victimizations transpire in a way that results in defensive gun use; guns certainly are not usable in all crime situations. Victim gun use is associated with lower rates of assault or robbery victim injury and lower rates of robbery completion than any other defensive action or doing nothing to resist. Serious predatory criminals perceive a risk from victim gun use that is roughly comparable to that of criminal justice system actions, and this perception may influence their behavior in socially desirable ways. Nevertheless, a deterrent effect of widespread gun ownership and defensive use has not been conclusively established, any more than it has been for activities of the legal system. Given the nature of deterrent effects, it may never be convincingly established.

Nevertheless, the most parsimonious way of linking these facts is to tentatively conclude that civilian ownership and defensive use of guns deters violent crime and reduces burglar-linked injuries. One cannot precisely calculate the social control impact of gun use and ownership any more than one can for the operations of the legal system, but the available evidence is compatible with the hypothesis that mass gun ownership could exert as much effect on violent crime and burglary as do CJS activities.

Does the widespread use of guns for defensive purposes constitute vigilantism? Certainly there are some parallels. Vigilantism, in the true sense of collective private force used for social control purposes, flourished where legal controls were weakest, such as frontier areas. And research on today's world indicates that private citizen crime prevention activities in general are more common where police are less numerous (Krahn and Kennedy 1985). It is commonplace to draw an analogy between conditions in the Western United States of the nineteenth century and high crime neighborhoods in today's cities. The analogy is especially close regarding the limited effectiveness of urban law enforcement agencies in controling crime.

However, it is also true that contemporary private efforts to collectively control crime, such as neighborhood crime watch organizations, are least effective and enduring in precisely those areas that most need them—disorganized high crime areas occupied largely by transient populations of socially isolated strangers (Greenberg et al. 1984). The social disorganization and lack of cultural consensus that encourage criminal behavior also hinder any kind of effective collective action to control crime. Under the anomic conditions characterizing large U.S. cities, it is no more possible to form lynch mobs than it is for ghetto residents to maintain stable neighborhood watch or patrol organizations or for the police to control crime. Instead, more individualistic efforts, whether violent or not, prevail. The late twentieth century substitute for vigilantism is individualistic resistance to criminals by those directly victimized.

It is a dispiriting fact of life that economic injustice, a history of racism, and other factors have created dangerous conditions in many places in America. Police cannot realistically be expected to provide personal protection for every American (and indeed are not even legally obliged to do so [Kates 1991]). Gun ownership is no more an all-situations, magical source of protection than the police are, but it can be a useful supplementary source of safety in addition to police protection, burglary alarms, guard dogs and all the other resources people exploit to improve their security. These sources are not substitutes for one another. Rather, they are complements, each useful in different situations. Possession of a gun gives its owner an additional option for dealing with immediate danger. If other sources of security are adequate, the gun does not have to be used; but where other sources fail, it can preserve bodily safety and property in at least some situations.

One can dream of a day when governments can eliminate violence and provide total protection to all citizens. In reality, the American legal system has never even approximated this state of

affairs, and is unlikely to do so in the foreseeable future. If predatory crime can be reduced, the private resort to violence for social
control purposes should decline. In the meanwhile, the widespread legal use of guns against criminals will persist as long as
Americans believe crime is a serious threat and that they cannot
rely completely on the police as effective guardians.

Implications for Crime Control Policy

Undesirable though such a state of affairs may be, much of social
order in America may depend on the fact that millions of people
are armed and dangerous to each other. The availability of deadly
weapons to the violence-prone may well contribute to violence by
increasing the probability of a fatal outcome of combat (but see
Kleck 1991, Chapter 5; Wright et al 1983, pp. 189-212). However,
this very fact may also raise the stakes in disputes to the point
where only the most incensed or intoxicated disputants resort to
physical conflict, with the risks of armed retaliation deterring
attack and coercing minimal courtesy among otherwise hostile
parties. Likewise, rates of commercial robbery, residential burglary injury, and rape might be still higher than their already high
levels were it not for the dangerousness of the prospective victim
population. Gun ownership among prospective victims may well
have as large a crime-inhibiting effect as the crime-generating
effects of gun possession among prospective criminals. This could
account for the failure of researchers to find a significant net
relationship between rates of crime, such as homicide and robbery,
and measures of gun ownership that do not distinguish between
gun availability among criminals and availability in the largely
noncriminal general public (for example, Cook 1979; Kleck 1984a;
Kleck and Patterson 1993; Kleck 1991, pp. 214-215); the two effects
may roughly cancel each other out (see also Bordua 1986).

   Guns are potentially lethal weapons whether wielded by
criminals or by victims. They are frightening and intimidating to
those they are pointed at, whether these be criminals or victims.
Guns thereby empower both those who would use them to victimize and those who would use them to prevent their victimization. Consequently, they are a source of both social order and

disorder, depending on who uses them, just as is true of the use of force in general.

The failure to fully acknowledge this reality can lead to grave errors in devising public policy to minimize violence through gun control. Some gun laws are intended to reduce gun possession only among relatively limited "high-risk" groups such as convicted felons through measures such as laws licensing gun owners or requiring permits to purchase guns. However, other laws are aimed at reducing gun possession in all segments of the civilian population, both criminal and noncriminal. Examples would be the aforementioned Morton Grove and Evanston handgun possession bans, near approximations of such bans (as in New York City, Chicago, and Washington, D.C.), prohibitions of handgun sales, and most laws regulating the carrying of concealed weapons. By definition, laws are most likely to be obeyed by the law-abiding, and gun laws are no different. Therefore, measures applying equally to criminals and noncriminals are almost certain to reduce gun possession more among the latter than the former. Because very little serious violent crime is committed by persons without previous histories of serious violence (Kleck and Bordua 1983), there are at best only modest direct crime control benefits to be gained by reductions in gun possession among noncriminals, whereas even marginal reductions in gun possession among criminals might have crime-reducing effects. Consequently, one has to take seriously the possibility that prohibitionist gun control measures could decrease the crime-control effects of noncriminal gun ownership more than they would decrease the crime-causing effects of criminal gun ownership. For this reason, more narrowly targeted gun control measures like bans on felon gun possession, instant background checks, gun owner licensing, and permit-to-purchase systems seem preferable (see Kleck 1991, chapter 8, for descriptions of these measures).

People skeptical about the value of gun control sometimes argue that although a world in which there were no guns would be desirable, it is also unachievable. The evidence presented here raises a more radical possibility — that a world in which no one had guns would actually be *less* safe than one in which nonaggressors had guns and aggressors somehow did not. As a practical matter, the latter world is no more achievable than the former, but the point is worth raising as a way of clarifying what the goals of rational gun control policy should be. If gun possession among noncriminal prospective victims tends to reduce violence, then reducing such gun possession is not, in and of itself, a social good. Instead, the best policy goal to pursue may be to shift the distribution of gun possession as far as practical in the direction of likely aggressors being disarmed and currently armed nonaggressors being left armed. To disarm noncriminals in the hope this might somehow indirectly help reduce access to guns among criminals (for example, by reducing theft) is not a cost-free policy.

These categories are, of course, simplifications. Some serious aggressors are also victims of serious aggression, and most generally noncriminal people are at least occasionally aggressors in some very minor way. However, it is clear these two groups overlap to some extent, but it is equally clear that they can and are routinely distinguished in law, for example, in statutes that forbid gun possession among persons with a criminal conviction and allow it among others. Further, although a great deal of violence is committed by persons without criminal convictions, it is also true that convicted felons are far more likely to be violent aggressors in the future than nonfelons. The idea that a significant share of serious violence is accounted for by previously nonviolent "average Joes," as in the "crime-of-passion" domestic homicide, is largely a myth (Kleck and Bordua 1983).

Consequently, a rational goal of gun control policy could be to tip the balance of power in prospective victims' favor, by reducing aggressor gun possession while doing nothing to reduce nonaggressor gun possession. This would contrast sharply with across-the-board restrictions that apply uniformly to aggressors and nonaggressors alike. In light of this chapter's evidence, prohibitionist policies would facilitate victimization because legal restrictions would almost certainly be evaded more by aggressors than nonaggressors, causing a shift in gun distribution that favored the former over the latter.

Note

1. It may help to place McDowall and Loftin's assessments of evidence on these issues in context by noting their views on the desirability of mass gun ownership for self-protection. In an article addressing the prevalence of handguns owned for self-protection, they expressed the opinion that "collective security requires the disarming and demobilizing of individual capabilities [for self-protection]" (1983, p. 1148).

References

Alviani, Joseph D., and William R. Drake. 1975. *Handgun Control . . . Issues and Alternatives.* Washington, D.C.: U.S. Conference of Mayors.

Bachman and O'Malley. 1981. "When Four Months Equal a Year: Inconsistencies in Student Reports of Drug Use." *Public Opinion Quarterly* 45: 536–543.

Bankston, William B., Carol Y. Thompson, and Quentin A.L. Jenkins. 1986. "Carrying Firearms: The Influence of Southern Culture and Fear of Crime." Paper presented at the 1986 annual meetings of the American Society of Criminology, Atlanta, Georgia.

Benenson, Mark K. 1982. Memorandum recording telephone conversation with Kennesaw, Georgia Police Chief Ruble, November 4, 1982.

Bensing, Robert C., and Oliver Schroeder. 1960. *Homicide in an Urban Community.* Springfield, Ill.: Charles Thomas.

Blackman, Paul H. 1985. "Carrying Handguns for Personal Protection." Paper presented at the annual meeting of the American Society of Criminology, San Diego, California.

Block, Richard. 1977. *Violent Crime.* Lexington, Mass.: Lexington Books.

_____. 1984. "The Impact of Victimization, Rates and Patterns: A Comparison of the Netherlands and the United States." Pp. 23–28 in *Victimization and Fear of Crime: World Perspectives,* edited by Richard Block. Washington, D.C.: U.S. Government Printing Office.

Blumstein, Alfred, Jacqueline Cohen, and Daniel Nagin (eds.). 1978. *Deterrence and Incapacitation: Estimating the Effects of Criminal Sanctions on Crimes.* Washington, D.C.: National Academy of Sciences.

Bordua, David J. 1982. Unpublished tabulations done for the author from 1977 statewide Illinois survey. Urbana: Department of Sciology, University of Illinois.

_____,1986. "Firearms Ownership and Violent Crime: A Comparison of Illinois Counties." Pp. 156–88 in *The Social Ecology of Crime,* edited by James M. Byrne and Robert J. Sampson. N.Y.: Springer-Verlag.

_____, Mark Beeman, and Debra Kelley. 1985. *Operation and Effects of Firearm Owner Identification and Waiting Period Regulation in Illinois.* Urbana: Department of Sociology, University of Illinois.

_____, Alan J. Lizotte, and Gary Kleck, with Van Cagle. 1979. *Pat-*

terns of Firearms Ownership, Regulation and Use in Illinois. Springfield, Ill.: Illinois Law Enforcement Commission.

Brearley, H.C. 1932. *Homicide in the United States.* Chapel Hill: University of North Carolina Press.

Britt, Chester, III, Gary Kleck, and David J. Bordua. 1996. "A Reassessment of the D.C. Gun Law: Some Cautionary Notes on the Use of Interrupted Time Series Designs for Policy Impact Assessment." *Law & Society Review* 30: 361–380.

Brown, Richard Maxwell. 1969. "The American Vigilante Tradition." Pp. 144–218 in *Violence in America,* edited by Hugh Davis Graham and Ted Robert Gurr. New York: Signet.

Bruce-Briggs, Barry. 1976. "The Great American War." *The Public Interest* 45: 37–62.

Cambridge Reports. 1978. *An Analysis of Public Attitudes Towards Handgun Control.* Cambridge, Mass.: Cambridge Reports, Inc.

Cohen, Lawrence E., and Marcus Felson. 1979. "Social Change and Crime Rate Trends: A Routine Activities Approach." *American Sociological Review* 44:588–608.

Conklin, John E. 1972. *Robbery and the Criminal Justice System.* Philadelphia: Lippincott.

Cook, Philip J. 1979. "The Effect of Gun Availability on Robbery and Robbery Murder." Pp. 743– *Policy Studies Review Annual,* edited by Robert Haveman and B. Bruce Zellner. Beverly Hills: Sage.

_____. 1985. "The Case of the Missing Victims: Gunshot Woundings in the National Crime Survey." *Journal of Quantitative Criminology* 1:91–102.

_____. 1986. "The Relationship Between Victim Resistance and Injury in Noncommercial Robbery." *Journal of Legal Studies* 15:405–16.

_____. 1991. "The Technology of Personal Violence." *Crime and Justice* 14:1–71.

_____, and Daniel Nagin. 1979. *Does the Weapon Matter?* Washington, D.C.: INSLAW.

Crocker, Royce. 1982. "Attitudes Toward Gun Control: A Survey." Pp. 229–67 in *Federal Regulation of Firearms,* edited by Harry L. Hogan. Washington, D.C.: U.S. Government Printing Office.

Curtis, Lynn A. 1974. *Criminal Violence: National Patterns and Behavior.* Lexington, Mass.: Lexington.

Davis, James A., and Tom W. Smith. 1984. *General Social Surveys, 1972–1984: Cumulative Codebook.* Chicago: National Opinion Research Center.

_____. 1994. *General Social Surveys, 1972–1994: Cumulative Codebook.* Chicago: National Opinion Research Center.

DIALOG. 1990; 1995. Computer search of DIALOG database, POLL file of public opinion survey results. Palo Alto, Calif.: DIALOG Information Services, Inc.

Dietz, Mary Lorenz. 1983. *Killing for Profit: The Social Organization of Felony Homicide.* Chicago: Nelson-Hall.

DMI (Decision-Making-Information). 1979. *Attitudes of the American Electorate toward Gun Control.* Santa Ana, Calif.: DMI.

Dodge, Richard. 1981. "The Washington, D.C. Recall Study." Pp. 12–15 in *The National Crime Surveys: Working Papers, Volume I: Current and Historical Perspectives,* edited by Robert G. Lehnen and Wesley G. Skogan. U.S. Department of Justice, Bureau of Justice Statistics. Washington, D.C.: U.S. Government Printing Office.

Field Institute. 1976. *Tabulations of the Findings of a Survey of Handgun Ownership and Access Among a Cross Section of the California Adult Public.* San Francisco: Field Institute.

Firman, Gordon R. 1975. "In Prison Gun Survey the Pros are the Cons." *The American Rifleman* 23(November):13.

Garin, Geoffrey. 1986. Telephone conversion with Geoffrey Garin of Peter D. Hart Research Associates, Inc., Washington, D.C., April 30, 1986.

Geller, William A., and Michael S. Scott. 1992. *Deadly Force: What We Know.* Washington, D.C.: Police Executive Research Forum.

Gibbs, Jack. 1975. *Crime, Punishment, and Deterrence.* N.Y.: Elsevier.

Gillespie, Cynthia. 1989. *Justifiable Homicide.* Columbus: Ohio State University Press.

Goode, William J. 1972. "Presidential Address: The Place of Force in Human Society." *American Sociological Review* 37:507–19.

Gove, Walter R., Michael Hughes, and Michael Geerken. 1985. "Are Uniform Crime Reports a Valid Indicator of the Index Crimes? An Affirmative Answer with Minor Qualifications." *Criminology* 23:451–501.

Green, Gary S. 1987. "Citizen Gun Ownership and Criminal Deterrence." *Criminology* 25:63–81.

Greenberg, Stephanie W., and William M. Rohe, and J.R. Williams. 1984. *Informal Citizen Action and Crime Prevention at the Neighborhood Level: Synthesis and Assessment of the Research.* National Institute of Justice. Washington, D.C.: Government Printing Office.

Hassinger, James. 1985. "Fear of Crime in Public Environments." *Journal of Architectural Planning Research* 2:289–300.

Hindelang, Michael J., Travis Hirschi, and Joseph G. Weis. 1981. *Measuring Delinquency.* Beverly Hills: Sage.

Inter-university Consortium for Political and Social Research (ICPSR). 1984. *Uniform Crime Reporting Program Data.* Study 9028, Parts 3, 7, 11, 15. Supplementary Homicide Reports, 1979–1982. Federal Bureau of Investigation. Ann Arbor: Inter-University Consortium [distributor].

———. 1985. Codebook for ICPSR Study 7633. *Mortality Detail Files 1969–1978, External Deaths Subfile.* National Center for Health Statistics. Ann Arbor, Mich.: ICPSR [distributor].

———. 1986. Codebook for ICPSR Study 8437. *Armed Criminals in America: A Survey of Incarcerated Felons.* Principal Investigators James Wright and Peter Rossi. Ann Arbor, Mich.:ICPSR [distributor].

———. 1987a. *National Crime Surveys: Victim Risk Supplement, 1983.* Study 8316 [MRDF]. Principal Investigator U.S. Department of Justice. Ann Arbor: ICPSR [distributor].

———. 1987b. *National Crime Surveys: National Sample, 1979–1985 (Revised Questionnaire).* Study 8608 [MRDF]. Principal Investigator U.S. Department of Justice. Ann Arbor: ICPSR [distributor].

Kates, Don B., Jr. 1983. "Handgun Prohibition and the Original Meaning of the Second Amendment." *Michigan Law Review* 82:204-273.

———. 1990. *Guns, Murders, and the Constitution.* Policy Briefing, Pacific Research Institute for Public Policy. San Francisco: Pacific Institute.

Kleck, Gary. 1984. "The Relationship Between Gun Ownership Levels and Rates of Violence in the United States." Pp 99–135 in *Firearms and Violence: Issues of Public Policy,* edited by Don B. Kates, Jr. Cambridge, Mass.: Ballinger.

———. 1988. "Crime Control Through the Private Use of Armed Force." *Social Problems* 35:1–21.

———. 1991. *Point Blank: Guns and Violence in America.* Hawthorne, N.Y.: Aldine de Gruyter.

———, and David J. Bordua. 1983. "The Factual Foundations for Certain Key Assumptions of Gun Control." *Law & Policy Quarterly* 5:271-298.

———, Chester Britt, and David J. Bordua. 1993. "The Emperor Has No Clothes: Using Interrupted Time Series Designs to Evaluate Social Policy Impact." Paper presented at the annual meetings of the American Society of Criminology in Phoenix, Arizona, October 30, 1993.

_____, and Miriam DeLone. 1993. "Victim Resistance and Offender
Weapon Effects in Robbery." *Journal of Quantitative Criminology*
9:55–82.

_____, and Marc Gertz. 1995. "Armed Resistance to Crime: The
Prevalence and Nature of Self-Defense with a Gun." *Journal of
Criminal Law & Criminology* 86:150–187.

_____, and Marc Gertz. 1996. "Carrying Guns for Protection: Results
from the National Self-Defense Survey." Unpublished paper.
School of Criminology and Criminal Justice, Florida State University, Tallahassee, Florida.

_____, and E. Britt Patterson. 1993. "The Impact of Gun Control and
Gun Ownership Levels on Violence Rates." *Journal of Quantitative
Criminology* 9:249–287.

_____, and Susan Sayles. 1990. "Rape and Resistance." *Social Problems* 37: 149–62.

Kochanek, Kenneth D., and Bettie L. Hudson. 1994. "Advance Report
of Final Mortality Statistics, 1992." *Monthly Vital Statistics Report.*
Volume 43, Number 6, Supplement. Hyattsville, Md.: National
Center for Health Statistics.

Krahn, Harvey, and Leslie W. Kennedy. 1985. "Producing Personal
Safety: The Effects of Crime Rates, Police Force Size, and Fear of
Crime." *Criminology* 23:697–710.

Krug, Alan S. 1968. "The Relationship Between Firearms Ownership
and Crime Rates: A Statistical Analysis." *The Congressional Record*
(January 30, 1968): H570–2.

Lee, Roberta K., Richard J. Waxweiler, James G. Dobbins, and Terri
Paschetag. 1991. "Incidence Rates of Firearm Injuries in
Galveston, Texas, 1979–1981." *American Journal of Epidemiology*
134:511–521.

Link, Mitchell. 1982. "No Handguns in Morton Grove — Big Deal!"
Menard Times (prison newspaper of Menard, Illinois Federal Penitentiary) 33:1.

Lizotte, Alan J. 1986. "Determinants of Completing Rape and Assault."
Journal of Quantitative Criminology 2:203–17.

_____, and David J. Bordua. 1980. "Firearms Ownership for Sport
and Protection: Two Divergent Models." *American Sociological Review* 45: 229–44.

Loftin, Colin, and Ellen J. MacKenzie. 1990. "Building National Estimates of Violent Victimization." Paper read at the National Research Council Symposium on the Understanding and Control of
Violent Behavior, Destin, Florida, April 1–6, 1990.

Los Angeles Times. 1981. *L.A. Times Poll Number 39*. Los Angeles: Los Angeles Times.

Luckenbill, David F. 1977. "Criminal Homicide as a Situated Transaction." *Social Problems* 25:176–86.

Lundsgaarde, Henry P. 1977. *Murder in Space City: A Cultural Analysis of Houston Homicide Patterns*. New York: Oxford.

Mauser, Gary A. 1990. Unpublished tabulations from a 1990 national survey, produced at the author's request.

_____. 1993. "Firearms and Self-Defense: The Canadian Case." Paper presented at the annual meetings of the American Society of Criminology, Phoenix, Arizona, October 28, 1993.

_____, and David B. Kopel. 1992. "'Sorry, Wrong Number': Why Media Polls on Gun Control Are Often Unreliable." *Political Communication* 9: 69–91.

Mayhew, Pat, Natalie Aye Maung and Catriona Mirrlees-Black. 1993. *The 1992 British Crime Survey*. London: Her Majesty's Stationary Office.

McCleary, Richard, and Richard A. Hay, Jr., with Errol E. Meidinger and David McDowall. 1980. *Applied Time Series Analysis for the Social Sciences*. Beverly Hills: Sage.

McDowall, David, Alan Lizotte, and Brian Wiersema. 1991. "General Deterrence Through Civilian Gun Ownership." *Criminology* 29:541–59.

_____, and Colin Loftin. 1983. "Collective Security and the Demand for Legal Handguns." *American Journal of Sociology* 88:1146–61.

_____, Colin Loftin, and Brian Wiersema. 1992. "The Incidence of Civilian Defensive Firearm Use." *Violence Research Group Discussion Paper 10*. College Park, Md.: Institute of Criminal Justice & Criminology.

_____, and Brian Wiersema. 1994. "The Incidence of Defensive Firearm Use by US Crime Victims, 1987 Through 1990." *American Journal of Public Health* 84:1982–1984.

_____, Brian Wiersema, and Colin Loftin. 1989. "Did Mandatory Firearm Ownership in Kennesaw Really Prevent Burglaries?" *Sociology and Social Research* 74:48–51.

McNamara, Joseph D. 1986. "Statement of Joseph D. McNamara, Chief of Police, San Jose, Ca." Pp. 981–93 *Hearing Before the Committee on the Judiciary*, House of Representatives, 994th Congress, 1st and 2nd Sessions on Legislation to Modify the 1968 Gun Control Act, Part 2. Testimony 2-19-86. Serial No. 131. Washington, D.C.: U.S. Government Printing Office.

Murphy, Linda R., and Richard W. Dodge. 1981. "The Baltimore Recall Study." Pp. 16–21 in *The National Crime Surveys: Working Papers, Volume I: Current and Historical Perspectives,* edited by Robert G. Lehnen and Wesley G. Skogan. U.S. Department of Justice, Bureau of Justice Statistics. Washington, D.C.: U.S. Government Printing Office.

National Safety Council. 1994. *Accident Facts – 1994 Edition.* Chicago: National Safety Council.

Newton, George D., and Franklin Zimring. 1969. *Firearms and Violence in American Life.* A Staff Report to the National Commission on the Causes and Prevention of Violence. Washington, D.C.: U.S. Government Printing Office.

O'Carroll, Patrick W., Colin Loftin, John B. Waller, David McDowall, Allen Bukoff, Richard O. Scott, James A. Mercy, and Brian Wiersema. 1991. "Preventing Homicide: An Evaluation of the Efficacy of a Detroit Gun Ordinance." *American Journal of Public Health* 81:576–81.

Ohio. 1982. *Ohio Citizen Attitudes Concerning Crime and Criminal Justice.* The Ohio Statistical Analysis Center, Division of Criminal Justice Services. Columbus, Ohio: Ohio Department of Development.

Pierce, Glenn L. and William J. Bowers. 1981. "The Bartley-Fox Gun Law's Short-Term Impact on Crime in Boston." *The Annals* 455:120–137.

Quinley, Hal. 1990. Memorandum reporting results from Time/CNN Poll of Gun Owners, dated 2-6-90. N.Y.: Yankelovich Clancy Shulman survey organization.

Rand, Michael. 1994. *Guns and Crime.* Crime Data Brief, Bureau of Justice Statistics. Washington, D.C.: U.S. Government Printing Office.

Reiss, Albert J., and Jeffrey A. Roth. 1993. "Firearms and Violence." Pp. 255–87 in Understanding and Preventing Violence, edited by Albert J. Reiss and Jeffrey A. Roth. Washington, D.C.: National Academy Press.

Rengert, George, and John Wasilchick. 1985. *Suburban Burglary: A Time and Place for Everything.* Springfield, Ill.: Charles Thomas.

Ronhovde, Kent M., and Gloria P. Sugars. 1982. "Survey of Select State Firearm Control Laws." Pp. 201–28 in *Federal Regulation of Firearms,* report prepared by Congressional Research Service for U.S. Senate Judiciary Committee. Washington, D.C.: U.S. Government Printing Office.

Rushforth, Norman B., Amasa B. Ford, Charles S. Hirsch, Nancy M. Rushforth, and Lester Adelson. 1977. "Violent Death in a Metropolitan County: Changing Patterns in Homicide (1958–74)." *New England Journal of Medicine* 297:531–8.

_____, Charles S. Hirsch, Amasa B. Ford, and Lester Adelson. 1975. "Accidental Firearm Fatalities in a Metropolitan County (1958–1975)." *American Journal of Epidemiology* 100: 499–505.

Schmidt, William E. "Town to Celebrate Mandatory Arms." *New York Times,* April 11, 1987, pp. 6–7.

Schneidman, Dave. 1982. "Gun-totin' Town Gets an Apology." *Chicago Tribune,* April 8, 1982, p. 15.

Schultz, Leroy G. 1962. "Why the Negro Carries Weapons." *Journal of Criminal Law, Criminology and Police Science* 53:476–83.

Sherman, Lawrence W., and Robert H. Langworthy. 1979. "Measuring Homicide by Police Officers." *Journal of Criminal Law and Criminology* 70:546–60.

Shields, Pete. 1981. *Guns Don't Die – People Do.* New York: Arbor House.

Skogan, Wesley. 1981. *Issues in the Measurement of Victimization.* U.S. Department of Justice, Bureau of Justice Statistics. Washington, D.C.: U.S. Government Printing Office.

Sudman, Seymour, and Norman M. Bradburn. 1974. *Response Effects in Surveys: A Review and Synthesis.* Chicago: Aldine.

Tonso, William R. 1984. "Social Problems and Sagecraft: Gun Control as a Case in Point." Pp. 71–95 in *Firearms and Violence: Issues of Public Policy,* edited by Don B. Kates, Jr. Cambridge: Ballinger.

Turner, Anthony G. 1981. "The San Jose Recall Study." Pp. 22–7 in *The National Crime Surveys: Working Papers, Volume I: Current and Historical Perspectives,* edited by Robert G. Lehnen and Wesley G. Skogan. U.S. Department of Justice, Bureau of Justice Statistics. Washington, D.C.: U.S. Government Printing Office.

U.S. Bureau of the Census. 1982; 1983; 1986; 1988; 1993; 1995. *Statistical Abstract of the United States 1981* (1982–83; 1984; 1987; 1989; 1995). Washington, D.C.: U.S. Government Printing Office.

_____. 1983d. *National Crime Survey: Interviewer's Manual.* NCVS-550. Part D – How to Enumerate NCS. Washington, D.C.: U.S. Government Printing Office.

U.S. Bureau of Justice Statistics. 1980. *Intimate Victims: A Study of Violence Among Friends and Relatives.* Washington, D.C.: U.S. Government Printing Office.

_____. 1981. *The Prevalence of Crime.* BJS Bulletin. Washington, D.C.: U.S. Government Printing Office.

_____. 1982a. *Criminal Victimization in the United States 1980.* Washington, D.C.: U.S. Government Printing Office.

_____. 1984. *Sourcebook of Criminal Justice Statistics 1983.* Washington, D.C.: U.S. Government Printing Office.

_____. 1985a. *Household Burglary.* BJS Bulletin. Washington, D.C.: U.S. Government Printing Office.

_____. 1985b. *The Risk of Violent Crime.* BJS Special Report. Washington, D.C.: U.S. Government Printing Office.

_____. 1985c. *Reporting Crimes to the Police.* BJS Special Report. Washington, D.C.: U.S. Government Printing Office.

_____. 1986. The Use of Weapons in Committing Crimes. Bureau of Justice Statistics Special Report. Washington, D.C.: U.S. Government Printing Office.

_____. 1987a. *Lifetime Likelihood of Victimization.* BJS Technical Report. Washington, D.C.: U.S. Government Printing Office.

_____. 1987b. *Imprisonment in Four Countries.* BJS Special Report. Washington, D.C.: U.S. Government Printing Office.

_____. 1990. *Handgun Crime Victims.* BJS Special Report. Washington, D.C.: U.S. Government Printing Office.

_____. 1991. *Capital Punishment 1990.* BJS Bulletin. Washington, D.C.: U.S. Government Printing Office.

_____. 1992. *Criminal Victimization in the United States 1990.* Washington, D.C.: U.S. Government Printing Office.

_____. 1994. *Criminal Victimization in the United States 1992.* Washington, D.C.: U.S. Government Printing Office.

U.S. Federal Bureau of Investigation (FBI). 1977; 1978; 1981; 1983; 1993; 1994; 1995. *Crime in the United States (year) – Uniform Crime Reports* (Covering years 1976, 1977, 1980, 1982, 1993, 1994). Washington, D.C.: U.S. Government Printing Office.

_____. 1980. *Uniform Crime Reporting Handbook.* Washington, D.C.: U.S. Government Printing Office.

_____. 1991. *Law Enforcement Officers Killed and Assaulted 1990.* Washington, D.C.: U.S. Government Printing Office.

_____. 1992. *Killed in the Line of Duty.* Washington, D.C.: U.S. Government Printing Office.

U.S. Law Enforcement Assistance Administration (LEAA). 1972. *The San Jose Methods Test of Known Crime Victims.* Statistics Division Technical Series, Report No. 1. Washington, D.C.: U.S. Government Printing Office.

U.S. National Center for Health Statistics (NCHS). 1982. *Public Use Data Tape Documentation: Mortality Detail 1979 Data.* Hyattsville, Md.: U.S. Public Health Service.

_____. 1983. *Public Use Data Tape Documentation: Mortality Detail*

1980 Data. Hyattsville, Maryland: U.S. Department of Health and Human Services.

_____. 1985. *Vital Statistics of the United States 1980*. Volume II—Mortality, Part A. Rockville, Md.: NCHS.

_____. 1994. *Vital Statistics of the United States 1990*. Volume II—Mortality, Part A. Rockville, Md.: NCHS.

_____. 1996. "Advance Report of Final Mortality Statistics, 1993." *Monthly Vital Statistics Report* Vol. 44, No. 1 (supp.), February 29, 1996.

U.S. Small Business Administration. 1969. *Crime Against Small Business*. Senate Document No. 91–14. Washington, D.C.: U.S. Government Printing Office.

Walker, Samuel. 1989. *Sense and Nonsense about Crime*. Pacific Grove. Calif.: Brooks/Cole.

Waller, Irvin, and Norman Okihiro. 1978. *Burglary: The Victim and the Public*. Toronto: University of Toronto Press.

Wilbanks, William. 1984. *Murder in Miami*. Lanham, Md.: University Press.

Wilson, James Q. 1976. "Crime and Punishment in England." *The Public Interest* 43:3–25.

Wilt, G. Marie, J. Bannon, Ronald K. Breedlove, John W. Kennish, Donald M. Snadker, and Robert K. Sawtell. 1977. *Domestic Violence and the Police: Studies in Detroit and Kansas City*. Washington, D.C.: U.S. Government Printing Office.

Wolfgang, Marvin E. 1958. *Patterns in Criminal Homicide*. Philadelphia: University of Pennsylvania Press.

Woltman, Henry, John Bushery, and Larry Carstensen. 1981. "Recall Bias and Telescoping in the National Crime Survey." Pp. 90–3 in *The National Crime Surveys: Working Papers, Volume I: Current and Historical Perspectives*, edited by Robert G. Lehnen and Wesley G. Skogan. U.S. Department of Justice, Bureau of Justice Statistics. Washington, D.C.: U.S. Government Printing Office.

Wright, James D., and Peter H. Rossi. 1985. *The Armed Criminal in America: A Survey of Incarcerated Felons*. National Institute of Justice Research Report. Washington, D.C.: U.S. Government Printing Office.

_____, and Peter H. Rossi. 1986. *Armed and Considered Dangerous: A Survey of Felons and Their Firearms*. New York: Aldine.

_____, Peter H. Rossi, and Kathleen Daly. 1983. *Under the Gun: Weapons, Crime and Violence in America*. New York: Aldine.

Yeager, Matthew G., Joseph D. Alviani, and Nancy Loving. 1976. *How*

Well Does the Handgun Protect You and Your Family? Handgun Control Staff Technical Report 2. Washington, D.C.: United States Conference of Mayors.

Ziegenhagen, Eduard A., and Dolores Brosnan. 1985. "Victim Responses to Robbery and Crime Control Policy." *Criminology* 23:675–95.

Zimring, Franklin E., and Gordon J. Hawkins. 1973. *Deterrence: The Legal Threat in Crime Control.* Chicago: University of Chicago Press.

_____, and James Zuehl. 1986. "Victim Injury Death in Urban Robbery: A Chicago Study." *The Journal of Legal Studies* 15:1–40.

PART IV

CONSTITUTIONAL ISSUES

Chapter 9

The Second Amendment and the Ideology of Self-Protection

Don B. Kates, Jr.

Introduction

From the enactment of the Bill of Rights through most of the 20th Century, the Second Amendment seems to have been understood to guarantee to every law-abiding responsible adult the right to possess arms. Until the mid-20th Century courts and commentaries (the two earliest having been before Congress when it voted on the Second Amendment) deemed that the Amendment "confirmed [the people] in their right to keep and bear their private arms," "their own arms," albeit 19th Century Supreme Court decisions held it subject to the non-incorporation doctrine under which none of the Bill of Rights were deemed applicable against the states.[1] In a 1939 case which is its only full treatment, the Supreme Court accepted that private persons may invoke the Second Amendment, but held that it guarantees them only freedom of choice of militia-type weapons, i.e., high quality handguns

This chapter is reprinted with permission from *Constitutional Commentary*, vol. 9, no. 1 (1992).

and rifles, but not "gangster weapons" like sawed-off shotguns, switchblade knives and (arguably) "Saturday Night Specials.[2]

In the 1960s this individual right view was challenged by scholars arguing that the Second Amendment guarantee extends only to the states' right to arm formal military units.[3] The states' right view attained predominance, being endorsed by the ABA, the ACLU and such texts as Laurence Tribe's *American Constitutional Law*. During the 1980s, however, a large literature on the Amendment appeared, most of it rejecting the states' right view as inconsistent with the text ("right of the people," not "right of the states") and with new research findings on the immediate legislative history, the attitudes of the authors, the meaning of the right to arms in antecedent American and English legal thought and the role that an armed citizenry played in classical liberal political philosophy from Aristotle through Machiavelli and Harrington to Sidney, Locke, Rousseau and their various disciples.[4] Indicative of the current Supreme Court's probable view is a 1990 decision which, though focussing on the Fourth Amendment, cites the First and Second as well in concluding that the phrase "right of the people" is a term of art used throughout the Bill of Rights to designate rights pertaining to individual citizens (in contrast to the states).[5]

Sanford Levinson speculates that the indifference of academia, and the legal profession generally, to the Amendment reflects

> a mixture of sheer opposition to the idea of private ownership of guns and the perhaps subconscious fear that altogether plausible, perhaps even "winning" interpretations of the Second Amendment would present real hurdles to those of us supporting prohibitory regulation.[6]

Surprisingly, perhaps, the converse is not the case; Levinson and others who reluctantly embrace the individual right view are by no means necessarily sympathetic to gun ownership, much less to the gun lobby's obnoxious pretension that the Amendment bars any gun control it happens to oppose, however moderate or rational.[7] This may help account for the fact that, though the availability of guns for self-defense is of great import to the gun lobby, that issue plays little part in modern academic exposition of the individual rights position. In contrast, proponents of the state's right view do focus on the issue of self-protection, straight-forwardly denying the existence of historical evidence that it was one of the concerns underlying the Second Amendment.[8]

The purpose of this article is to explore the numerous and protean ways in which the concept of self-protection related to the Amendment in the minds of its authors. For self-defense is indeed at the core of the Second Amendment and an element in the Founders' political thought generally. At the same time it is important to realize that the Founding Fathers' view of self-protection was not only more favorable but also more inclusive than the concept as disfavored by many modern thinkers. To the Founders and their intellectual progenitors, being prepared for self-defense was a *moral* imperative as well as a pragmatic necessity; moreover, its pragmatic value lay less in repelling usurpation than in deterring it before it occurred.

Self-Protection as a Core Concept of Classical Liberal Political Philosophy

The underpinnings of the classical liberal belief in an armed people are obscure to us because we are not accustomed to thinking about political issues in criminological terms. But the classical liberal worldview was criminological, for lack of a better word. It held that good citizens must always be prepared to defend themselves and their society against criminal usurpation—a characterization no less applicable to tyrannical ministers or pillaging foreign or domestic soldiery (who were, in point of fact, largely composed of criminals inducted from gaols[9]) than to apolitical outlaws.

To natural law philosophers, self-defense was "the primary law of nature," the primary reason for man entering society.[10] Indeed, it was viewed as not just a right but a positive duty: God gives Man both life and the means to defend it; the refusal to do so reviles God's gift; in effect it is a Judeo-Christian form of hubris. Indicative of the intellectual gulf between that era and our own is that Montesquieu could rhetorically ask a question that today might be seriously posed, "Who does not see that self-protection is a duty superior to every precept?"[11]

Radiating out directly from this core belief in self-defense as the most self-evident of rights came the multiple chains of reasoning by which contemporary thinkers sought to resolve a multitude of diverse questions. For instance, 17th and 18th Century treatises on international law were addicted to long disquisitions on individual self-protection from which they attempted to deduce a law of nations.[12] More important for present purposes, John Locke adduced from the right of individual self-protection his justification of the right(s) of individuals to resist tyrannical officials and, if necessary, to band together with other good citizens in overthrowing tyranny: God gives Man life, liberty, and property. Slavers, robbers and other outlaws who would deprive him of these rights may be resisted even to the death because their attempted usurpation places them in a "state of war" against the honest man; likewise, when a King and/or his officials attempts to divest the subject of life, liberty or property, they dissolve the compact by which he has agreed to their governance and enter into a state of war with him—wherefore they may be resisted the same as any other usurper. Likewise Algernon Sidney declared: "Swords were given to men, that none might be Slaves, but such as know not how to use them;" a tyrant is "a public Enemy;" every man may rightfully use his arms rather than submit to "the violence of a wicked Magistrate, who having armed a Crew of Lewd Villains" subjects him to murder and pillage. "Nay, all Laws must fall, human Societies that subsist by them be dissolved, and all innocent persons be exposed to the violence of the most wicked, if men might not justly defend themselves against injustice."[13]

From these premises it followed, as Thomas Paine wrote, that "the good man," had both right and need for arms; moreover, no law would dissuade "the invader and the plunderer" from having them. So, "since some *will not*, others *dare not* lay them aside. . . . Horrid mischief would ensue were" the law-abiding "deprived of the use of them; . . . the weak will become a prey to the strong."[14] Similarly did Cesare Beccaria assail arms bans as a paradigm of simplistic legislation reflecting "False Ideas of Utility." His discussion deserves quotation in full, *inter alia* because Thomas Jefferson translated and laboriously copied it in long-hand into his personal compilation of great quotations:[15]

> False is the idea of utility that sacrifices a thousand real advantages for one imaginary or trifling inconvenience; that

would take fire from men because it burns, and water because one may drown in it; that has no remedy for evils, except destruction. The laws that forbid the carrying of arms are laws of such a nature. They disarm those only who are neither inclined nor determined to commit crimes. Can it be supposed that those who have the courage to violate the most sacred laws of humanity, the most important of the code, will respect the less important and arbitrary ones, which can be violated with ease and impunity, and which, if strictly obeyed, would put an end to personal liberty — so dear to men, so dear to the enlightened legislator — and subject innocent persons to all the vexations that the quality alone ought to suffer? Such laws make things worse for the assaulted and better for the assailants; they serve rather to encourage than to prevent homicides, for an unarmed man may be attacked with greater confidence than an armed man. They ought to be designated as laws not preventive but fearful of crimes, produced by the tumultuous impression of a few isolated facts, and not by thoughtful consideration of the inconveniences and advantages of a universal decree.

Self-Protection as Benefit to the Whole Community. The ideas underlying the Second Amendment are also obscured to us by the distinction we tend to draw between self-protection as a purely private and personal value and defense of the community, which we tend to conceptualize as a function and value of the police. Modern Americans tend to see incidents in which a violent criminal is thwarted by a police officer as very different from similar incidents in which the defender is a civilian. When the police defend citizens it is conceptualized (and lauded) as defense of the community. In contrast, when civilians defend themselves and their families the tendency is to regard them as exercising what is, at best, a purely personal privilege serving only the particular interests of those defended, not those of the community at large. Such influential and progressive voices in American life as Garry Wills, Ramsey Clark and the *Washington Post* go further yet, declaring those who own firearms for family defense "anti-citizens," "traitors, enemies of their own *patriae*," arming "against their own neighbors" and denouncing "the need that some homeowners and shopkeepers believe they have for weapons to defend themselves" as representing "the worst instincts in the human character," a return to barbarism, "anarchy, not order under law—a jungle where each relies on himself for survival."[16]

The notion that the truly civilized person eschews self-defense, relying on the police instead, or that private self-protection disserves the public interest, would never have occurred to the Founding Fathers since there were no police in 18th Century America and England. As addressed *infra*, in the tradition from which the Second Amendment derives it was not only the unquestioned right, but a crucial element in the *moral* character, of every free man that he be armed and willing to defend his family and the community against crime both individually and by joining with his fellows in hunting criminals down when the hue and cry went up, and in more formal posse, and militia patrol duties, under the control of justices of the peace or sheriffs.[17] In this milieu, individuals who thwarted a crime against themselves or their families were seen as serving the community as well. If the right to possess and use arms "against robbers and plunderers was taken away, then would follow a vast license of crime and a deluge of evils" averred Hugo Grotius.[18]

This failure to distinguish the value of self-protection to individuals as opposed to the community helps account for what modern readers may deem a remarkable myopia in 17th-19th Century liberal discourse on crime, self-protection and community interest. Without apparent consciousness of any difference, liberal discourse addressed issues of community defense as if it were only individual self-protection writ large. Thus, Montesquieu confidently asserted that "The life of governments is like that of man. As the former has a right to kill in case of natural defense, the latter have a right to wage war for their own preservation." Likewise, Thomas Paine cited the (to his compeers) indubitable right and need for "the good man" to be armed against "the vile and abandoned" as irrefutable evidence of the right and need of nations to arm for defense against "the invader and plunderer"; for, if deprived of arms, "the weak will become a prey to the strong."[19] As we have seen, Algernon Sidney and John Locke adduced from the right of individual self-defense their justification of the right(s) of individuals to resist tyrannical officials and, if necessary, to band together with other good citizens to overthrow tyranny.

Thus a crucial point for understanding the Second Amendment is that it emerged from a tradition that viewed general possession of arms as a positive social good, as well as an indispensable adjunct to the premier individual right of self-defense. Moreover, arms were deemed to protect against every species of criminal usurpation, including "political crime," a phrase that the Founding Fathers would have understood in its most literal sense. Whether murder, rape and theft be committed by gangs of assassins, tyrannous officials and judges or pillaging soldiery, rather than outlaw bands, was a mere detail; the criminality of the "invader and plunderer" lay in his violation of natural law and rights, regardless of the guise in which he violated them. The right to resist and to possess arms therefor — and the community benefit from such individual and/or concerted self-protection — remained the same.

Political Functions of the Right to Arms

The views of Locke and Sidney — so controversial in their own time that they were the basis of the prosecution's case in the trial that resulted in Sidney's execution — had became settled orthodoxy by the mid-18th Century. Thus we find Edward Gibbon, a Tory M.P. in the circle of George III casually remarking, in the course of defining "monarchy":

> [U]nless public liberty is protected by intrepid and vigilant guardians, the authority of so formidable a magistrate will soon degenerate into despotism. [A]lthough the clergy might effectively oppose the monarch they have] very seldom been seen on the side of the people. A martial nobility and stubborn commons, *possessed of arms*, tenacious of property, and collected into constitutional assemblies, form the only balance capable of preserving a free constitution against enterprises of an aspiring prince.[20]

Similar sentiments were expressed by Gibbon's somewhat more liberal contemporary, Sir William Blackstone, in analyzing the right to arms. Significantly, the way in which he described that right emphasizes both the individual self-protection rationale, and the criminological premises, which are so foreign to the terms of the modern debate over the Second Amendment.

For Blackstone placed the right to arms among the "absolute

rights of individuals at common law" — those rights he saw as
preserving to England its free government and to Englishmen
their liberties. Yet, unquestionably, what Blackstone was referring
to was individuals' rights to have and use personal arms for
self-protection. The right to arms' he describes as being "for self-
preservation and defense," and self-defense as being "the primary
law of nature which [cannot be] taken away by the law of society" — the "natural right of resistance and self-preservation, when
the sanctions of society and laws are found insufficient to restrain
the violence of oppression." But, just as clearly, Blackstone saw
this right to personal arms for personal self-defense as a political
right of fundamental importance. For his discussion of the "absolute rights of individuals" ends with the following:

> In these several rights consist the rights, or, as they are fre-
> quently termed, the liberties of Englishmen. . . . So long as
> these remain inviolate, the subject is perfectly free; for
> every species of compulsive tyranny and oppression must
> act in opposition to one or [an]other of these rights, having
> no other object upon which it can possible be employed. . . .
> And, lastly, to vindicate these rights, when actually vio-
> lated or attacked, the subjects of England are entitled, in the
> first place, to the regular and free course of justice in the
> courts of law; next, to the right of petitioning the King and
> parliament for redress of grievances; and, *lastly, to the right
> of having and using arms for self-preservation and defense.*[21]

To readers with modern sensibilities this inevitably raises
two questions to which the remainder of this article is devoted:
Why did Blackstone regard the right to possess arms for self-protection as a political matter? How could he have grouped (what
we at least conceive as no more than) a privilege to have the means
of repelling a robber, rapist or cutthroat with such political rights
as access to the courts and to petition for redress of grievances?

The Armed Freeholder Ideal of Virtuous Citizenship

The final section of this article describes several historical situations in which the possession (or prohibition) of arms for personal self-protection had concrete political effects. But no less

important in the classical liberal worldview was the moral and symbolic significance of the right to arms.

Arms possession for protection of self, family and polity was both the hallmark of the individual's freedom and one of the two primary factors in his developing the independent, self-reliant, responsible character that classical liberal political philosophers deemed necessary to the citizenry of a free state. The symbolic significance of arms as epitomizing the status of the free citizen represented ancient law. From Anglo-Saxon times "the ceremony of freeing a slave included the placing in his hands of" arms "as a symbol of his new rank." Likewise in Norman times, "the *Laws of Henry I* stipulate[d] that a serf should be liberated by" a public ceremony involving "placing in his hands the arms suitable to a freeman." Anglo-Saxon law forbade anyone to disarm a free man, and Henry I's laws applied this even to the man's own lord.[22] Such precedents were particularly important to theorists like Blackstone and Jefferson to whom the concept of "natural rights" had a strongly juridical tinge relating to the English legal heritage.

The Anglo-American legal distinction between free man/armed and unfree/disarmed flowed naturally into the classical liberal view that the survival of free and popular government required citizens of a special character—and that the possession of arms was one of two keys in the development of that character. From Machiavelli and Harrington classical liberal philosophy derived the idea that arms possession and property ownership were the keys to civic *virtu*. In the Greek and Roman republics from whose example they took so many lessons, every free man had been armed so as to be prepared both to defend his family against outlaws and to man the city walls in immediate response to the tocsin warning of approaching enemies. Thus did each citizen commit himself to the fulfillment of both his private and his public responsibilities.[23]

The very survival of republican institutions depended upon this moral (as well as physical) commitment—upon the moral and physical strength of the armed freeholder: sturdy, independent, scrupulous, and upright, the self-reliant defender of his life, liberty, family, and polity from outlaws, oppressive officials, despotic government, and foreign invasion alike. That the freeholder might never have to use his arms in such protection mattered naught. (Indeed, one basic tenet classical political theory took from its criminological premises was that of deterrence: if armed and ready the free man would be least likely ever to actually have to defend. Simply to be armed, and therefore able to protect one's own, was enough; this moral commitment both developed and exemplified the character of the virtuous republican citizen.)

Commitment, duty, responsibility is also viewed as a positive right (at least when challenged) because, naturally enough, to the virtuous citizen the carrying out of responsibilities to family and duties to country are a right. And this right/obligation to be armed inevitably will be challenged for it is the nature of absolutism to want to disarm the people. Nor is this simply for the physical security despotism gains in monopolizing armed power in the hands of the state, thereby rendering the people helpless. Disarmament also operates on the moral plane. The tyrant disarms his citizens in order to degrade them; he knows that being unarmed

> palsies the hand and brutalizes the mind: an habitual dis-
> use of physical force totally destroys the moral; and men
> lose at once the power of protecting themselves, and of dis-
> cerning the cause of their oppression.[24]

Thus, when Machiavelli said that "to be disarmed is to be contemptible," he meant not simply to be held in contempt, but to deserve it; by disarming men tyrants render them at once brutish and pusillanimous.

It was in this tradition of civic virtue through armament that Thomas Jefferson (who believed that every boy of ten should be given a gun as he had been) advised his 15-year-old nephew:

> A strong body makes the mind strong. As to the species of
> exercises, I advise the gun. While this gives a moderate ex-
> ercise to the body, it gives boldness, enterprise and inde-
> pendence to the mind. Games played with the ball, and
> others of that nature, are too violent for the body and stamp
> no character on the mind. Let your gun therefore be the
> companion of your walks.[25]

The Efficacy of Arms and Self-Defense. Of course the reasons for the Founding Fathers' belief in arms possession were not limited to purely moral premises. Indeed, the Founders and their intellectual progenitors had an almost boundless faith in the pragmatic, as well as the moral, efficacy of widespread arms possession. They would be not at all surprised that no 20th Century military has managed to suppress an armed popular national insurgency, a fact which accounts for the modern histories of Afghanistan, Algeria, Angola, Cuba, Ireland, Israel, Madagascar, Nicaragua, Vietnam and Zimbabwe, to name only the most prominent examples. Classical liberal thought espoused an almost boundless faith in the efficacy of civilian arms possession as deterrent and defense against outlaws, tyrants and foreign invaders alike. Madison confidently assured his fellow-countrymen that a free people need not fear government "because of the advantage of being armed, which the Americans possess over the people of almost every other nation."[26] Arming the people is, according to Locke's followers Trenchard and Moyle,

> the surest way to preserve [their liberties] both at home and abroad, the People being secured thereby as well against the Domestick Affronts of any of their own [fellow] Citizens, as against the Foreign Invasions of ambitious and unruly Neighbors.[27]

This faith in the efficacy of arms buoyed up Locke and his English and American followers against their opponents' charge that their advocacy of a right to resistance and even revolution would lead to sanguinary and internecine disorders. To the contrary, they replied, that is what will come from disarming the people. Unchecked by the salubrious fear of its armed populace, government will follow its natural tendency to despotism. Tyrannous ministers will push their usurpations to the point that even an unarmed people will arise *en masse* to take their rights back into their bloody hands regardless of casualties.[28] But where the people are armed it would rarely, if ever, come to this for, as Thomas Paine asserted, "arms like laws discourage and keep the invader and plunderer in awe and preserve order in the world as well as property."[29] To avoid domestic tyranny, wrote Trenchard and Moyle, the people must be armed to

> stand upon [their] own Defense; which if [they] are able to do, [they] shall never be put upon it, but [their] Swords will grow rusty in [their] hands; for that Nation is surest to live in Peace, that is most capable of making War; and a Man

that hath a Sword by his side, shall have least occasion to
make use of it.[30]

Whatever the merits of this deterrence theory, in other respects the Founders also carried their belief in the right to arms to
absurdly utopian extremes. Writers like Timothy Dwight and Joel
Barlow airily dismissed the dangers inherent in widespread possession of arms:

> [T]heir conscious dignity, as citizens enjoying equal rights,
> [precludes armed citizens having any desire] to invade the
> rights of others. The danger (where there is any) from
> armed citizens, is only to the *government*, not to the *society*;
> as long as they have nothing to revenge in the government
> (which they cannot have while it is in their own hands)
> there are many advantages in their being accustomed to the
> use of arms and no possible disadvantage.[31]

Even more outlandish to modern eyes is the explanation
which the early English liberal Francis Place gave of how hatred
and violence against the Jews were erased in 18th Century England:

> Dogs could not be used in the streets in the manner many
> Jews were treated. One circumstance among others put an
> end to the ill-usage of the Jews. About the year 1787 Daniel
> Mendoza, a Jew, became a celebrated boxer and set up a
> school to teach the art of boxing as a science. The art soon
> spread among young Jews and they became generally ex-
> pert at it. The consequence was in a very few years seen
> and felt too. It was no longer safe to insult a Jew unless he
> was an old man and alone. But even if the Jews were un-
> able to defend themselves, the few who would now be dis-
> posed to insult them merely because they are Jews, would
> be in danger of chastisement from the passers-by and of
> punishment from the police.[32]

The First, Second, Third and Fourth
Amendments as Connected Guarantees

The Founding Fathers' reasons for guaranteeing a right to arms
for individual self-protection were not limited to abstruse moral

or philisophical precepts. The Amendment reflects concrete historical circumstances known to them, which help explain why the right to arms in our Bill of Rights follows immediately upon the First Amendment and precedes the Third and Fourth.

Probably the most obvious political ramification of the right to defensive arms is the deterrent effect of the power to disarm dissenters in a violence-ridden society. Until the early 19th Century England was an enormously violent country overrun with cutthroats, cutpurses, burglars and highwaymen and in which rioting over social and political matters was endemic. Moreover, until 1829 it had no police. So when the 17th Century Stuart Kings began selectively disarming their enemies the effect was not simply to safeguard the throne, but to severely penalize dissent. Those who had opposed the King were left helpless against either felons or rioters—who, by the very fact, were encouraged to attack them. The *in terrorrem* effect upon dissent of knowing that to speak out might render one's family defenseless while targeting them for every felon, and every enemy who might want to whip up riotous public sentiment against them, is obvious.

Caucasian readers in well-policed modern America may find it difficult to see riot either as a socio-political phenomenon or as something to which personal self-protection is relevant. Yet over many years riot and nightrider attacks—perpetrated while police stand by—have served to undercut or destroy civil rights gains, strike back at racial and ethnic minorities, and exclude blacks from white neighborhoods. It has been suggested that the availability of firearms for protection against private, retaliatory violence was a key to the Civil Rights Movement's survival in the southern United States of the 1950's and 1960's. Comparison might be made to South Africa where blacks, though an overwhelming majority, are subject to one of the world's most effective gun control campaigns.[33]

The disarmament of minorities or dissenters in a climate in which they may be subject to private violence (often encouraged by government) has been a well-established policy in many countries including Nazi Germany and the Soviet Union. The leading example is the Krystallnacht (Nov. 9, 1938) in which thousands of Jews were beaten, raped and/or murdered and a billion reichsmarks of Jewish property was looted or destroyed in nationwide riots orchestrated by the Nazi Party after the Jews had been excluded from gun ownership under German law.[34] It is dubious that many German Jews wanted to own arms—or that it would have made any difference to their eventual fate. But it is an item of faith in Israel that Jews persevered and triumphed in the Middle East—where they were during the 1930's a far smaller minority, and subject to far more violence, than in Europe—because they took steps to obtain and use arms.

Rioters and vigilantes are not the only kinds of villains against whom the necessity of protection may be less clearly perceived today than it was in the age of Blackstone. No less a menace than rioters or outlaws was the pillaging soldier, loosed not only on foreign populations but in his own country for political, religious or social reasons or because of the King's inability to pay, and thus control, him. Generally speaking, there was no difference of character between rioters, felons and soldiers—who were often one and the same. Often the soldier was a common criminal inducted directly out of jail and unleashed on the King's enemies, whether foreign or domestic. The perpetration of such outrages upon his critics by Charles I engendered the Petition of Right of 1628 and helped eventually to bring him to the headsman. But of innumerable such examples that might be cited from European history in this period, probably the one most remembered by 18th Century Englishmen and Americans would have been the persecution that drove the Huguenots to their shores by the thousands. As a modern historian has noted, among the numerous tribulations visited in the 1690's upon the Huguenots in order to compel them to convert, the

> most atrocious—and effective—were the dragonnades, or billeting of dragoons on Huguenot families with encouragement to behave as viciously as they wished. Notoriously rough and undisciplined, the enlisted troops of the dragoons spread carnage, beating and robbing the householders, raping the women, smashing and wrecking and leaving filth.[35]

As Englishmen and Americans were well aware from their reading of Bodin, Beccaria and Montesquieu, the Huguenots had been rendered incapable of resisting either individually or as a group by the Continental policy of disarming all but the Catholic nobility.

The need to be armed for individual protection had been brought home to late 18th Century Americans by their own experience with the "licentious and outrageous behavior of the military" Britain sent among them during the decade of protest and turmoil that preceded the Revolution.[36] As in England itself, the people's unwillingness to enforce smuggling laws upon themselves required the state to use soldiers to perform the duties of the non-existent police. Committed to the folly of "asserting a right [to tax the colonists] you know you cannot enforce,"[37] during the 1760's and early 1770's England dispatched ever-increasing numbers of troops as the Stamp Tax was added to the Navigation Acts and then succeeded by the Townshend Acts, the Tea Tax, etc. These soldiers (eventually operating under a specially appointed British Customs Board) executed both ordinary warrants and the notorious Writs of Assistance under which they made wholesale searches of vessels, homes, vehicles, and warehouses, perusing goods, documents and records — in a tumultuous process in which even those not seized were often destroyed along with the surrounding furnishings.[38]

By 1768 the people of Massachusetts, the most radical and impatient of the colonies, had had enough: rendered over confident by military reinforcements, the Customs Board had seized John Hancock's ship *Liberty* — and then fled to a British warship for safety in the resulting tumult; seven years of protest had resulted in the colonies feeling the yoke of ever-increased military occupation; Massachusetts' latest protest (a circular letter to the other colonial legislatures urging non-payment of the taxes) had been met by an official demand that the letter be repudiated on pain of dissolution of the Massachusetts Assembly; the Customs Board's intention to continue the searches was evident and General Gage was calling in troops for that purpose from all over the colonies and Canada.

So leading figures in Boston, and the town officially, advised the citizens that their only recourse was to arm themselves for the protection of their liberty and property. An article reprinted in newspapers throughout the colonies alleged abuses by the soldiers carrying out searches "of such nature" and "carried to such lengths" that for "the inhabitants to provide themselves with arms for their defence, was a measure as prudent as it was legal. . . ." As to the legality of personal armament, the article went on to invoke

Blackstone himself in terms that emphasize the political nature of the right and yet its relationship to the right of self-defense:

> It is a natural right which the people have reserved to themselves, confirmed by the [English] Bill of Rights, to keep arms for their own defence; and as Mr. Blackstone observes, it is to be made use of when the sanctions of society and law are found insufficient to restrain the violence of oppression.[39]

The denouement, of course, was an ever-escalating series of incidents between the colonists and troops attempting to enforce the taxes and customs duties and suppress protest of them. The Boston Massacre, General Gage's confiscation of the arms stored at Lexington and Concord, and his subsequent attempt to disarm the entire populace of Boston are among the most important of the things that propelled the colonies into revolution.

The desirability of citizens arming themselves against illegal search—or of revolution, for that matter—may seem dubious to modern Americans enjoying the benefits of a vigilant judiciary and police of a character far better than the soldiery known to our forefathers. But to 18th Century Americans, the course of pre-Revolution British policy only confirmed the necessity of every free citizen having access to arms: "to disarm the people"; that, said George Mason, "was the best and effectual way to enslave them."[40] This imagery of "enslavement" and the possession of arms as the guarantee against it appears throughout the writings of Sidney, Locke and their disciples up to and including the Founding Fathers forming a consistent theme consisting of the following propositions: every free man has an inalienable right to defend himself against robbery and murder—or enslavement, which partakes of both; the difference between a slave and a free man is the latter's possession of arms, which allows him to exercise his right of self-defense; for government to disarm the citizen is not just to rob him of his property and liberty; it is the first step toward "enslaving" him, i.e., robbing him of all his property and all his liberties—which will inevitably follow once he has been disarmed. In America from the immediate pre-Revolutionary period through the debates over the Constitution, this equation of personal self-protection with resistance to tyranny—of self-protection against the slave trader to self-protection against "en-slavement" by government — recurs again and again.[41]

In evaluating how such statements relate to the concept of self-protection it is also essential to remember that the imagery of a man defending himself against abduction by a slaver was not the mere figure of speech it might seem to us. Locke, Sidney and their contemporaries lived in a world in which human slavery was a grotesque reality; the Founding Fathers lived among, and upon the labor of, a people many of whom were being held under duress. The Founding Fathers were acutely conscious of the inconsistency between their noble declamations about their own freedom and their actual conduct regarding the enslavement of others. In invoking the right to resist "enslavement" they were analogizing to a situation conceived quite literally in terms of a right and need for direct personal self-defense.

It may be time now to rhetorically restate (and thereby answer) the questions posed earlier: Does this background suggest why Blackstone saw political overtones in the right to arms, coupling his discussion of it to rights that are plainly political in nature? Does it help explain why in the Bill of Rights arms follows religion, expression, press and petition — and is followed by the Third Amendment guarantee against quartering of soldiers and the Fourth against unreasonable searches and seizures? In view of this background, two other connections between the Fourth, Third, and Second Amendments merit mention: First, in both French and English experience, searches and seizures would generally have been carried out by soldiery rather than by civil authorities; second, the castle doctrine, which the Fourth Amendment enunciates ("a man's home is his castle and his defense"), originated in caselaw exonerating freeholders who had killed intruders.[42] In short, not only are these rights phrased in substantially identical terms (the First, Second, and Fourth Amendments all speak in terms of rights "of the people"), but their roots, and the situations in which they were visualized as operating, are closely identified.

Conclusion

The self-defense origins of the Second Amendment are many and

complex. Natural law philosophers saw self-defense as the premier natural right. From it they adduced a variety of other rights
(for both individuals and collectivities), the most obvious and
closely related being the right to arms. These connections were
particularly important to Lockeans and their progeny down to and
including the Founding Fathers. They saw killings, maimings,
assaults, despoilation and rapine as equally criminal whether the
perpetrators were apolitical outlaws or "lewd Villains" serving a
"wicked Magistrate." Viewing despotic impositions and terrori-
zation of the people as a species of *criminal* usurpation, the Founders saw the rights of individual arms possession and resistance,
and of collective revolution where necessary, as aspects of the
right to self-defense. At the same time the Lockeans believed
widespread popular possession of arms to be a powerful deterrent
to political and apolitical crime alike.

No less important in shaping the Amendment was the Anglo-
American legal tradition (as the Founders understood it) which
was influential both in its own right and as support for the view
of the right to arms the Founders took from classical liberal political philosophy. In that tradition there were no police, and the very
idea of empowering government to place an armed force in constant watch over the populace was vehemently rejected as a paradigm of abhorrent French despotism.[43] Notwithstanding the
evident need for municipal police, it would be another 40 to 50
years before police were commissioned in either English or American cities. Even then they were specifically forbidden arms, under
the view that if these were needed they could call armed citizens
to their aid. (Ironically, the only gun control in 19th Century
England was the policy forbidding police to have arms while on
duty.[44])

In the absence of a police, the American legal tradition was
for responsible, law-abiding citizens to be armed and see to their
own defense and for most military age males to chase down
criminals in response to the hue and cry and to perform the more
formal police duties associated with their membership in the *posse
comitatus* and the militia. It was the possession of arms in these
contexts that the Second Amendment constitutionalized. "The
right" to arms refers to that which pre-existed in American common and statutory law, i.e., the legal right to possess arms that was
enjoyed by all responsible, law-abiding individuals, including

both militiamen and those exempt from militia service (the clergy, women, conscientious objectors and men over the age of militia service).

Nor should it be thought that the Founding Fathers would have repudiated their belief in the right of self-defense—and of individuals to be armed for self-defense—if they had anticipated the replacement of the militia and *posse comitatus* by modern police agencies. They knew of the Stuarts' attempts to penalize dissent by disarming their opponents in an era of rampant crime and violence. Nor would it have seemed prudent to rely on the state as protector (rather than exploiter) of its unarmed citizens, given the examples of the Customs Board, and of General Gage's troops and the soldiery generally, in 18th Century America or Stuart England and Bourbon France. Rather those examples confirmed both the criminologically based worldview of classical liberal philosophy and its foundation in the even more ancient dictum that just and popular governments rest upon widespread popular possession of arms, whereas basic to tyrants is "mistrust of the people; hence they deprive them of arms."[45]

Notes

1. In addition to the cases and earlier commentaries quoted and discussed in Kates, "Handgun Prohibition and the Original Meaning of the Second Amendment," 82 *Mich. L.Rev.* 204, 224 and 241-51 (1983) (hereinafter "Original Meaning") see *Pomeroy's Constitutional Law* 152-3 (1870), 5 H. von Holst, *The Constitutional and Political History of the United States* 307 (1885), *Black's Constitutional Law* 403 (1895), J. Schouler, *Constitutional Studies: State and Federal* (1897), 2 J. Tucker, *The Constitution of the United States* § 327 (H. Tucker, ed. 1899), A. Putney, *United States Constitutional History and Law* 363 (1908) and 1 *J. of Crim. L., Crimin. & Pol. Sci.* 794 (1911).
2. *United States v. Miller*, 307 U.S. 174 (1939).
3. See, e.g., Levin, "The Right to Bear Arms: The Development of the American Experience," 48 *Chi-Kent L. Rev.* 148 (1971); Weatherup, "Standing Armies and Armed Citizens: An Historical Analysis of the Second Amendment," 2 *Hast. Const. L.Q.* 961 (1972).
4. See, e.g. Shalhope, *The Ideological Origins of the Second Amendment*, 69 *J. Am. Hist.* 599 (1982), and other works cited in the appendix to Chapter 2, above.
5. *United States v. Verdugo-Uriquez* 494 U.S. 259, 110 S.Ct. 1056, 108 L.Ed. 2d 222, 232–33 (1990).
6. *The Embarrassing Second Amendment*, 99 *Yale L. J.*, supra at 642.
7. Cf. a debate between the NRA's primary exponent of the Amendment and myself as to the extent to which various moderate, sensible gun controls are allowable under the individual right view we both endorse. Halbrook, *What the Framers Intended: A Linguistic Analysis of the Right to "Bear Arms"* 49 *Law & Contemp. Probs.* 151 (1986) vs. Kates, *The Second Amendment*, 49 *Law & Contemp. Probs.* 143 (1986).
8. See, e.g., G. Newton & F. Zimring, *Firearms and Violence in American Life* 259 (1969) (characterizing the Second Amendment "as a scheme dealing with military service, not individual defense").
9. R. Weighley, *History of the United States Army* 19 (1967). See infra in the section titled "The First, Second, Third, and Fourth Amendments as Connected Guarantees" for discussion of the billeting of criminous troops on the king's enemies as a punishment and means of surveillance. Throughout the 18th Century, criminal offenses by English soldiers and sailors in the colonies were a constant occurrence, and a subject of constant antagonism between Americans and the English military, which refused either to punish their men or to turn them over to local justice. See generally P.

Maier, *From Resistance to Revolution: Colonial Radicals and the Development of American Opposition to Britain.*

10. 3 W. Blackstone, *Commentaries* *4; see generally, T. Hobbes, *Leviathan*, ch. XIII (1952).

11. Montesquieu, 2 *Spirit of the Laws* 60.

12. See, e.g. 2 Burlamqui, *The Principles of Natural and Politic Law* 121 (xix; Nugent transl.), Vattel, *Law of Nations: Principles of the Law of Nature* 22 (J. Chitty ed.).

13. J. Locke, *Concerning Civil Government* (2nd essay) 72–73, 79 (1952), A. Sidney, *Discourses Concerning Civil Government* 175, 180–1, 266–7, 270 (1698).

14. *Writings of Thomas Paine* 56 (M. Conway ed. 1894) (emphasis in original).

15. *The Commonplace Book of Thomas Jefferson* 314 (G. Chinard ed. 1926) quoting C. Beccaria, *An Essay on Crimes and Punishments* 87–8 (1764).

16. Wills, "Handguns that Kill," *Washington Star*, Jan. 18, 1981 and "John Lennon's War," *Chicago Sun Times*, Dec. 12, 1980 and "Or Worldwide Gun Control," *Philadelphia Inquirer*, May 17, 1981; *Washington Post* editorial: "Guns and the Civilizing Process," Sept. 26, 1972, R. Clark, *Crime in America* 88 (1971).

17. *Original Understanding*, supra, 82 *Mich. L. Rev.* at 214–6, Malcolm, supra, 10 *Hast. Const. L. J.* at 290–2.

18. H. Grotius, 1 *De Jure Belli Et Pacis* 54 (W. Whewell trans. 1853). See generally, *Original Meaning*, supra 82 *Mich. L. Rev.* at 214–6, Morn, *Firearms Use and Police: A Historic Evolution in American Values*, in D. Kates (ed.), *Firearms and Violence* (1984).

19. See, respectively, *Spirit of the Laws* and *Writings of Thomas Paine*, supra.

20. 1 *Decline and Fall of the Roman Empire* 53 (Mod. Lib. ed.).

21. 1 *Commentaries* *121, *143–4; see also 3 *Commentaries* *4.

22. A. Norman, *The Medieval Soldier* 73 (1971), 1 *English Historical Documents* c. 500–1042, 427 (D. Whitelock ed. 1955), The Assize of Arms 416 (1181), reprinted in II *English Historical Documents* (D. Douglas & C. Greenaway eds. 1953).

23. *Original Meaning*, supra 82 *Mich. L. Rev.* at 230–2.

24. J. Barlow, *Advice to the Privileged Orders in the Several States of Europe: Resulting from the Necessity and Propriety of a General Revolution in the Principle of Government, Parts I and II* at 45 (London, 1792, 1795 & reprint 1956).

25. *The Jefferson Cyclopedia* 318 (Foley, ed., reissued 1967).

26. *The Federalist*, # 46 at 371.

27. J. Trenchard & W. Moyle, *An Argument Shewing, that a Standing*

Army Is Inconsistent with a Free Government, and Absolutely Destructive to the Constitution of the English Monarchy 7 (London, 1697).

28. Kates "Minimalist Interpretation of the Second Amendment," in E. Hickok (ed.), *The Bill of Rights: Original Meaning and Current Understanding* (U. Va. Press, 1991) at p. 132.

29. *Writings of Thomas Paine*, supra.

30. Trenchard & Moyle, supra 12.

31. J. Barlow, *Advice to the Privileged Orders in the Several States of Europe: Resulting from the Necessity and Propriety of a General Revolution in the Principle of Government, Parts I and II* at 17 (London, 1792, 1795 & reprint 1956). See also 1 T. Dwight *Travels in New England and New York* xiv (London, 1823).

32. F. Place, *Improvement of the Working Classes* (1834) as quoted in R. Webb, *Modern England: From the 18th Century to the Present* 115, n. 14 (1970).

33. Robert J. Cottrol and Raymond T. Diamond, "The Second Amendment: Toward an Afro-Americanist Reconsideration," 80 *Georgetown L.J.* 309–361 (1990); John Salter, "Civil Rights and Self-Defense," *Against the Current*, July-August 1988; D. Kates, "Toward a History of Handgun Prohibition in the United States," D. Kates (ed.) *Restricting Handguns* (1979) at 12–15 and 18–19.

34. *Restricting Handguns*, supra at 185 (quoting official commentary on the German Firearms Act of 1937 that explicitly excluded gun permit applications by Jews). See id. at 188 (statement by Hermann Goering, then head of the German police): "Certainly I shall use the police—and most ruthlessly—whenever the German people are hurt; but I refuse the notion that the police are protective troops for Jewish stores. The police protect whoever comes into Germany legitimately, but not Jewish usurers."

35. B. Tuchman, *The March of Folly* (1984)

36. This description is taken from *A Journal of the Times* (1768–1769), a Boston publication expressing the Whig point of view that was reprinted throughout the colonies and in England. Excerpted in D. Dickerson, *Boston Under Military Rule* 61 (D. Dickerson ed. 1936).

37. Lord Chesterfield as quoted in Tuchman, supra, at 158.

38. For a detailed discussion of the events detailed in this and the following paragraphs, see Halbrook, *Encroachments of the Crown on the Liberty of the Subject: Pre-Revolutionary Origins of the Second Amendment*, 15 U. Dayton L. Rev. 91 (1989).

39. From *A Journal of the Times* (1768–1769), a Boston publication expressing the Whig point of view that was reprinted throughout the colonies and in England. Excerpted in D. Dickerson, *Boston Under Military Rule* 61 (D. Dickerson ed. 1936).

40. 3 J. Eliott, *Debates in the Several State Conventions* 380 (2d ed. 1836).

41. P. Maier, *From Resistance to Revolution: Colonial Radicals and the De-velopment of American Opposition to Britain.*

42. *Anonymous,* 21 Hen. VII, fol. 39, pl. 50. Earlier cases included *Dhutti's Case,* Northumberland Assize Rolls (1255), 88 Publications of Surtees Society 94 (1891) (household servant privileged to kill nocturnal intruder); *Rex v. Compton,* 22 Liber Assisarum pl. 55 (1347) (homicide of burglar is no less justifiable than of criminal who resists arrest under warrant); and *Anonymous* 1353, 26 *Liber Assisarum,* (Edw. III), fol. 123, pl. 23 (householder privileged to kill arsonist).

43. See expressions of opposition and horror cited in B. Tuchman, *The March of Folly* 148 (1984) and R. Webb, supra at 184.

44. The British tradition of unarmed policing persists to this day be-cause crime, particularly violent crime, fell rapidly throughout 19th Century England; in contrast, as American violence increased police seized the right to be armed by refusing to patrol unarmed. C. Greenwood, *Firearms Control: A Study of Armed Crime and Fire-arms Control in England and Wales* ch. 1 (1971), Morn, supra.

45. Aristotle, *Politics* 218 (J. Sinclair trans. 1962).

Index